# OUR BROKEN ELECTIONS

## HOW THE LEFT CHANGED THE WAY YOU VOTE

### JOHN FUND *AND* HANS VON SPAKOVSKY

VOTE HERE

BALLO

Encounter
BOOKS

New York • London

First American edition published in 2021 by Encounter Books, an activity of Encounter for Culture and Education, Inc., a nonprofit, tax-exempt corporation. Encounter Books website address: www.encounterbooks.com

Manufactured in the United States and printed on acid-free paper. The paper used in this publication meets the minimum requirements of ANSI/NISO Z39.48–1992 (R 1997) (*Permanence of Paper*).

FIRST AMERICAN EDITION

LIBRARY OF CONGRESS CATALOGING-IN-PUBLICATION DATA

Names: Fund, John H., 1957—author. | von Spakovsky, Hans, 1959—author.
Title: Our Broken Elections: How the Left Changed the Way You Vote / John Fund and Hans von Spakovsky.
Description: First American edition. | New York: Encounter Books, 2021. Includes bibliographical references and index.
Identifiers: LCCN 2021022484 (print) | LCCN 2021022485 (ebook)
ISBN 9781641772082 (hardcover) | ISBN 9781641772099 (ebook)
Subjects: LCSH: Elections—Corrupt practices—United States.
Classification: LCC JK1994 F857 2021 (print) | LCC JK1994 (ebook)
DDC 324.60973—dc23
LC record available at https://lccn.loc.gov/2021022484
LC ebook record available at https://lccn.loc.gov/2021022485

1 2 3 4 5 6 7 8 9 20 21

# CONTENTS

# INTRODUCTION

The two of us have each been writing about and studying voting rights and election integrity for over twenty years.

Until the November 2020 election, we didn't feel compelled to update our 2012 book, *Who's Counting? How Fraudsters and Bureaucrats Put Your Vote At Risk*. We were happy to address the topic in our articles, media interviews, and speeches. But since bitter tribal warfare broke out over voting issues in the aftermath of the 2020 election, we have changed our minds.

First, a word on what this book *is not* about. We will not be going into great detail about allegations that election reform bills introduced in state legislatures represent "voter suppression" or, in the words of President Joe Biden, "a return to Jim Crow." If people actually read the bills in question, in almost all instances they would agree that is absolutely not the case and is simply partisan propaganda of the worst kind intended to scare voters and score political points.

We will examine the debate over Georgia's election integrity bill because it became such a rallying cry for Stacey Abrams and other mythmakers. They were able to fool or intimidate several major corporations into opposing the bill even though some of them had actually helped craft it and had supported it behind the scenes before the intimidation game began.

Second, this book is *not* about the clumsy, counterproductive, and often exaggerated claims made by lawyers claiming to speak for Donald Trump. The former president and lawyers such as Rudy Giuliani, Sidney Powell, and Lin Wood did real damage to those who were trying to examine the 2020 election with a critical eye and point out clear procedural shortcomings and illegal voting in key swing states. Fighting for election integrity measures must begin and end with a belief that voters deserve to have confidence in the fairness and accuracy of the system. The anger of a candidate or his supporters over election irregularities must also be accompanied by some restraint in making allegations that can't be backed up or are supported by unreliable evidence.

Last, for some of the above reasons, this book will not go into detail about allegations that electronic voting machines were manipulated and shifted or created large numbers of votes. President Trump tweeted frequently about a news report on the conservative news channel One American News Network (OAN). "Elections systems across the country are found to have deleted millions of votes cast for President Trump," it said. The OAN report referred to an "unaudited analysis of data" obtained from an election monitoring group called Edison Research.

However, the company's president, Larry Rosin, said: "Edison Research has produced no such report and we have no evidence of any voter fraud." OAN did not provide any evidence to back up its claim.[1]

There was a significant computer problem in Antrim County, Michigan, where Dominion voting machines were used. The suggestion was made by numerous individuals that it was only the most visible of a series of serious software problems that were also appearing elsewhere around the country.

We believe Dominion and other electronic voting machines are vulnerable to unauthorized entry—as proven repeatedly by hackers at computer security conferences—and that that problem should be studied carefully. Where at all possible, software programs for voting machines should be made public with greater transparency into the contracts given by state election officials along with a paper trail for every electronic machine. We will be discussing Antrim's Dominion voting machine controversy but will not go into great detail about others. We will note that Fox News, Fox Business Channel, Newsmax, and OAN have had to step away from and apologize for allegations against Dominion machines that aired on their networks.[2]

This book tries to step back from personalities and punditry and make simple points. Our system is broken. Many of the problems we cite were ignored by the media in 2020. The media used to win prizes for investigative reports on election fraud, and *60 Minutes* used to highlight the issue on television.[3] No more. Now there is a blinkered media narrative that sees every allegation of voter fraud as an attempt at voter suppression. "Every time a media narrative runs all in one direction you know it's time to question it," says Glenn Garvin, a columnist for the *Miami Herald*.[4] That paper won the 1999 Pulitzer Prize for Investigative Journalism for its reporting on a corrupt mayoral race in Miami that was overturned by the courts and led to the indictment of fifty-seven people.

If the country remains solely wrapped up in angry arguments about who won the last election and who is trying to take advantage of whom, we will continue to erode confidence in our government and our ability to solve problems.

Now that a year has passed since the passions of the 2020

election, we hope this book makes a contribution to a quieter, more reasoned discourse. We hope the facts we put down provide the basis for an honest debate. If we ignore the systemic problems of our election system and don't fix them, we will—to paraphrase the philosopher George Santayana—be condemned to repeat our mistakes.

We have to get beyond the divisiveness and anger of the 2020 election. This is a time when our country can afford that kind of division even less than before.

## THE WAY FORWARD

Election integrity is a fundamental requirement of a functioning democratic republic.

In the freest nation in the world, our system of government and our very liberty depend on free and fair elections. Whether selecting a mayor or the president of the United States, every American must be able to trust the process, or the democratic system itself breaks down.

When someone commits election fraud, the process is no longer fair, everyone's vote gets diluted, and in some cases election results are changed. Problems can arise not only from intentional misconduct by individuals trying to take advantage of the vulnerabilities in our voter registration and election process, which is largely an honor system, but also from administrative errors made by election and other government officials.

Contrary to the claims of many on the left, election fraud is a very real problem. When the Supreme Court upheld Indiana's voter ID law in 2008, John Paul Stevens, the most liberal justice on the court at the time, wrote for the 6–3 majority that "flagrant examples of such fraud...have been documented throughout this Nation's history by respected historians and journalists...that demonstrate that not only is the risk of voter fraud real but that it could affect the outcome of a close election."

The National Commission on Federal Election Reform chaired by former President Jimmy Carter and former Secretary of State James Baker similarly concluded that fraud "could affect the outcome of a close election." Cases of local elections getting overturned because of fraud have occurred in California, Florida, New Jersey, North Carolina, Indiana, and other states.

Although hundreds of people have been convicted in recent years, election fraud often goes undetected. And even when it's discovered, overburdened prosecutors rarely prioritize these cases.

Fraudsters can steal votes and change election outcomes in many ways, including the following:

- Forging voter signatures on candidate ballot qualification petitions
- Voting in someone else's name in person or through absentee ballots
- Registering and voting under a false identity or in a district where the individual does not actually reside
- Submitting fraudulent, altered, or forged absentee ballots
- Registering in multiple locations within a state or in different states to vote multiple times in the same election
- Voting even though they're not eligible because they're felons or noncitizens
- Paying, coercing, or intimidating people to vote for certain candidates

Unfortunately, many on the left are attempting to make election fraud easier by fighting laws that require an ID, a common-sense reform overwhelmingly supported by the American public.

They've pushed to get noncitizens and jailed inmates to vote, and they oppose all efforts by election officials to certify the citizenship of registered voters through federal databases and other means. And they've sued states that have tried to clean up their voter rolls by removing individuals who have died, moved away, or are registered multiple times in several states.

The changes that were rammed through for the 2020 "COVID" election, including switching to universal all-mail elections or dramatically increasing the use of absentee mail-in ballots, are unwise and dangerous. Absentee ballots are the tools of choice for vote thieves because they are the only ballots cast outside the supervision of election officials and outside the observation of poll watchers, destroying the transparency of the election process that is a fundamental hallmark of a healthy democracy.

Absentee or mail-in ballots also have a much higher rejection rate than votes cast in a polling place since there are no election officials present in someone's home to answer questions or resolve any problems a voter may be having. When you add the problems of missed delivery, delayed delivery, and other errors made by the postal service, it seems obvious that mail-in ballots are not a good alternative to voting in person.

Preserving this great experiment that is America depends on having free and fair elections where all Americans can trust the process and the results.

Something as critical as election integrity can't be left to a simple honor system or the delivery of ballots by unknown third parties. One of the most important roles of government is to safeguard the electoral process and ensure that every voter's right to cast a ballot is protected and not diluted by fraud or administrative errors.

There are two fundamental civil rights when it comes to voting. First, the right not to be intimidated, blocked, or otherwise prevented from voting. We fought a great struggle to pass a Voting Rights Bill in the 1960s to end discriminatory state laws. We have to preserve those gains and build on them.

Second, everyone has the right not to have their vote cancelled out by someone who shouldn't be voting, whether that person is dead, has moved out of state, is a noncitizen, is underage, hasn't paid their full debt to society after imprisonment, or doesn't even exist.

Protecting both rights is how we safeguard the future of our republic.

## CHAPTER ONE

# A CONFLICT OF VISIONS

I t's clear that Americans are separated not just by political disagreements but by a basic difference in how we regard voting.

Democrats gravitate toward the view that the most important value is empowering people to exercise their democratic rights, regardless of security issues, and they worry about people being denied that right.

The Democratic National Committee's Voting Rights Institute emphasizes the need "to remove every barrier that impedes or denies an eligible vote." High in the Democratic Party's pantheon of heroes (unlike fifty years ago when the party had many segregationist leaders) are "activists from all over America who converged on Mississippi in the summer of 1964 to help educate and register tens of thousands of previously disenfranchised American citizens." What they do not want to acknowledge is that the barriers that existed then are long gone and that it is easier to register and vote today than ever before in modern history.

Republicans tend to pay more attention to the rule of law and the standards and procedures that govern elections. Conservative legal scholars have noted that voters as well as election officials have an obligation to ensure that democracy works. Republicans worry publicly about elections but not with the same emphasis as Democrats. They often emphasize election integrity rather than access to the polls, but that is because they assume—correctly—that guaranteeing the security of elections does not hinder access.

In his classic 1988 book *A Conflict of Visions: Ideological Origins of Political Struggles*, the economist and sociologist Thomas Sowell outlined the important role that social "visions" play in our thinking. By "vision," he meant a fundamental sense of how the world works.

Competing visions or worldviews are particularly powerful in determining how people regard issues because, unlike "class interests" or other motivating forces, they are largely invisible, even—or especially—to those who harbor them. They explain how so often in life the same people continually line up on the same sides of different issues.

For decades, public opinion researchers sought the perfect polling question that best correlated with whether someone considered himself a Republican or a Democrat. In the 1960s, Gallup finally came up with the question that has had the most consistent predictive power over the last half century: "In your opinion, which is more often to blame if a person is poor? Lack of effort on his own part, or circumstances beyond his control?" Today, as might be expected of a divided nation, these two competing views on what creates poverty are equally strong in their hold on American public opinion.

Sowell maintains that conflicts of visions dominate history. "We will do almost anything for our visions, except think about them," he concludes. Sowell identifies two distinct visions that shape the debate on controversial issues. The first he calls the "unconstrained" vision of human nature, and the second he terms the "constrained" vision.

Those with an unconstrained vision think that if we want a society where people are enlightened, prosperous, and equal, we must develop programs to accomplish those goals and work to implement them. The focus is on results or outcomes. That would include making sure that as many people as possible vote, thus animating the ideals of democracy.

But sometimes the desire to expand voting opportunities takes on unrealistic qualities. San Francisco narrowly approved allowing noncitizens to vote in school board elections in 2018. Then in 2019, a *majority* of House Democrats voted to lower the federal voting age from eighteen to sixteen. A number of high-profile Democrats voted in favor of the legislation, including California Reps. Adam Schiff and Maxine Waters, New York Rep. Alexandria Ocasio-Cortez, Michigan Rep. Rashida Tlaib, and Minnesota Rep. Ilhan Omar.[1]

"Young people are at the forefront of some of our most existential crises," said the bill's cosponsor Rep. Ayanna Pressley of Massachusetts. "The time has come. Our young people deserve to have the opportunity to exercise their right to vote." Apparently, these representatives think sixteen-year-olds are mature enough to make important decisions and judgments about the political life of the country even though they are not legally considered an adult in any state, cannot sign leases or contracts, cannot be trusted to purchase alcohol, and are barely old enough in most states to get a license to drive a car.

Those with a "constrained" vision of human nature believe that the goal of reason should be not to remodel society but rather to identify "natural laws" and work within them. Such people focus on general rules and processes. In regard to elections, the constrained vision would favor setting up procedures ensuring that votes are counted accurately and fairly but not bending those procedures to increase voter participation at the cost of the integrity and security of the process.

"I run into two kinds of people," says Mischelle Townsend, the former registrar of Riverside County, California. "The first is focused on making sure everything is geared to increasing turnout and making sure no one is disenfranchised. The other is more interested in making sure things get done right, are secure, and the law is followed." She vividly remembers the 2003 recall that put Arnold Schwarzenegger in office as governor of California.

The ACLU, the NAACP, and other liberal groups convinced a three-judge panel of the U.S. Court of Appeals for the Ninth Circuit to cancel the election because six counties still used punch card ballots, which according to the anti-recall plaintiffs had a higher error rate than other forms of voting. The argument was that some minority voters would thus be disenfranchised. But an eleven-member panel of the Ninth Circuit unanimously rejected that view, contending that postponing a recall election was tantamount to disenfranchising *all* voters.[2]

An excessively cramped view of elections holding that rules and procedures must be interpreted in such a way as to guarantee that absolutely no improper vote is cast would be regarded as unfairly denying some people the right to vote. Anti-fraud efforts that cross the line, like stationing off-duty cops at polling places—as some Republican campaigns did in the 1980s—invite a response such as that from Steven Hill, a senior analyst for the Center for Voting and Democracy: "There must be something about certain types of voters that Republicans don't trust."

At the other extreme, a loose and lax approach toward the law can lead to unacceptable attempts to cheat the system, such as the one that created thousands of suspect voter registrations during a South Dakota photo-finish U.S. Senate race in 2002.

Maka Duta, the woman at the heart of that scandal, admitted duplicating signatures on registration forms and applications for absentee ballots. But she asked for understanding: "If I erred in doing so, I pray that Attorney General Mark Barnett will agree with me that I erred on the side of angels."[3] In other words, doing the devil's work of forging voter signatures is somehow understandable given her angelic goal of increasing voter turnout.

What Duta is completely missing, as do others who think like her, is that in order to preserve the fairness and integrity of our election process, we must have both access and security. Contrary to the claims constantly made by liberals and many in the media, there is no conflict between providing both access and security; one does not prevent the other.

And the American people agree with that vision of how our elections should be conducted. Polling by the Honest Elections Project in 2021 revealed that

> Most voters (64%) want to strengthen voting safeguards to pre-vent fraud, rather than eliminate them to make voting "easier." Fifty-one percent of Black voters and 66% of Hispanics agree, as do 59% of Urban voters and 61% of Independents. Only 21% want to make voting "easier" by getting rid of the precautionary measures that prevent fraud.[4]

When it comes to the constant propaganda by the media and leftists that election fraud doesn't exist or is inconsequential, the public also disagrees with them. The same polling shows that "eighty percent of voters believe that election fraud disenfran-chises voters and casts doubt on the legitimacy of the democratic process, including majorities across all gender, racial, age, and income demographics."

Similarly, polling by the Honest Elections Project found that

77 percent of Americans support voter ID requirements, including 64 percent of Black voters and 78 percent of Hispanic voters. Nearly two-thirds of voters want ID requirements for in-person voting extended to absentee ballots. Moreover, 62 percent of voters believe that "it should be illegal for political operatives and paid organizers to have direct access to absentee voters as they vote, and then take unsupervised possession of their ballots." So Americans disagree with one of the fundamental changes that leftists are pushing: vote trafficking of absentee ballots by third-party strangers.[5]

The bottom line according to the polling is that 87 percent of voters "agree that protecting the right to vote is about more than casting ballots, it is about protecting a fair and honest election system that ensures every lawful ballot is counted, and guards against fraud."[6] So while there may be a conflict of visions when it comes to election integrity, those opposed to security in the election process are on the wrong end of that vision according to the overwhelming majority of the public.

Last April, a poll by the University of Massachusetts Amherst and WCBV-TV on election reform had the same kind of disturbing news for liberals.[7]

"To the chagrin of Democratic officials, the most popular reform is to require all voters to show ID to vote, with 67% of voters supporting this, and roughly a majority saying they strongly support it," said Jesse Rhodes, associate director of the poll.

In fact, even though critics often claim that young people and members of minority groups are hardest hit by the ID requirement, the poll found that both groups "overwhelmingly favor requiring that voters show government issued identification in order to vote on Election Day."

Social thinker Jonathan Haidt, whose books include *The*

*Righteous Mind*, isn't surprised by this. "People are very sensitive to procedural fairness. They really hate processes that are being gamed or tricked. They want those people to be punished. I think people see the requirement to show ID as something really basic to prevent cheating. It's not a big deal at all. You have to show your ID to buy beer, rent a car, get on an airplane, or do anything official," he wrote in an email to colleagues and friends. In fact, in an April 2021 poll by *The Economist*, people even favored requiring a photo ID in order to vote by absentee ballot by 52 percent to 31 percent.[8]

Haidt noted that a friend of his shared a video showing white liberals telling an interviewer that requiring an ID to vote is racist, but the black residents of Harlem that are interviewed all say that of course they have ID's, everyone does, and they clearly do not think an ID requirement is a problem.[9]

Opponents of voter ID laws refuse to acknowledge that the public doesn't think it is a problem, and they refuse to recognize a decade of hard data on turnout that shows it is not a problem. It is a partisan political tactic used to oppose all election reforms and to try to unfairly and fraudulently paint reformers as racists.

Opponents also claim that voter ID is a solution in search of a problem because in-person voter impersonation fraud doesn't really exist.

But how would they know? It's almost the perfect crime since it can't be detected without an ID requirement. It is easy for fraudsters to commit it without getting caught. In 2013, New York City's Department of Investigations detailed how undercover agents claimed at sixty-three polling places to be individuals who were in fact dead, had moved out of town, or were in jail. In sixty-one instances, 97 percent of the time, they were allowed to vote. (To avoid skewing results, they voted only for nonexistent write-in candidates.)[10]

How did the city's Board of Elections respond? Did it immediately probe and reform their sloppy procedures? Not at all. It instead demanded that the investigators be prosecuted. Most officials don't want to admit how vulnerable election systems are, but privately they express worry that close elections could be flipped by fraud. In any event, the fraud deniers refuse to acknowledge that, in addition to impersonation fraud, an ID requirement can also potentially prevent voting by aliens, individuals who actually live in another state, and individuals who don't actually live where they are registered.

## BREAKING THE IMPASSE

Is there any way to break the stalemate on voter ID between liberals and conservatives?

Yes. At a voting summit in Texas in 2015, former Presidents Bill Clinton and Jimmy Carter endorsed the idea of adding a picture ID to Social Security cards. Carter said he would "support the idea in a New York minute." Clinton said, "The idea behind this agreement is to find a way forward that eliminates error and makes the best possible decision that we can all live with."

The two former Democratic presidents were joined by Andrew Young, former U.N. ambassador, mayor of Atlanta, and confidante of Martin Luther King, Jr. Young told the summit: "It is our obligation to make sure that every citizen has the ability to obtain a government-issued photo ID, and the Social Security administration is ideal for making that happen effectively and efficiently." Social Security has 1,300 offices around the country, and adding a photo option for cardholders would cost just 10 cents a card, he said.

Young has said voter ID doesn't have to be a symbol of discrimination but instead could be a "freedom card," a natural extension of President Lyndon Johnson's efforts to elevate the poor and disadvantaged. "In today's world, you can't board an airplane or get into most buildings or cash a check without predatory fees or get Medicare without a photo ID," Young said. "Ensuring people have one allows them to enter the mainstream of American life and would be a help to them."[11]

Martin Luther King III, son of the civil rights leader, added, "If we embrace Andy's idea, we help marginalized citizens secure independence from predators and ensure them our nation's most fundamental right to vote. My father used to talk about ending the silence of good people. I cannot emphasize enough the positive impact a free and easy-to-obtain photo ID will have for those who are marginalized."

On the other side of the political spectrum, Republicans also see promise in a photo ID Social Security card. "This would help tone down the debate over who is trying to manipulate the system and actually get real ID into the hands of whoever doesn't have one—something we should all agree on," said Don Palmer, the former secretary of the Virginia Board of Elections who is now a member of the U.S. Election Assistance Commission.[12] Former presidents George W. Bush and Donald Trump have also expressed support for the concept of the Freedom Card.

Election law experts say more safeguards might be necessary to curb identity theft. The Social Security Administration warns people that they should "not routinely carry your card or other documents that display your number" because "someone illegally using your number and assuming your identity can cause a lot of problems."[13] A photo ID Social Security card would thus be limited mostly to those people without any other form of ID. But it would be cheap: in the 1990s, the Clinton administration estimated that producing a Social Security card with an embedded photo would cost only eight cents a card.

So if both sides agree, why isn't the photo ID Social Security card already available? For one thing, President Obama proved to be of no help on the issue. Justice Department lawyers, who automatically oppose any voter ID requirement, and the Rev. Al Sharpton, who was Obama's liaison to the black community, killed the idea.

When one of us discussed the Freedom Card idea in testimony on voting-rights issues before the U.S. Commission on Civil Rights in 2018, we were greeted by a stony silence. No questions were asked. One civil rights attorney in the audience admitted privately that the groups in the room were interested more in victory than in a political solution. But average Americans should be looking for solutions.

In 2011, Rhode Island Secretary of State Ralph Mollis, a Democrat, persuaded his state's overwhelmingly Democratic legislature to pass a photo ID bill to address problems of voter fraud in Providence and other cities. The bill was passed with the support of the state's leading minority legislators. The effort included extensive outreach efforts, with members of Mollis's office going to senior centers, homeless shelters, and community centers to process free IDs. The law was implemented smoothly, Mollis says, and at the time he viewed it as a potential national model. (He sadly did not anticipate the current polarized political environment).

"When the day is done, my job is to maintain the integrity of elections," Mollis told us. "Even if a state doesn't have an immediate problem with fraud, doesn't it make sense to take sensible precautions rather than wait for someone to abuse the system, and then it's too late?"[14]

The same thinking should apply across the country. All citizens should be able to become full participants in American life. Many on both left and right occupy common ground on the issue. Voter ID laws improve the honesty and efficiency of elections. They can also empower people on the margins of society. In public policy, we should grab the chance of a win-win solution when we can.

## THE VOTING EQUIPMENT AND SOFTWARE ISSUE

There is another election issue that represents a conflict of visions: whether or not electronic voting machines can be trusted to count our votes accurately and fairly.

Both parties have many activists who are convinced that sinister forces use voting machines to steal elections. President Trump for a while endlessly repeated allegations by his former lawyer Sidney Powell that computer algorithms had shifted votes from him to Joe Biden in key states. A majority of House Republicans voted not to accept the Electoral College votes of several states on January 6, just before the infamous riot by Trump supporters that engulfed the U.S. Capitol. Some members as well as many of the protestors cited computer manipulation of the vote in key states.

In 2004, many Democrats became obsessed with the Diebold voting machines in Ohio and believed they'd been tampered with enough to swing the state to George W. Bush. The House conducted a two-hour debate on the alleged irregularities before voting to accept Bush's Ohio victory. The late Christopher Hitchens wrote a lengthy piece on the purported conspiracy for *Vanity Fair*.[15]

In January 2017, seven House Democrats objected to certifying the Electoral College in several key states narrowly won by Trump the previous November. In fact, they objected to more states than Republicans did when they sought to block the Electoral College votes for Joe Biden on January 6.[16]

California Rep. Barbara Lee of California cited malfunctioning voting machines when she objected to the counting of Michigan's Electoral College votes.

There is a clear "conflict of vision" between those who have a high degree of confidence in the accuracy and security of voting machines and those who believe they are a disaster waiting to happen.

Individual voting machines are easy to hack, but since they are not connected to other machines in a network, large-scale fraud is difficult. Some critics worry about algorithms that could alter results, but in the real world there has never been a proven case of a significant computer manipulation of votes going back to the days of optical scan ballots in the 1970s.

Nonetheless, there has been a growing and welcome trend to replace paperless electronic voting machines with devices that record votes on paper ballots. Such paperless machines have been eliminated in Georgia, Michigan, Pennsylvania, and Wisconsin, all states Trump supporters focused on after the November election. Wherever paper ballots are used, officials can use recounts and audits to find out whether the software was honest. The hand audits done in Georgia, plus recounts in some counties in Wisconsin and in Antrim County, Michigan, found no evidence of hacking. However, as discussed later in this chapter, there were computer glitches in Antrim County.

White House economic adviser Peter Navarro wrote a report in which he claimed massive computer irregularities but said they involved "process fouls" that made it impossible to actually check the results.

Despite the large numbers of dubious claims about the dangers of electronic voting machines, it is certainly true that millions of people still cast ballots on sometimes unreliable and aging machines.

"No one is using a computer they purchased in the 1990s," says Warren Stewart, a senior editor and data specialist for Verified Voting, a nonprofit advocacy group tracking election systems.[17]

But such concerns are a far cry from some of the bizarre claims that have been tossed out by both Democrats and Republicans in recent elections. Sidney Powell was publicly exiled from the Trump camp after she appeared with Rudy Giuliani at a news conference hosted by the Republican National Committee. She claimed to have identified "massive influence of Communist money through Venezuela, Cuba and likely China in the interference with our elections here in the United States."

Without official backing, Powell then went on to file lawsuits on Trump's behalf in Georgia, Michigan, Arizona, and Wisconsin. None went anywhere.

After the election, Powell was sued by Dominion Voting Systems for defamation. In a motion to dismiss the complaint, her lawyers argued that the conspiracies she laid out constituted legally protected First Amendment speech. In a truly unfortunate choice of words, her lawyers wrote:

"No reasonable person would conclude that the statements were truly statements of fact."[18] They concluded with the statement that Powell still believed her statements were true. Not exactly a confidence-building measure.

## THE ANTRIM AUDIT

Now let's examine one of most scrutinized controversies in the 2020 election: the vote totals in Antrim County, Michigan. They raised questions about election equipment and software produced by the Dominion Voting Systems company, and some feared that fraud, collusion, or intentional misconduct occurred in Antrim County, where a little over sixteen thousand votes were cast.

A report by Allied Security Operations Group, a Dallas-based organization run by Trump supporters, claimed that voting machines in Antrim County had error rates of over 68 percent that year. Trump later tweeted the same figure. The implication was that the errors went uncorrected, skewing the result. The county had indeed misreported results in the presidential election, initially showing that Joe Biden had beaten Donald Trump in a normally GOP county.[19]

In Antrim County, the machines were misconfigured in a way that led to errors in combining vote totals from different precincts but not in recording the votes. A hand recount in the county in December found that Trump's vote total was underreported by eleven votes and that Joe Biden lost one vote.

As summarized in an audit report published on March 26, 2021, "totals in the presidential race and other contests were initially misreported by up to several thousand votes, and over the next three weeks, the county restated the results four times to correct this and other errors."[20] Donald Trump actually won the county with 9,748 votes to Joe Biden's 5,960 votes, according to the final election totals of the Michigan secretary of state, a result confirmed by a complete hand count of the optical scan paper ballots cast in the election.

What happened in Antrim was so concerning that the Michigan secretary of state and the attorney general hired Prof. J. Alex Halderman to audit the Dominion Voting Systems election software used by Antrim and to analyze what happened. Halderman is a well-known expert on computer security and the director of the Center for Computer Security and Society and the Software Systems Laboratory at the University of Michigan. He has testified before numerous congressional committees on cybersecurity and U.S. elections.

In 2012, Prof. Halderman came to national attention when

he issued a scathing report on the security vulnerabilities of the Internet voting system developed by the District of Columbia. During a mock election that the district staged to demonstrate the supposedly invincible security of its new system, Halderman described how he and his team penetrated the system within forty-eight hours and "gained near-complete control of the election server" without detection by district election officials and "successfully changed every vote and revealed almost every secret ballot." As a result of his work, the district cancelled its Internet voting project.[21]

As Halderman says in his Antrim report, his analysis was intended to answer several questions: What caused the errors? Are they evidence of a cyberattack or other foul play? Have they been fully corrected? Could similar problems affect other localities? What should be done to prevent such issues in the future?[22]

Halderman not only examined the software in the county's Dominion election management system, including the important activity logs, he also looked at the memory cards used in the county's ballot scanners. He was able to reconstruct what had happened that "led to the initially erroneous results" and was able to "precisely account for the discrepancies and identify the underlying causes." His conclusion? The "inaccurate results were a consequence of human errors" that were "compounded by gaps in election procedures and their adherence."[23] As Halderman himself has demonstrated throughout his career, "the vulnerabilities in election technology are well documented," but he concluded that "the Antrim County incident was not caused by a security breach," nor was there "credible evidence that it was caused deliberately." He does say "the election software also could have done more to help election staff avoid making mistakes that could lead to erroneous results."[24]

For those who still have doubts about the election software,

Halderman's report is well worth reading in its entirety. He goes into great detail to describe what happened. In summary, the incident was

> due to the county's mishandling of last-minute ballot design changes…Several layers of protection that are supposed to ensure accuracy broke down due to human errors on multiple layers, including mistakes by county and township staff while operating the election technology, procedural missteps while processing ballots in some localities, and the failure of the county canvassers to detect lingering discrepancies.[25]

He recommends "greater oversight of county and local election administration" as well as a series of improvements to "election technology, training, and procedures in order to better guard against similar problems in future elections."[26]

Prof. Halderman also goes into great detail analyzing a report released by Russell James Ramsland, Jr. of Allied Security Operations Group, "Antrim Michigan Forensics Report-Revised Preliminary Summary, v2," on December 13, 2020. Ramsland claimed in his report that "the Dominion Voting System is intentionally and purposefully designed with inherent errors to create systemic fraud and influence election results." However, according to Halderman, the Ramsland analysis "contains an extraordinary number of false, inaccurate, or unsubstantiated statements and conclusions" that Halderman then proceeds to refute.[27]

Halderman points out errors that he says are made by Ramsland over everything from error rates to the adjudication of ballots. Halderman also says that Ramsland misinterprets the "election system logs," that he "mischaracterizes" certain changes as "software updates," and that he did not apparently realize that Antrim's Dominion scanners had no Internet connectivity because

Antrim "did not purchase and does not use the Dominion wireless results transmission functionality."[28]

Even though he concluded that what had happened in Antrim was due to human error and not intentional misconduct, such as a cyberattack, Halderman does not give Dominion a free pass. He says that Dominion's election management system "lacks important security updates, has weak authentication and access control mechanisms, and is vulnerable to compromise if an attacker has physical access to the computer." He classifies these as "serious vulnerabilities that should be mitigated on a priority basis, but there is no evidence that any of these problems was ever exploited in Antrim County."[29]

What all of this portends is simply that we need to ensure that the state agencies that evaluate the voting equipment and software that is sold in their states do a better job of evaluating, testing, and assessing it before it is qualified for use in elections. That includes making sure that it cannot be compromised by insiders or outside cybercriminal and hackers and that, as the Halderman report makes clear, election officials and workers have the training they need to actually use the equipment without making the kind of mistakes that occurred in Antrim County.

States should also conduct audits after every election to ensure that their election equipment was functioning properly and that all applicable rules, regulations, and procedures were strictly followed to the letter by election officials. Given that private companies and businesses routinely undergo audits to ensure their compliance with legal and financial requirements, there is no credible justification for anyone to oppose such audits other than for partisan, political reasons.

As this book was being written, the results were not yet available from the audit being conducted by the Arizona legislature of the 2020 election in Maricopa County despite partisan opposition from Democrats and some local election officials. But there were early reports from a similar audit being conducted in Windham, New Hampshire, of a local race. Preliminary reports revealed that problems in the computer scanners used to count votes led to the winning candidates not being credited with over two hundred votes, while the losing candidate got over a one hundred fewer votes. These discrepancies did not change the outcome of the election, but without the audit, local election officials would never have known they had a problem with their election equipment that needs to be fixed before it changes the results of a future election.[30]

## CHAPTER TWO

# TAKING ADVANTAGE OF THE COVID PANDEMIC TO CHANGE THE WAY WE VOTE

R ahm Emanuel, the former mayor of Chicago and chief of staff for President Barack Obama, famously said in 2008 that you should never let "a serious crisis go to waste" because it is "an opportunity to do things that you think you could not do before." Liberals in 2020 took Emanuel's political tenet to heart and used the COVID pandemic to try to implement through litigation and executive actions by state government officials the reckless changes in voting and election procedures that they had been wanting for years.

That effort involved voiding basic security protocols on election procedures, including absentee ballots, and pushing for the equivalent of all-mail elections, which would give their activists a free hand in pressuring, coercing, and influencing voters in their homes in ways they are unable to do in polling places. To force these changes, they ended up filing more election-related lawsuits than had ever been filed in an election year in U.S. history. The prior record was almost two hundred lawsuits before and after the 2000 election when George W. Bush beat Al Gore; by late October 2020, more than four hundred election-related lawsuits had been filed across the nation, the overwhelming majority by the left.[1]

It is important to understand that almost all the changes sought were unnecessary, particularly the huge increase in mail-in ballots and the short-circuiting of security requirements on absentee ballots because of the supposed danger of voting in person. The United States lived through the 1968 Hong Kong influenza pandemic without shutting down the country or radically changing election procedures for the November presidential election that year. The country also did not shut down due to the Swine Flu pandemic in 2009. COVID-19 is a different disease with different infection and fatality rates, but the history of elections conducted during epidemics, including this one, shows it can be done safely.

Liberia did it in 2014 in the midst of the Ebola epidemic sweeping West Africa.[2] Liberian election officials worked closely with health experts to "integrate a range of practical health measures, such as social distancing and revised processing, to ensure the safe exchange of ballot papers, ID cards, pens, and other common voting materials."[3] Poll workers were also trained in the "roll of queue controllers," and there was an extensive voter education effort.

In other words, Liberia did the very same thing during the election that we did in dealing with the coronavirus in 2020. Businesses open to the public (such as grocery stores, drug stores, and chains like Lowes and The Home Depot) incorporated social distancing and the use of face masks, gloves, and cleaning supplies into their business models—just as Liberia had incorporated the same tools, sanitation procedures, and distancing to minimize possible contamination.

Using all of the recommended precautions of health officials, Liberia held its election on December 20, 2014, in the midst of the epidemic.[4] It was only the third election since the end of what the U.N. secretary general, who was in Liberia the day before the election, called a "brutal war."[5] That election was conducted with *in-person voting*—not an all-mail election—and the U.N. congratulated Liberia on organizing a successful election "under challenging circumstances, particularly in the midst of difficulties posed by the Ebola crisis."[6]

South Korea held a national election on April 15, 2020, in the midst of COVID-19, in which 29 million South Koreans voted in their national elections in person using safety procedures and protocols recommended by health experts. South Korea's health authorities reported that there were "no infections" that resulted from that general election.[7]

Wisconsin held its primary election on April 7, 2020, shortly after the nation started shutting down. Although there was a significant increase in absentee ballots, several hundred thousand state residents voted in person in their regular polling places. Just like in South Korea, the Wisconsin Election Commission implemented stringent safety procedures. That included social distancing in voter lines, hand washing and sanitizing stations for all voters when entering and leaving polling places, and regular sanitizing of all tables, door handles, voting booths, voting equipment, and everything else touched or handled in the polling place. They even had curbside voting for those who did not want to come inside.[8]

A report released by analysts from the World Health Organization and Stanford University after the Wisconsin election found "no detectable surge" in COVID-19 transmission due to the April 7 election.[9] Similarly, the Centers for Disease Control and Prevention (CDC), the federal agency that led the nation's response to COVID-19, issued a report looking at the experience of Milwaukee, the largest city in Wisconsin. It concluded that there was no "increase in cases, hospitalizations, or deaths" from COVID-19 due to the election. In fact, there were fewer cases reported during the "incubation period" after the election—April 9–21—than in the thirteen days preceding the election.[10]

The CDC issued a series of guidelines for conducting in-person voting safety in June 2020, which included everything from social distancing in voter lines to cleaning and disinfecting of equipment and voting materials used in a polling location. In fact, the CDC recommended that jurisdictions "maintain or increase the total number of polling places" to "improve the ability to social distance."[11]

The point is that there was no need to vastly increase the number of absentee ballots or to push the public to vote by mail. We could have held a regular election by implementing the same safety precautions Americans were used to when they went shopping at their local grocery stores and pharmacies. But that would not benefit the left's objective of overriding state election laws aimed at ensuring security, so they instead fed the hysteria over the supposed danger of voting in person.

The many lawsuits filed by organizations like the Democratic National Committee and their nonprofit political allies like the ACLU attacked state laws governing absentee ballots, such as those requiring a witness or notarization, a copy of a voter identification document, comparison of voter signatures, and an excuse to use an absentee ballot. They also pushed states to mail out absentee ballot request forms or absentee ballots themselves to all registered voters and to extend the deadlines for the receipt of absentee ballots. Even if more individuals wanted to vote absentee because of their fear of the pandemic, there was still no justification for relaxing the security protocols put in place by state legislatures to protect the integrity of the absentee balloting process.

Typical of this lawfare was the lawsuit filed in Wisconsin by the Democratic National Committee. The DNC convinced a liberal federal judge appointed by Barack Obama, William Conley, to extend both the deadline for registering to vote by a week and the Election Day deadline for the receipt of absentee ballots by six days to Nov. 9 as long as the ballots were postmarked by Election Day, November 3. There was no valid COVID-related reason for either of these extensions. Fortunately, he was overruled by the U.S. Court of Appeals for the Seventh Circuit, which chastised Conley for violating Supreme Court precedent, reminding him that "the Supreme Court has insisted that federal courts not change electoral rules close to an election date" and that "the design of adjustments during a pandemic" is not a "judicial task."[12]

The DNC unsuccessfully filed an emergency appeal to the U.S. Supreme Court, which rejected the appeal just a week before the election. Justice Neil Gorsuch wrote a concurrence emphasizing that "the Constitution provides that state legislatures—not federal judges, not state judges, not state governors, not other state officials—bear primary responsibility for setting election rules…and the Constitution provides a second layer of protection, too. If state rules need revision, Congress is free to alter them."[13]

The very same thing happened in Indiana, where the Seventh Circuit Court continued the reasoning of the Wisconsin case. It stayed and "summarily reversed" an Indiana-based federal judge's order "requiring the state to count all absentee ballots received by November 13, 2020, ten days after Election Day" even though the deadline for the receipt of absentee ballots under Indiana law is noon on Election Day. Another important point that too many seemed to ignore, particularly the plaintiffs, Common Cause, and the NAACP, is that, as the Seventh Circuit Court said, "as long as the state allows voting in person, there is no constitutional right to vote by mail." The fact that there is a pandemic, said the court, is still "not a good reason for the federal judiciary to assume tasks that belong to politically responsible officials."[14]

Alabama saw a similar litigation tactic used against it. The state was sued by a host of liberal groups that obtained an injunction from another liberal federal judge appointed by Barack Obama, Abdul Kallon. Kallon told the state it could not—because of COVID—enforce either its ID or its witness-or-notarization requirement for absentee ballots.[15] This case also ended up in front of the Supreme Court, which fortunately overruled Kallon.

But Justice Sonia Sotomayor filed a dissent, which Justices Stephen Breyer and Elena Kagan joined. The dissenting opinion made it clear that they would have had no hesitation in substituting their "expert" judgment on how to deal with the health issues raised by the COVID-19 pandemic and to override the judgment of the state legislature. This is a task far outside the boundaries of what judges and justices should be doing in their roles as interpreters of laws and the Constitution.[16]

The Supreme Court also dealt with an emergency appeal from South Carolina only a month before the 2020 election. South Carolina asked the court to overturn an injunction issued by another Obama appointee, District Court Judge J. Michelle Childs, which would have prevented South Carolina from applying its requirement for a witness signature to absentee ballots.[17] The court granted a stay of the order without an opinion. The only explanation given for the Supreme Court's stay was a concurrence by Justice Brett Kavanaugh. In it, he pointed out two reasons for overturning the decision by Childs, which she claimed was based on the dangers posed by COVID-19.

First, Kavanaugh said the Constitution entrusts the safety and health of a state's residents principally to the "politically accountable officials" of that state. Thus, "a state Legislature's decision either to keep or to make changes to election rules to address COVID-19" should "not be subject to second-guessing by an 'unelected federal judiciary,' which lacks the background, competence, and expertise to assess public health and is not accountable to the people."

Second, Kavanaugh made clear that "for many years, this

Court has repeatedly emphasized that federal courts ordinarily should not alter state election rules in the period close to an election," citing a 2006 precedent, *Purcell v. Gonzalez.*[18]

In a not-so-subtle criticism of the Obama judge, Kavanaugh said that "by enjoining South Carolina's witness requirement shortly before the election," Childs "defied that principle and this Court's precedents." Child's injunction had already been stayed by a three-judge panel of the U.S. Fourth Circuit Court of Appeals in a 2–1 decision on Sept. 24, 2020.[19] But a majority of the entire Fourth Circuit, which is controlled by liberal judges, had overturned the panel decision almost immediately and reinstated the unjustified injunction.[20]

The two judges on the panel who had originally dissolved Childs's injunction, J. Harvie Wilkinson and Steven Agee, issued a stinging dissent to the full court decision. They pointed out that the court's action represented "a stark interference with South Carolina's electoral process right in the middle of the election season" and that the plaintiffs who sued had "a legally unsupportable case."[21]

Wilkinson and Agee added that under Article I, Section 4, Clause 1, the "Constitution makes it clear that the principal responsibility for setting the ground rules for elections lies with the state legislatures." Thus, the Constitution "provides States—not unelected federal judges—the ability to choose among many permissible options when designing elections."

Childs's decision, they said, "upends this whole structure and turns its back upon our federalist system."

Wilkinson, appointed by Ronald Reagan, and Agee, appointed by George W. Bush, also criticized their fellow judges on the Fourth Circuit for reinstating Childs's injunction, saying that their "disregard for the Supreme Court is palpable." The Supreme Court, they said, "has repeatedly cautioned us not to interfere with state election laws in the 'weeks before an election.'" According to Wilkinson and Agee, the "pandemic does not give judges 'a roving commission to rewrite state election codes.'"[22]

In fact, requiring the signature of a witness on an absentee ballot is "commonplace and eminently sensible." The two judges said it is "designed to combat voter fraud, a fight which 'the State indisputably has a compelling interest' in winning." Wilkinson and Agee clearly were surprised by Childs's suggestion, often repeated by the mainstream media, that South Carolina's "interest in preventing voter fraud" was "not legitimate" because there is "an utter dearth of absentee voter fraud." As Wilkinson and Agee pointed out in their dissent: "Just last year, the election in North Carolina's 9th Congressional District was overturned on the basis of absentee ballot fraud."[23]

But South Carolina was "not required to produce evidence of voter fraud to demonstrate it has a legitimate interest in maintaining the integrity of its elections" since the Supreme Court "has *repeatedly* held that a State 'indisputably has a compelling interest' in combatting voter fraud."

The two dissenting judges also noted "all the areas in which law requires witnesses and notaries to inspire trust in official documents and acts and to convey their authenticity." Therefore, they wrote, it is "unsurprising that the courts of appeal have resisted overturning these laws," citing cases from other federal appeals courts.

Wilkinson and Agee also said that all three branches of South Carolina's government "have addressed whether absentee voters should be required to have a witness," and all have answered in the affirmative. Yet, they wrote, a federal district judge and the Fourth Circuit had taken it upon themselves to overturn those decisions:

> No member of our Court now holds elected office, much less an elected or appointed office of the State of South Carolina. By

substituting its own policy choice for that of the representatives of the Palmetto State, the district court's injunction robs South Carolina of its sovereign prerogative to determine the rules for its elections.[24]

To show how bogus the claim was that COVID justified getting rid of the witness signature requirement for absentee ballots, South Carolina produced testimony from the director of the infectious diseases division of the Medical University of South Carolina. She said that the witness requirement did not "pose a significant risk" because "it takes little time and can be done with facemasks, social distancing, and proper hygiene."[25]

Finally, Wilkinson and Agee pointed out a stark truth about the unprecedented number of lawsuits filed in 2020 trying to overturn laws governing the election process and the danger they pose to the judiciary. In concluding that the injunction was "not in the public interest," they said it appeared "more and more" that

political parties seem to be bringing these election law challenges in an effort to gain partisan advantage. This trend is deeply disturbing. Selective interventions by the courts in these cases will create the appearance of partisanship. They undermine our most valued asset, the public's trust and confidence in the judiciary. They also create confusion and make it more difficult for the States to run their elections.[26]

With that conclusion, Wilkinson and Agee accurately summarized the tactics employed by the left in 2020 with the seemingly endless number of lawsuits filed against states officials.

States like Wisconsin, Indiana, Alabama, and South Carolina were successful in resisting these meritless lawsuits and defending their election laws by spending substantial time and money in contentious court battles, overcoming many poor decisions by liberal federal judges. But other states were not as successful. Others had partisan government officials who engaged in collusive litigation, in which state officials used lawsuits filed by their friends and political allies to subvert laws implemented by state legislatures that they did not like or that were passed by their political opposition.

Once a lawsuit is filed in collusive litigation, the relevant state officials, rather than defending the state law, will agree to a settlement giving the plaintiffs everything they want and enter what is called a "consent decree" with the court. This process avoids litigation (and the usual fact-finding), makes the new rules enforceable with regular legal procedures and keeps the legislature and other parts of the state government out of the decision making.

That is what happened in another North Carolina case, where the liberal Fourth Circuit Court of Appeals refused to stay a six-day extension during which mail-in ballots could be received and counted by election officials.[27] This extension was the result of a state court consent decree entered into by the North Carolina Alliance for Retired Americans, a liberal group headquartered in Washington, DC, and affiliated with the AFL-CIO,[28] and the North Carolina Board of Elections, which is controlled by Democrats. A lower court judge, William J. Osteen, found that the board had "secretly" negotiated the settlement without consulting the legislature, which was controlled by Republicans, and "showed little or no interest" in defending state law against the lawsuit.[29]

Judge James A. Wynn, another Obama appointee, wrote the opinion for the entire Fourth Circuit upholding the extension of the absentee ballot deadline over the vigorous dissent (once again) of Judges J. Harvie Wilkinson III and G. Steven Agee as well as Paul Niemeyer. The dissenters pointed out that "we are faced with nonrepresentative entities changing election law immediately preceding or during a federal election. In making those changes, they have undone the work of the elected state legislatures, to which the Constitution clearly and explicitly delegates the power to prescribe the times, places, and manner of holding elections."[30]

In a scathing rebuke of their fellow judges on the Fourth Circuit, they said that "Whether it is a federal court...or a state election board—as it is here—does not matter; both are unaccountable entities stripping power from the legislatures. They are changing the rules of the game in the middle of an election— exactly what *Purcell*...counsels against." In fact, the Fourth Circuit majority was changing the rules when "well over 1,000,000" North Carolinians had already voted.[31]

The dissenters once again warned that the action of the federal appeals court "disrespects the Supreme Court's repeated and clear command not to interfere so late in the day. This pernicious pattern is making the courts appear partisan, destabilizing federal elections, and undermining the power of the people to choose representatives to set election rules."[32] Inexplicably, however, unlike with the South Carolina and Alabama cases, Chief Justice John Roberts refused to accept an appeal of this erroneous decision by the Fourth Circuit that allowed a collusive settlement abrogating state law to stay in place.[33]

Justices Clarence Thomas, Neil Gorsuch, and Samuel Alito would have granted the appeal. Gorsuch was clearly dismayed by the refusal of the chief justice to accept the case, saying that this case was even more "egregious" than other election cases that were coming before the Supreme Court, "given that a state court and the [Election] Board worked together to override a carefully tailored legislative response to COVID. Indeed, the president *pro tempore* of the North Carolina Senate and the speaker of its House of Representatives have intervened on behalf of the General Assembly to oppose revisions to its work."

The same type of collusive litigation happened in Minnesota.

There, as in North Carolina, Steve Simon, the Minnesota secretary of state and a former Democratic state legislator, entered into a consent decree with liberal groups to settle a state court lawsuit, agreeing that he would not enforce Minnesota's statutorily mandated absentee ballot receipt deadline of 8:00 P.M. on Election Day, November 3, 2020. Instead, election officials would count ballots postmarked by November 3 if they were received within a week of Election Day. Again, there was no possible COVID-19 justification for simply changing the deadline set by the state legislature.

Two Republican Party presidential electors sued in federal court, challenging the collusive consent decree and the state court order approving it and claiming it was unconstitutional. However, a federal district court dismissed their lawsuit, saying the electors did not have standing or the ability to pursue these claims in federal court because they had not been injured by the change in election procedures.[34] This was a bizarre claim and legally wrong given that it is presidential electors who are elected by voters when they cast ballots, not the presidential candidates themselves. Fortunately, the Eighth Circuit U.S. Court of Appeals agreed and reversed the district court's mistaken opinion.[35]

In Michigan, the state court of appeals turned back an attempt by liberal organizations to extend the deadline for the receipt of absentee ballots. Only two weeks before the election, the appeals court overruled a lower Michigan court judge who was ordering the state to accept mail-in ballots up to fourteen days *after* Election Day as well as telling the state it was prohibited from enforcing its laws relating to who, other than the voter, could handle and deliver his or her ballot. The appeals court made clear that "designing adjustments to our election integrity laws is the responsibility of our elected policymakers, not the judiciary."[36]

In fact, the court said:

> Our legislature has addressed the expected increase in [absentee] voter ballots by empowering clerks to begin processing [absentee] voter ballots earlier in an effort to provide a final vote tally after polls close for the 2020 election....
>
> While plaintiffs may view these efforts as inadequate first steps, there is no reason to believe that these specific efforts are constitutionally required, even in the midst of a pandemic.
>
> Instead, they reflect the proper 'exercise of discretion, the marshaling and allocation of resources, and the confrontation of thorny policy issues' that the people have reserved exclusively for our Legislative and Executive branches to exercise.

Besides the union front organization that was the lead plaintiff, one of the others was the A. Phillip Randolph Institute. This is the same far-left organization that lost a 2018 Supreme Court decision in which it tried to prevent Ohio from cleaning up its voter registration list by removing individuals who had died or moved out of the state.[37] Its participation in the 2020 litigation reveals what this lawsuit was really about, which had nothing to do with responding to the pandemic and everything to do with weakening the security rules governing absentee ballots.

Unfortunately, a directive severely limiting the effectiveness of signature comparison on absentee ballots that was issued just prior to the 2020 election by Michigan's secretary of state, Jocelyn Benson, was not found invalid until March 2021, long after the election. Benson, who in our opinion may be one of the worst and most partisan secretaries in the country, ordered local clerks to "presume" that the signatures on absentee ballots and absentee ballot request forms were valid and also to treat the signatures as valid unless there were "multiple, significant and obvious" differences. "Dissimilarities" were to be resolved in favor of the voter "whenever possible." A state judge found that Benson violated state law when she issued this directive, which made it very difficult for election officials to reject absentee ballots that may have had forged voter signatures.[38]

In Iowa, the state supreme court issued a decision in mid-October that brought up the other action that liberals were trying to push: sending out pre-completed, absentee ballot request forms to all registered voters, supposedly because of COVID-19. No one ever adequately explained why this was necessary or why COVID-19 somehow prevented voters from requesting a form if they wanted to vote absentee or from filling it out on their own.

The secretary of state, Paul Pate, directed county officials to only send blank absentee ballot request forms, but three counties were mailing request forms with voter information already printed on the form, including the voter's registered name, registration address, date of birth, and state verification number. The Democratic Senatorial Campaign Committee, the Democratic Congressional Campaign Committee, and the Iowa Democratic Party sued Pate to support the three Iowa counties that were violating his directive. The lower court issued an injunction preventing Pate from enforcing his directive, which the Iowa Supreme Court overturned as an abuse of discretion.[39]

While the state supreme court said that while "reasonable people can disagree on whether sending out blank or prepopulated absentee-ballot request forms is better policy," it was true that "blank forms help ensure that the person submitting the request is the actual voter." The court also held that issuing the directive was within the authority of the secretary of state.[40]

But contrary to the court's comment about "reasonable people," knowledgeable election officials understand that sending out absentee ballot request forms that are already populated with a voter's registration information, rather than requiring the voter to provide that information, cuts out one of the safety protocols for authenticating absentee ballot requests. The court was entirely correct that "blank forms" help ensure it is really the voter filling out the form. The fact that the state Democratic Party and the two major Democratic organizations whose purposes are electing members of the U.S. Senate and House of Representatives were pushing for action that makes fraud easier to commit says everything you need to know.

Democratic-allied groups filed numerous other lawsuits in other states, with mixed results. Probably one of the worst partisan abuses of the election process in terms of state officials changing the law unilaterally without legal authority was in Pennsylvania. They did so with the connivance of The Supreme Court of Pennsylvania, which is dominated by very political, liberal Democrats, who were elected to office in 2015 with their campaigns "fueled by cash provided largely by organized labor and Philadelphia trial lawyers."[41] And the U.S. Supreme Court refused to do anything about it. More on that in a moment.

In addition to the lawsuits filed by the Democratic Party and its liberal allies to persuade courts to change election rules and the collusive settlements of some of these cases, there were unilateral actions by partisan officials in the executive branch of state governments that violated the U.S. Constitution as well as state laws.

Probably the best and most succinct description of this parade of events is contained in the well-written and well-researched motion and complaint that Texas attempted to file with the Supreme Court on Dec. 8, 2020, against Pennsylvania, Georgia, Michigan, and Wisconsin over their "rampant lawlessness." Texas was asking the court for permission to file the lawsuit and issue an order that would temporarily prevent those states from certifying their election results. Under applicable Supreme Court rules, a state suing another state first must receive permission from the court.[42]

Unfortunately for the rule of law and the administration of elections as directed by the U.S. Constitution, the court dodged what might have been one of the most politically volatile but vitally important cases it has ever handled. It issued what we believe was an unjustified opinion on Dec. 11 refusing to give Texas permission to file the lawsuit, claiming Texas had no standing and no "judicially cognizable interest" in how other states conducted their elections.[43] This despite the fact that numerous other states filed amicus briefs supporting the claims made by Texas, including Missouri, Alabama, Arkansas, Florida, Indiana, Kansas, Louisiana, Mississippi, Montana, Nebraska, North Dakota, Oklahoma, South Carolina, South Dakota, Tennessee, Utah, and West Virginia.

It is important to note that under the Electors Clause of the Constitution, Art. II, Sec. 1, Clause 2, state legislatures, not state governments in general, are given the specific authority to decide how presidential electors will be appointed.[44] Thus, it is state legislatures that have the sole power to establish the laws for how a presidential election will be conducted in their states, not the governor, not the secretary of state, not a state or local board of elections, and not state courts. State courts can interpret how the laws should be applied but cannot simply override, change, or amend the law because they disagree with the policies implemented by the state legislatures. Yet that is exactly what happened in the four states Texas tried to sue.

As Texas summarized in its complaint:

- In Pennsylvania, the Democratic Secretary of State Kathy Boockvar "unilaterally abrogated several Pennsylvania statutes requiring signature verification for absentee ballots," then quickly settled a lawsuit filed by the League of Women Voters (which is a very partisan organization these days) that claimed signature verification was unlawful. In the settlement, Boockvar claimed that state law did not allow absentee ballots to be rejected based on "signature analysis" by boards of elections, a statement that was categorically untrue. In essence, Boockvar enabled election fraud with absentee ballots in Pennsylvania.

Then the Democratic-controlled state supreme court stepped in. Despite the fact that state law clearly and unambiguously sets 8:00 P.M. on Election Day as the deadline for the receipt of absentee ballots, the Pennsylvania court in a supreme act of judicial arrogance extended the deadline to three days *after* Election Day in a case filed by the Pennsylvania Democratic Party.[45] And it ordered that "even non-postmarked ballots were presumptively timely."[46] Their justification? A provision of the state constitution that says that "Elections shall be free and equal." No, really that is the legal excuse the Democratic judges on the court gave.

On Oct. 19, 2020, an evenly divided Supreme Court deadlocked 4–4 and refused an emergency request for a stay filed by the Republican Party of Pennsylvania and state legislators, with Chief Justice John Roberts joining the liberals on the court to deny the appeal.[47]

On Oct. 28, it happened again when an appeal was filed on the merits, and the court again refused to take the case.[48] Samuel Alito, joined by Justices Thomas and Gorsuch, criticized the court for its mishandling "the important constitutional issue raised by this matter" that "has needlessly created conditions that could lead to serious post-election problems." Alito added that this issue had "national importance" and that there was a "strong possibility" that what the state supreme court did "violates the Federal Constitution."

As if all of this were not enough, Secretary of State Boockvar also told election officials to start opening absentee ballots prior to Election Day, which is not allowed under state law, so that officials could contact voters to give them a chance to "cure" any defects, even though state law does not provide for any such cure process. Election officials in Democratic counties like Philadelphia and Allegheny took advantage of this, while election officials in other areas refused to violate state law. And election officials in both Philadelphia and Allegheny County also illegally blocked observers from being able to observe the processing of these absentee ballots. All of this resulted in absentee ballots being, according to Texas, "evaluated under an illegal standard regarding signature verification," with voters in certain parts of the state (Democratic strongholds) being given the ability to cure absentee ballots that should have been rejected and absentee ballots being counted that also should have been rejected because they were received late.

- In Georgia, Secretary of State Brad Raffensperger agreed to settle a lawsuit filed by the Democratic Party of Georgia in March 2020 without putting up any real defense. Without the approval of the state legislature, he agreed to change the signature verification requirement on absentee ballots required by state law, making it much more difficult for election officials to reject an absentee ballot when the signature did not match. The settlement agreement, said Texas, even included requiring state election officials to issue "guidance and training materials drafted by an expert retained by the Democratic Party of Georgia" on this unilateral and unauthorized change to state law. Texas said this benefited Joe Biden since he "had almost double the number of absentee ballots" as President Trump.[49]

- In Michigan, Secretary of State Jocelyn Benson sent absentee ballot request forms to all registered voters even though she had no authority to do so under state law. Additionally, in violation of state law, she allowed voters to request absentee ballots online without a signature, resulting in the "dissemination" of millions of absentee ballots "in violation of Michigan's statutory signature-verification requirements." Local election officials in one large Democratic stronghold, Wayne County, which includes Detroit, even went so far as to ignore the signature verification requirement for completed absentee ballots received from voters. As Texas said, these unauthorized changes to Michigan's election statutes "resulted in a number of constitutionally tainted votes that far exceeds the margin of voters separating the candidates in Michigan."[50]

- In Wisconsin, the Wisconsin Election Commission and the mayors of Democratic strongholds Green Bay, Kenosha, Madison, Milwaukee, and Racine, in violation of state law, "undertook a campaign to position hundreds of drop boxes to collect absentee ballots" that were unmanned and unsecured. Wisconsin law requires that absentee ballots can only be mailed back or delivered in person to the local clerk, and state law specifies that absentee ballots returned any other way "may not be counted." Furthermore, the commission and local officials also encouraged voters to falsely assert they were "indefinitely confined," an exception to Wisconsin's statutory ID and signature requirement for absentee ballots that requires a voter to be hospitalized or disabled due to illness.[51]

As Texas pointedly concluded:

Using the COVID-19 pandemic as a justification, government officials in the defendant states...usurped their legislatures' authority
and unconstitutionally revised their state's election statutes. They
accomplished these statutory revisions through executive fiat or
friendly lawsuits, thereby weakening ballot integrity. Finally, these
same government officials flooded the Defendant States with
millions of ballots to be sent through the mails, or placed in drop
boxes, with little or no chain of custody and, at the same time,
weakened the strongest security measures protecting the integrity
of the vote—signature verification and witness requirements.[52]

What Texas correctly argued was that "non-legislative actors"
amended "duly enacted" state election laws in violation of the
Electors Clause. This violation resulted in "intrastate differences
in the treatment of voters, with more favorable [treatment] allot-
ted to voters...in areas administered by local government under
Democrat control with populations with higher ratios of Democrat votes than other areas of Defendant States." When combined
with the "appearance of voting irregularities...consistent with
the unconstitutional relaxation of ballot-integrity protections,"
it diminished the value of the votes of the citizens of Texas and
other states and may have unlawfully changed the outcome of
the election.[53] Yet the Supreme Court refused to allow Texas to
file its lawsuit.

The one case remaining at the U.S. Supreme Court after the
Texas filing was dismissed was the Pennsylvania case, which had
been refiled in the court after the 2020 election. Yet on Feb. 22,
2021, the Supreme Court rejected the appeal for the third and final
time and refused to do anything to stop the unilateral changes in
Pennsylvania election law made before the November 2020 elec-

tion in violation of the U.S. Constitution.[54] The only dissenting justice was Clarence Thomas. As he pointed out,

> The Constitution gives to each state legislature authority to determine the "Manner" of federal elections. Yet both before and after the 2020 election, nonlegislative officials in various States took it upon themselves to set the rules instead.... That decision to rewrite the rules [in Pennsylvania by the state supreme court] seems to have affected too few ballots to change the outcome of any federal election. But that may not be the case in the future. These cases provide us with an ideal opportunity to address just what authority nonlegislative officials have to set election rules, and to do so well before the next election cycle. *The refusal to do so is inexplicable.*[55]

One important point that Justice Thomas noted is that a change made by the Pennsylvania Supreme Court after Election Day in another case *had* altered an election result. The state supreme court, again without any legal authority to do so, nullified a state law requirement that a voter write the date on their mail-in ballots:

> According to public reports, one candidate for a state senate seat claimed victory under what she contended was the legislative rule that dates must be included on the ballots. A federal court noted that this candidate would win by 93 votes under that rule...A second candidate claimed victory under the contrary rule announced by the Pennsylvania Supreme Court. He was seated.[56]

It probably comes as no surprise that the candidate who was declared the winner in that Pennsylvania state senate race under the rule created by the state supreme court out of its fertile imagination was a Democrat, James Brewster. The candidate who lost but would have won under the applicable state law before the court unilaterally voided it was a Republican, Nicole Ziccarelli.

Thomas's dissent foretells a problematic future in the election realm. As he concluded, what happened in 2020

> is not a prescription for confidence. Changing the rules in the middle of the game is bad enough. Such rule changes by officials who may lack authority to do so is even worse. When those changes alter election results, they can severely damage the electoral system on which our self-governance so heavily depends. If state officials have the authority they have claimed, we need to make that clear. If not, we need to put an end to this practice now before the consequences become catastrophic.[57]

We can expect liberals to work even harder in future elections to change the rules to make it easier to cheat and easier to manipulate election results. That is what they tried to do, with some success, in the 2020 election. We should expect them to do it through legislation, litigation, and unconstitutional, unilateral executive actions by their political allies in state government. The results may be, as Justice Thomas said, catastrophic to the integrity and security of the election process.

# THE MEDIA AND PRESIDENT'S TRUMP PRESIDENTIAL ADVISORY COMMISSION ON ELECTION INTEGRITY

One of the biggest problems in the area of election integrity is the constant attacks by the "mainstream" media, which the late Rush Limbaugh more accurately termed the leftstream media, on anyone (including the authors) who attempts to expose election fraud or make efforts to remedy the vulnerabilities in the registration and voting process that make fraud possible.

The media has become a propaganda machine that pushes the false premise of the progressive left's leadership that election fraud does not exist and that any attempts to implement reforms are unnecessary and intended only to "restrict" the ability to vote. Even the supposedly nonpartisan Associated Press (AP), which now disguises its opinion commentaries as news articles, has joined the left's propaganda machine, falsely claiming that election reforms proposed by Republicans are a "campaign to place new restrictions" on voting.[1] That is no surprise since, according to the AP itself, its "coverage of voting rights" is funded by "the Carnegie Corporation of New York," which for years has been funding left-wing advocacy organizations that fight election reforms and deny the existence of election fraud.[2]

The media's attitude today is quite a contrast from what it used to be. The *Miami Herald*, for example, as we explain in our chapter on absentee ballot fraud, won a Pulitzer Prize in 1999 for its extensive investigation into the 1997 Miami mayor's race that uncovered widespread fraud. The *New York Times*, which today routinely asserts that "voter fraud is extremely rare,"[3] had quite a different attitude in 1984 when it reported on a wide-ranging New York City election fraud conspiracy that had successfully cast thousands of fraudulent ballots for fourteen years. The title of its story then was "Boss Tweed Is Gone, But Not His Vote," a reference to one of the most infamous vote-stealing machines in American history, rivaled only by Mayor Richard Daley of Chicago.[4]

The *New York Times* has gone so far down the road of irrationality when it comes to this issue that it actually published an article claiming that a law passed in Arizona's 2021 legislative session was a "voting restriction" that rolls "back access to voting." The bill it attacked "requires the secretary of state to compare death records with voter registrations," according to the *Times*.[5] Apparently, "rolling back access" for the ability of people who are dead to vote is now a "voting restriction." If this were not such a serious topic, it would be laughable.

Quin Hillyer, a columnist for the *Washington Examiner* and a former editor at the *Washington Times*, points out the fantasyland that the *New York Times* lives in. A staffer for the newspaper, David Leonhardt, "sneered" (according to Hillyer) in April 2021 that "there is no reason to believe [voter fraud] has determined the outcome of a single U.S. election in decades." Hillyer was flabbergasted that Leonhardt could make such an easily disprovable claim.[6] Hillyer gave just a brief listing of recent elections that had been overturned due to fraud. It included several elections in North Carolina in 2013, 2016, and 2018; in Mississippi in 2021;

and numerous other races in Alabama, California, Louisiana, New Jersey, and Georgia. As Hillyer said, "the narrative-obsessed media can't admit" that election fraud exists or that it has changed election outcomes.

The propagandists of the left include former President Barack Obama, former Secretary of State Hillary Clinton, and former Attorney General Eric Holder, who have created a false hue and cry about a supposed loss of voting rights in recent years.[7] They claim that the support of state legislatures and particularly Republicans, including former Pres. Donald Trump, for reforms intended to improve integrity and stop election fraud amounts to widespread, systemic "voter suppression" of minority voters.

The progressive left seems to label almost any election rule or regulation they dislike as "voter suppression." That includes voter ID laws, not counting ballots cast outside an assigned precinct, any steps taken by states to maintain the accuracy of voter registration rolls by removing ineligible voters, and even the requirement that has been in place for decades in the overwhelming majority of states that requires an individual to register prior to election day. According to the founder of iVote, a partisan "advocacy group that campaigns to elect Democratic secretaries of state," "voter registration itself is a voter-suppression tool."[8]

In fact, there is no "voter suppression" epidemic, as demonstrated by, among other things, the enforcement record of the Voting Section of the Civil Rights Division of the U.S. Department of Justice. The Civil Rights Division is responsible for enforcing all federal voting rights laws such as the Voting Rights Act that prohibit discrimination, intimidation, and other efforts intended to prevent individuals from voting as well as federal requirements imposed on the states for offering voter registration opportunities and maintaining those records' accuracy.

These new state regulations and laws addressing the security of our elections, such as requiring voter identification or participation in programs that compare state voter registration lists, cannot be validly termed "voter suppression." They comply with existing federal voting laws, and there is overwhelming evidence that such reforms have not hurt turnout or prevented eligible individuals from being able to vote. Moreover, the Justice Department has seen a steady *decrease* in the number of voting discrimination enforcement cases, even during the Obama administration, due to decreasing violations of federal law.

The Bush administration, which was constantly accused of not enforcing federal voting rights law by left-wing organizations, filed sixteen cases to enforce Section 2 of the Voting Rights Act, which prohibits racial discrimination in the voting context. By contrast, the Obama administration, despite all its fabricated bombast about "voter suppression," filed only four cases to enforce Section 2 in its entire eight years in office.[9] If there really was a wave of "voter suppression" as claimed, why did the Obama Justice Department not file dozens of enforcement cases against all the states that were supposedly suppressing votes? The answer is obvious.

"Voter suppression" is not even a legitimate, defined legal term under the statutes that protect voters, including the Voting Rights Act and the National Voter Registration Act of 1993.[10] It is a faux term artificially created to unfairly condemn any election reform with which critics disagree, including perfectly legal reforms. The term is a linguistic trick designed to lump reasonable, legal, and common-sense actions by states meant to safeguard the integrity of the election process with illegal activities like poll taxes and literacy tests, thereby tainting the legal actions taken by states to protect voters and elections.

The critics of these reform efforts allege that maintaining

accurate voter registration rolls to ensure that only eligible individuals cast ballots, prosecuting actual cases of election fraud, and implementing basic security reforms such as voter identification requirements that the American people overwhelmingly support is somehow "voter suppression." Nothing could be further from the truth. They even falsely label it as a new form of "Jim Crow," a patronizingly race-baiting and dishonest categorization that trivializes and insults Americans who actually suffered under the real Jim Crow laws of the last century.

Michael Lancaster, the Georgia state director of the Frederick Douglass Foundation, responded to the claims by Pres. Joe Biden and others that the election reforms passed by the Georgia legislature in 2021, which included extending the state's in-person voter ID requirement to absentee ballots, were Jim Crow 2.0. Lancaster said that a "civil debate about voting rights is an important conversation to have, but comparing Georgia's election reform legislation to Jim Crow is insulting to my Black ancestors who suffered those dehumanizing segregation laws.[11] He added that "comparing absentee ballot changes and ID requirements to banning Black people from restaurants and drinking fountains is absurd." Similarly, Wilfred Reilly, an associate political science professor at historically black Kentucky State University, said the "Jim Crow claim passes through 'nonsensical' into offensiveness."[12]

The claim that voter ID laws are all "aimed at disenfranchising Black voters" is an especially pernicious lie that is constantly repeated by the media and Democratic lawyers and activists like Marc Elias, the lawyer for the Democratic National Committee and many other Democratic and liberal organizations.[13] This despite the fact that such laws have now been in place for more than a decade. And not only have they not suppressed any votes, turnout of voters, including minority voters, increased in states after their ID laws became effective.

Georgia, which was the target of so many vicious lies about its 2021 election reform legislation,[14] is a good example of that. Georgia's requirement that anyone voting in person provide a government or tribal-issued photo ID became effective in the 2008 presidential election. But from the criticism launched against its 2021 election reform legislation that extended the ID requirement to absentee ballots, you would have thought the state had legalized racially segregated water fountains and lynching. The media totally ignored the actual language of the amendment as well as the turnout evidence from ten years of the state's experience with voter ID that totally disproves the voter suppression claims.

When a federal judge threw out the lawsuit filed by Common Cause, the NAACP, and a host of other so-called civil rights organizations against the ID law in 2007 (amid similar "Jim Crow" comparisons), he specifically noted that in two years of litigation, the challengers could not produce a single resident of the state who would be unable to vote because of the new ID requirement.[15] The ID law included providing a free photo ID to anyone who does not already have one.

So what happened in the 2008 presidential election when the ID requirement was implemented for the first time? The turnout of black residents of Georgia increased 42 percent over the turnout in the 2004 presidential election! The turnout of Hispanics increased by a whopping 140 percent, while the turnout of white voters only increased by 8 percent.[16]

In the 2010 congressional elections, the turnout of black Georgians increased by 44.2 percent over the 2006 congressional elections. Hispanic turnout went up 66.5 percent, and white turnout went up 11.7 percent. The same advocates who lost their lawsuit against the ID law had claimed there were hundreds of thousands of Georgians who would be unable to vote because they did not have an ID. So how many Georgians applied for the free ID provided by the state? In 2009, only 2,473 individuals applied for (and received) the free ID, representing 0.05 percent of the over 5 million registered voters in Georgia.[17]

Other states that have implemented ID laws have had similar results. In 2019, the National Bureau of Economic Research released a study on what the researchers termed "strict" voter ID requirements that reviewed turnout across the nation from 2008 to 2018. Its conclusion? That "strict ID laws have no significant negative effect on registration or turnout, overall or for any subgroups defined by age, gender, race, or party affiliation."[18] In other words, the whole "voter suppression" claim constantly repeated by the media is a total myth.

And the heated criticism of the Georgia extension to absentee ballots? The new law does not even require voters to provide a photocopy of their ID. Instead, the voter can simply write "the number of his or her Georgia driver's license or identification card" on the application for the absentee ballot. Moreover, if the voter does not have such a Georgia ID card, she can "provide a copy of a form of identification listed" in another code section of Georgia law. That code section says you can satisfy the ID requirement with a "copy of a current utility bill, bank statement, government check, paycheck, or other government document that shows the name and address of such elector."[19]

Now, where do you think the Georgia Legislature got that language? It got it from federal law, the Help America Vote Act of 2002.

Section 303(b) of that law requires an individual who registered to vote by mail and who is voting for the first time in a federal election (whether in person or by mail) to provide "a copy of a current utility bill, bank statement, government check, paycheck, or other government document that show the name and address of the voter" if he doesn't have a "current and valid photo identification."[20] The language on voter IDs for absentee ballots in the new Georgia law is thus identical to the language in federal law, promulgated through the Help America Vote Act.

Guess who voted to approve this federal law in 2002? Why, then-Sen. Joe Biden of Delaware, who as president called the new Georgia law "un-American" and "sick, sick."[21] In fact, the vote approving the Help American Vote Act was 92 to 2 in the Senate, and included in the "yes" votes were Sens. Dianne Feinstein (D-Calif.), Dick Durbin (D-Ill.), Harry Reid (D-Nev.), and Patrick Leahy (D-Vt.). Yet not a single reporter mentioned in their coverage of the Georgia reform bill that Joe Biden had voted for an "un-American" voting requirement in 2002.

Another provision in the Georgia reform package that was hysterically and deceitfully attacked was one that critics claimed was intended to prevent voters standing in line from being given water. Pres. Biden said this was a "punitive" measure "design[ed] to keep people from voting."[22] This was totally untrue.

Like almost every state, Georgia prohibits electioneering inside or within 150 feet of a polling place or within 25 feet of any voters waiting in line to vote. The prior law prohibited the solicitation of "votes in any manner or by any means or method, nor shall any person distribute or display any campaign material" within such distances.[23]

Section 33 of the new bill simply added "nor shall any person give, offer to give, or participate in the giving of any money or gift, including, but not limited to, food and drink, to any elector" within such distances.

In other words, a candidate and his campaign staffers cannot show up at a polling place with a truckload of pizzas and sodas and start giving them to voters standing in line. The clear intent here is to prevent campaigns, candidates, and political operatives from unduly influencing or bribing voters with money or gifts, including food and drink. A Democratic candidate for the state house, Matthew Wilson, was accused of doing exactly that in 2018 at a polling place in north Atlanta, handing out pizzas to voters waiting in line to vote.[24]

Similarly, federal law also prohibits paying or offering to pay anyone to register to vote or to vote. In fact, this ban was part of the original Voting Rights Act of 1965.[25] According to the U.S. Justice Department's handbook on "Federal Prosecution of Election Offenses," this statute has been broadly interpreted to apply to "anything having monetary value, including cash, liquor, lottery chances, and welfare benefits such as food stamps."[26] Moreover, New York, a blue state, has a similar provision that bans giving voters "any meat, drink, tobacco, refreshment or provision."[27]

The idea that Georgia is somehow doing something nefarious by preventing gift giving at the polls is bizarre, and it ignores the unfortunate, long history of this type of corruption and undue influence being used in our elections. Unmentioned in the hysterical criticisms is new language making it OK for poll officials to make "self-service water from an unattended receptacle" available to "an elector waiting in line."

Even Reuters, which like the Associated Press is simply supposed to report the news instead of editorializing, has joined in spreading the left's false narrative on election fraud and election reform. In September 2020 just before the November election, Reuters published a three-thousand-word hit piece written by Simon Lewis and Joseph Tanfani going after those who raise concerns about election fraud, including one of the authors (von Spakovsky); J. Christian Adams, the president and general counsel of the Public Interest Legal Foundation; Christopher Coates, a voting rights lawyer with an outstanding record who works with Judicial Watch; and Cleta Mitchell, a prominent Washington, D.C. lawyer.[28]

Mitchell was driven out of her law firm, Foley Lardner, where she was a partner, after the 2020 election for doing what lawyers are supposed to do: vigorously representing their clients. But because her client was Donald Trump, that was apparently considered unacceptable. You can represent terrorists at Guantanamo Bay who killed Americans and be honored for your work, but represent a former president hated by the media and liberal establishment in an election case, and you are supposed to be blacklisted. John Eastman, a constitutional scholar and distinguished law professor—the former dean of the law school no less—was also forced out of Chapman University School of Law.[29]

Democratic Michigan Governor Gretchen Whitmer, Michigan Attorney General Dana Nessel, and Michigan Secretary of State Jocelyn Benson—probably three of the most partisan elected officials in the country—actually filed a grievance with the Michigan Bar Association requesting that three Michigan lawyers who represented Donald Trump's presidential campaign be disbarred. In response to this revenge tactic by the Democratic political establishment, one of the targeted lawyers, Greg Rohl, called it a "witch hunt run amok" and leveled the accusation that the attempt to censure him and his colleagues "is reminiscent of the dark age of Nazi Germany."[30]

The Reuters hit piece was riddled with errors, but what it *did not* mention was just as telling. For example, it raised the alarm that a network" of "right-wing donors" gave a handful of conservative groups about $6.5 million to support election integrity and election reform efforts but failed to mention that left-wing donors gave scores of radical liberal groups $600 million to *attack* state election integrity laws.[31]

As for what Reuters got wrong, the story started by repeating a false claim that the presidential advisory panel commissioned by Pres. Trump to research problems in our election system "disbanded after less than a year without finding evidence of significant fraud."

Here is what really happened. On May 11, 2017, Pres. Trump issued an executive order establishing the bipartisan Presidential Advisory Commission on Election Integrity.[32] Its purpose, as outlined in the executive order, was to "study the registration and voting process used in Federal elections" and to identify "those laws, rules, policies, activities, strategies, and practices" that "undermine" and "enhance the American people's confidence in the integrity of the voting processes." The commission was also directed to identify "those vulnerabilities...that could lead to improper voter registration and improper voting, including fraudulent voter registrations and fraudulent voting."

All of this sounds very innocuous, like a logical, reasonable effort to prepare a report that determines what problems, if any, exist in our registration, voting, and election system and to recommend solutions. Pres. Barack Obama appointed a similar bipartisan commission, the Presidential Commission on Election Administration, to identify best practices in election administration and make recommendations to improve the voting experience, very similar to the stated objectives of the Trump commission. Obama's commission presented him with a report in 2014. Among its recommendations was "having all states update and exchange their voter registration lists to create the most accurate lists possible to increase registration rates, reduce costs, and protect against fraud."[33]

The reaction by the media and left-wing advocacy groups was as if the Trump commission were the coming of the Antichrist. Keep in mind that a presidential commission has no executive authority; all it can do is study a problem and make recommendations. Yet the media world was immediately filled with claims that the work of the commission would be "used to suppress the vote."[34] The ACLU called on all "Governors and Secretaries of State to refuse" to cooperate with the commission, particularly with respect to any request from the commission for voter registration information from each state that could be used to establish the extent of multiple registrations as well as registrations by ineligible individuals like aliens.

Unfortunately, numerous states followed that lead and refused to provide the commission with any information or data, including voter registration information that almost all states routinely provide to political parties, candidates, and third-party organizations. Among those refusing to cooperate was then-Gov. Terry McAuliffe (D) of Virginia (and former head of the Democratic National Committee), who bizarrely claimed that providing information for research was "a tool to commit large-scale suppression."[35] McAuliffe did that despite the fact that Virginia's Department of Elections provides its voter registration list and voter history to candidates, political parties, political action committees, nonprofit organizations that "promote voter participation and voter registration," and "members of the public seeking to promote voter participation and registration."[36]

People For the American Way was so scared of what this commission might find that it paid several hundred thousand dollars for a full-page ad in the July 23, 2017, Sunday edition of the *New York Times* attacking the commission and four of its members: then-Kansas Secretary of State Kris Kobach, former Ohio Secretary of State Ken Blackwell, J. Christian Adams, and Hans von Spakovsky.[37] The ad made one false, defamatory claim after another about each of the commission members and urged readers to not "let these extremists get away with un-American voter suppression." The result of this polemical attack was that each of these commission members started receiving a flood of hate mail and threats, which was clearly the intent behind the ad.

Even more damaging to the work of the commission was the fact that radical advocacy groups like the ACLU immediately filed nearly a dozen meritless lawsuits to keep the commission from operating. They did not want anyone even talking about election fraud much less looking for it or reporting on the problems in our election system. They were helped in their efforts by certain members of the commission like then-Maine Secretary of State Matt Dunlap (D), who began trying to undermine the commission from the day he was appointed. He actually sued the commission and issued his own "report" claiming the commission found no evidence of voter fraud.[38]

The commission was dissolved by another presidential order on Jan. 3, 2018, after holding only two hearings, not because it failed to find anything but because it never had the chance to conduct any kind of investigation due to a lack of cooperation from states and the left's lawfare, which ate up all the time of the small staff assigned to the commission.[39] No research was done and no report was issued because the commission never got any of the data it requested from the states. Yet one media source after another, including the AP, PBS, and the *Los Angeles Times*, published totally false stories claiming the commission found no widespread fraud.[40]

Other misrepresentations in the Reuters piece were almost comical, such as calling the uber-leftist Brennan Center "nonpartisan." And then there was the reporters' decision to give Ike Brown a platform.

If you do not know Brown, he is the first African American found to have violated the Voting Rights Act of 1965. A law that stopped Jim Crow decades later saw the tables turned when Brown blatantly and unapologetically engaged in racial discrimination in a black-majority county in Mississippi to keep whites out of power. Reuters stooped so low as to give this man a platform to call the Justice Department case against him a scam.

Both a Mississippi federal district court and the Fifth Circuit U.S. Court of Appeals ruled that Brown masterminded a racially discriminatory scheme to use vote harvesters to steal votes—from black voters—and to systematically disenfranchise white voters by canceling and voiding their ballots.[41] Brown's behavior was so bad that the federal court stripped him of any role in county elections, but you would not know any of this by reading the Reuters piece.

Reuters mentions The Heritage Foundation's Election Fraud Database, which contains over 1,300 proven cases of fraud, but tried to minimize the problem by comparing that number to the "billions of votes cast" during the period the database covers. Reuters failed to mention, of course, the cautionary note, prominently posted on the database, that it presents only "a sampling of recent proven instances of election fraud."

Using the "billions" comparison is also absurd, although it is constantly used by the election fraud deniers. A single case of fraud may involve several conspirators and hundreds of votes. Moreover, billions of votes are not cast in individual local, county, or state elections. As both the U.S. Supreme Court and the Carter-Baker Commission on Election Reform said, fraud could make a difference in a close election, and it has.

We have close elections all the time, like the congressional race in North Carolina's Ninth District in 2018. It was overturned by the State Board of Elections because of fraud and illegal vote harvesting. It seems that Tanfani and Lewis did not read Reuters's own coverage of that case, in which the margin of victory was only nine hundred votes, since they never mentioned it in their story.

When can we expect a story from Reuters or the Associated Press about how dozens of left-wing groups pour huge amounts of money into pushing the myth of "voter suppression" and opposing every effort and every reform intended to secure the integrity of the election process? Probably about the same time we can expect an unbiased, accurate story about the election fraud that unfortunately happens all too often in our elections, fraud that dilutes and steals the legitimate votes of Americans of every political stripe and color.

## CHAPTER FOUR

# THE TOOL OF CHOICE FOR VOTE THIEVES: ABSENTEE BALLOT FRAUD

N o one disputes the need for absentee or mail-in ballots for people who cannot make it to their neighborhood polling places on Election Day for legitimate reasons, such as being sick, being physically disabled, or serving the country abroad. But changing the U.S. election system to no-fault absentee balloting (where anyone can vote with a mail-in ballot without a reason) or to mail-only elections (where voters are simply mailed ballots and they no longer vote in person) is an unwise and dangerous policy that will make fraud far easier.

The many cases of proven absentee ballot fraud in The Heritage Foundation's Election Fraud Database show that mail-in ballots are susceptible to being stolen, altered, and forged. They make voters vulnerable to being pressured and coerced. In fact, a 1998 report by the Florida Department of Law Enforcement concluded that the "lack of 'in-person, at-the-polls' accountability makes absentee ballots the 'tool of choice' for those inclined to commit voter fraud."[1]

All states have bans on electioneering in and near polling places. In contrast, there are no prohibitions on electioneering in voters' homes.[2] This makes voters vulnerable to intimidation and unlawful "assistance" as well as pressure by candidates, campaign staffers, political party activists, and political consultants—all of whom have a stake in the outcome of the election—to vote in the campaign's interests, not the voter's own. Thus, it also potentially destroys the secrecy of the ballot process, another basic and important hallmark of American elections for more than a century.

This is a particular problem in the twenty-seven states and the District of Columbia that allow vote trafficking (what liberals call "vote harvesting.") Those jurisdictions expressly allow any third party to pick up a completed absentee ballot from the voter and deliver it to election officials.[3]

Vote trafficking is such a common practice in some states that traffickers (or ballot brokers) are paid by campaigns to collect absentee ballots from voters and "even have their own region-specific names. In Florida, they are known as 'boleteros.' In Texas, they're called 'politiqueras.'"[4]

Mail-in ballots certainly make illegal vote-buying easier since the buyer can ensure that the voter is voting the way he is being paid to vote, something that cannot happen in a polling place. This is illustrated by the 2019 conviction of a city council candidate in Hoboken, New Jersey. Frank Raia was convicted for "orchestrating a widespread scheme" that targeted and bribed low-income residents for their absentee ballots in a 2013 election. Sources told a local reporter that "the operation began in 2009, when changes in state law eased requirements for voting by mail. Prior to that a resident needed to provide a reason why they couldn't make it to the poll in order to get an absentee ballot."[5]

To understand the vulnerabilities of absentee or mail-in ballots to fraud and coercion, here are four cases that illustrate many of these issues.[6]

## 1. School Board Election, Fresno County, California, November 5, 1991

California, where vote trafficking is now legal, seems to have forgotten the lessons it should have learned from *Gooch v. Hendrix*, a 1993 decision by the Supreme Court of California.[7] The court in that case overturned the results of consolidated school board elections in Fresno County due to fraud and "tampering" with absentee ballots.[8]

The November 5, 1991, election was for school board positions in one high school and four elementary school districts. In essence, a local political organization, the Fresno chapter of the Black American Political Association of California (BAPAC), took over the voter registration and absentee balloting process, completely controlling the application for, delivery of, completion of, and return of absentee ballots for minority voters. Additionally, a trial court found evidence of "fraud and tampering" with the absentee ballots by BAPAC.

BAPAC had an elaborate strategy orchestrated by Frank Revis, who headed BAPAC's Voter Education Project, to deliver the absentee ballots necessary to win the thirteen seats it had targeted in these school districts. The trial court found out the following:

- BAPAC volunteers and paid staff visited registered and unregistered voters' residences to get them to sign both a voter registration form and an absentee ballot request form under the proviso that BAPAC would deliver those forms to election officials and that the requested ballots would be sent to BAPAC, not to the voter.
- Voters were told to leave blank the part of the absentee ballot request form where it asked for the address to which the absentee ballot should be sent.
- BAPAC took the forms to its headquarters and filled

in the address to which the absentee ballot should be sent—the address for the Voting Education Project, the home residence of Frank Revis.[9]

- When BAPAC received the absentee ballots from election officials, BAPAC staff delivered the ballots to voters' homes.
- Voters were "encouraged to vote in the presence" of the BAPAC vote harvesters, who then collected the completed ballot for delivery to election officials.[10]

Given BAPAC's unsupervised access to all of these absentee ballots, it is unsurprising that the group took advantage of voters who, according to the BAPAC president, were targeted through a "highly selective process."[11] Numerous witnesses testified at a five-day trial about their experiences with BAPAC that illustrate all the problems with and vulnerabilities of the absentee balloting process. The trial included the testimony of the following people:

- A voter who did not sign the absentee ballot request form nor the envelope for the absentee ballot, which had been sent to BAPAC. Her signatures had been forged.
- A voter who was "urged" by a BAPAC solicitor (through a translator) to "sign for the schools" and was told that it was "all right" for his daughter to sign his absentee ballot application.
- Another voter who said that three BAPAC staffers came to his door late at night, "told him for whom to vote," and "were emphatic that he not seal his ballot." They returned to his house when he was not home because he had not signed the ballot and had told his wife "to sign her husband's name for him."

- A voter who was told to sign a "petition for a free breakfast" that was actually an absentee ballot request form. An absentee ballot was later mailed to election officials by BAPAC "ostensibly by him."
- A voter who was visited by a candidate supported by BAPAC along with a BAPAC staffer. The staffer filled out an absentee ballot without the voter's consent, permission, or consultation.[12]

Election officials sent almost 1,300 "requested" absentee ballots to BAPAC, 269 of which were never returned, and BAPAC could not account for what had happened to them. Of the remaining 1,023 ballots, 63 were disqualified for invalid signatures (signatures that did not match voter signatures on file), 93 were disqualified because there "had been fraud and tampering" with those ballots, and the rest were disqualified due to unlawful and illegal conduct by BAPAC, including using its own address for the absentee ballot delivery address instead of voters' addresses.[13]

One of the problems noted by the court, which applies to many election fraud cases, is that "once illegal ballots are cast and comingled with the legal ballots, they cannot be traced to reveal for whom they were cast."[14] In other words, it is impossible to determine which candidate received the illegal votes. But the election ended up being overturned by the California Supreme Court because the "widespread illegal voting practices that permeated this election—including fraud and tampering" with absentee ballots and other "illegal votes affected the outcomes of the consolidated elections."[15]

### 2. Mayoral Election, Miami, Florida, November 4, 1997

In the Miami mayoral election held on November 4, 1997, Joe Carollo won a plurality in a field of five candidates but was

155 votes short of winning a majority. Carollo won a majority of the in-person precinct votes, but his challenger, Xavier Suarez, won a majority of the absentee ballots. Carollo "would have won outright on Nov. 4" if not for "Suarez's lopsided advantage in absentees."[16] Carollo then lost the run-off election on November 13 when Suarez received two-thirds of the absentee votes cast in the election. However, the Nov. 13 election was voided, the Nov. 4 election was overturned, and Carollo was returned to office after a court found evidence of widespread, massive fraud involving five thousand absentee ballots in the original election.[17] A Miami-Dade County grand jury in 2012 summarized what happened:

> In 1997, the City of Miami had one of its most memorable elections. The mayoral election for that year was plagued with widespread absentee ballot fraud. Many absentee ballots were filled out by *boleteros* and even one absentee ballot was cast in the name of a voter who was already dead.... Charges were filed against fifty-five (55) persons, including a City of Miami Commissioner (charged with being Accessory After the fact to Voter Fraud), his Chief of Staff, and the Chief of Staff's father. The Commissioner, Chief of Staff and the father were all convicted and sentenced to jail. Collectively, findings of guilt were entered against fifty-four (54) of the fifty-five (55) defendants and one was sent to a pretrial diversion program. On the civil side in a lawsuit filed by the mayoral candidate who lost the election, the judge found that fraud was involved in so many of the absentee ballots that he threw them out. That action resulted in the losing candidate being declared the winner of that mayoral election.[18]

As the grand jury explained in a footnote, and as previously mentioned, *boleteros*, "roughly translated, means 'ticket-person' and is used for a person who assists in collecting absentee ballots, primarily helping elderly and disabled voters." As case after case proves, all too often these boleteros do not just assist voters—they fill out the voters' ballots or intimidate and pressure voters to vote for the candidates who are paying the boleteros to collect the ballots. Others go even further and alter the choices of the voters or forge witness and voter signatures, much of which seemed to have happened in the Miami case.

The Florida state court of appeals that upheld the findings of the trial court noted that the 1997 election was overturned because the evidence showed an extensive "pattern of fraudulent, intentional and criminal conduct that resulted in such an extensive abuse of the absentee ballot laws that it can fairly be said that the intent of these laws was totally frustrated."[19] The fraud was so pervasive that "the integrity of the election was adversely affected."[20]

Miami Commission District 3 was the focal point of the fraud; in fact, the district "was the center of a massive, well-conceived and well-orchestrated absentee ballot voter fraud scheme."[21] The scheme included stolen ballots, ballots cast by voters using false registration addresses, ballots falsely witnessed, and hundreds of ballots cast that violated state statutory requirements or were "procured or witnessed by the 29 so-called 'ballot brokers' who invoked their privilege against self-incrimination instead of testifying at trial."[22]

One of the Suarez volunteers criminally charged in the case was caught "trying to buy fake absentee ballots that used the names of dead people" who were still on the voter registration roll, demonstrating the mischief that can be caused by the failure of election officials to maintain the accuracy of their voter rolls.[23] The ruling by the trial court also cited "witness after witness" who testified to "a catalogue of abuses that included ballots cast by persons who did not ask for an absentee ballot, who did not live in [Miami] or did not know the person who supposedly witnessed their signatures."[24]

In a description that correctly summarizes the effect that fraud has on all the voters in an election, the trial court concluded that the absentee ballot fraud in the Miami mayor's race "literally and figuratively, stole the ballot from the hands of every honest voter in the City of Miami."[25]

Much of the wrongdoing in the election was uncovered through investigative reporting by the *Miami Herald*, which won a Pulitzer Prize in 1999 for this reporting—quite a contrast to the work of so many media today, which seem to spend most of their time trying to deny that election fraud occurs.[26]

Among the findings of the *Miami Herald's* extensive, in-depth investigation were the following:[27]

- Volunteers, including a former food stamp worker, pressured elderly food stamp recipients into voting for Suarez.
- Inner-city, "poor and homeless" voters were transported in "white vans and beat-up cars" to County Hall to vote by absentee ballot[28] and then to the "back lot at St. John Baptist Church," where they were paid $10 apiece for their votes by "a man with a wad of cash."
- Among the numerous witnesses to this vote-buying operation was one who lived in an apartment overlooking the church lot (and took $10 himself) and who estimated that the operation, which went on all day, paid off "300 or 400 people."
- The man "with a wad of cash" admitted that he had participated in "two or three" such vote-buying schemes in the past, a clear indication that this type of fraud was not unique to the 1997 mayor's race.

- Fraudulent absentee ballots came from the homes of supporters of a commissioner involved in the fraud.
- A man signed as a witness the absentee ballot of a voter who had been dead for four years and gathered dozens of other fraudulent ballots. That same dead voter had "voted three other times since his burial in a pauper's grave."
- Other dead Miamians voted, including a Haitian immigrant (and U.S. citizen) who voted in his first and only election in 1996. He died in May 1997, and his registration was cancelled by election officials. However, his name was "resurrected" at a polling place in the mayor's race when his name was "handwritten on...the precinct voter roll, along with an obvious forgery of his signature."
- Many nonresidents voted, including employees of the city, "even though their homes are miles outside city limits." "Records show that many had been voting for years, in election after election—cancelling the votes of real Miami residents and taxpayers."
- Campaign workers "registered people to vote at addresses where they didn't live...punched[29] voters' absentee ballots without permission...cast ballots in the names of people who insist they did not vote...[and] signed dozens of ballots as witnesses even though they weren't present when the voters signed the envelopes."
- A nonprofit organization that had received $2 million in grants from city officials and was barred by law from engaging in political activity carried out similar behavior, including completing absentee ballots without the permission of voters.
- Some elderly voters said "someone cast ballots in their names," and other voters said that "they didn't vote"

and that the "signatures on the [absentee] ballots are forgeries."

- Six adult members of the same family and registered at the same address in Miami voted in the election even though only one of them lived in Miami (this was just one of numerous such examples).
- Votes were cast by convicted felons who had not yet regained their right to vote, including muggers, con artists, car thieves, robbers, drug traffickers, murderers, a flasher who beat his cellmate to death, and a former Miami detective who "covered up the murder of a drug dealer."

Although this case concentrated on absentee ballots, the *Miami Herald*'s investigation found that dozens of "ineligible voters came and voted at the poll" too.

One poignant story uncovered by the *Miami Herald* demonstrates how elderly and disabled voters can easily be manipulated and pressured in their homes, hospitals, or nursing homes where there are no election officers or poll watchers to supervise or observe the voting process. "I was taken advantage of," Ada Perez told the investigative reporters. A campaign operative tracked down Perez, age seventy, at the hospital where she was recovering from a severe stroke. She described how the operative "badgered her to vote for Suarez, then finally took her ballot and punched it for her." Her "eyes welling with tears," Perez said her "vote was stolen...They know our eyesight is not good and we are not well. What kind of person would take advantage of the elderly?"[30]

The court of appeals reinstated Carollo as the mayor since he won a majority of the votes once the fraudulent ballots were discounted. The court said the proper remedy "and the public policy of the State of Florida" in the face of "massive absentee voter fraud" was "to not encourage such fraud" by holding a new election:

> Rather, it must be remembered that the sanctity of free and honest elections is the cornerstone of a true democracy... Were we to approve a new election as the proper remedy following extensive absentee voting fraud, we would be sending out the message that the worst that would happen in the face of voter fraud would be another election....
>
> Further, we refuse to disenfranchise the more than 40,000 voters who, on November 4, 1997, exercised their constitutionally guaranteed right to vote in the polling places of Miami... Public policy dictates that we not void those constitutionally protected votes... A candidate who wins an election by virtue of obtaining a majority of the votes cast is entitled to take office as a result thereof, and not be forced into a second election... when the said second election only comes about due to absentee ballot fraud, in the first election, that favored one of his or her opponents.[31]

### 3. Democratic Mayoral Primary Election, East Chicago, Indiana, May 6, 2003

The absentee ballot fraud that occurred in the 2003 mayoral primary in East Chicago, Indiana, was so pervasive that the U.S. Supreme Court cited it as an example of proven fraud when it upheld Indiana's new voter ID law in 2008. In *Crawford v. Marion County Election Board*, the Supreme Court noted that "Indiana's own experience with fraudulent voting in the 2003 Democratic primary for East Chicago Mayor—though perpetrated using absentee ballots and not in-person fraud—demonstrate[s] that not only is the risk of voter fraud real but that it could affect the outcome of a close election."[32]

That is certainly what happened in East Chicago, and it is why the Indiana Supreme Court overturned the results of the election.[33] George Pabey was challenging the incumbent mayor, Robert Pastrick. Of the 8,227 votes cast on Election Day, Pabey received 199 more votes than the incumbent mayor. But of the 1,950 absentee ballots cast, the mayor had 477 more votes than Pabey, giving the incumbent a victory with a margin of 278 votes.[34]

However, after a week-and-a-half trial, and after hearing from 165 witnesses, the trial judge concluded that the mayor and his cronies had "perverted the absentee voting process and compromised the integrity and results of that election." The judge found "direct, competent, and convincing evidence that established the pervasive fraud, illegal conduct, and violations of elections law" that proved the "voluminous, widespread and insidious nature of the misconduct."[35] The fraud "compromised the integrity and results of that election."[36]

As the judge noted, the "pervasive fraud and illegal conduct" included but was not limited to the following:

- "A predatory pattern" by Pastrick supporters of "inducing voters that were first-time voters or otherwise less informed or lacking in knowledge of the voting process, the infirm, the poor, and those with limited skills in the English language, to engage in absentee voting."
- "Providing compensation [bribes] and/or creating the expectation of compensation to induce voters to cast their ballot via the absentee process."
- "Assisting" voters in completing their ballots, that is, pressuring people to vote for Pastrick, and directly watching the voters while they "marked and completed their absentee ballots."

- "The use of vacant lots or the former residences of voters on applications for absentee ballots."
- "The possession of unmarked absentee ballots by Pastrick supporters and the delivery of those ballots to absentee voters."
- "The possession of completed and signed ballots" by Pastrick operatives even though they were not authorized by law to have those ballots.
- "The routine completion of substantive portions of absentee ballot applications by Pastrick supporters to which applicants simply affixed their signatures," which were then delivered to Pastrick's campaign headquarters and photocopied before delivery to election officials.
- Votes cast by city employees "who simply did not reside in East Chicago."[37]

The trial judge said this primary provided a "textbook" example of the "chicanery that can attend the absentee vote cast by mail…instances where the supervision and monitoring of voting by Pastrick supporters and the subsequent possession of ballots by those malefactors are common." The judge also determined that Pastrick supporters preyed on "the naïve, the neophytes, the infirm and the needy," subjecting them to "unscrupulous election tactics."[38]

This case illustrates that, all too often, those targeted by absentee ballot vote thieves are the most vulnerable in society. In 2012, Anthony DeFiglio, a local Democratic committeeman in Troy, New York, pleaded guilty to falsifying business records in a case involving absentee ballot fraud in a 2009 primary election. Voters' signatures were forged on absentee ballot request forms and submitted without their knowledge, then their absentee ballots were fraudulently completed and submitted without their knowledge.[39]

The voters whose ballots had been stolen lived in low-income housing. When investigators asked DeFiglio why he targeted them, he said that those voters were "a lot less likely to ask any questions."[40] Another Democratic operative who admitted to forging absentee ballot applications said that he had "been present when 'ballots were voted correctly' by party operatives. Voted correctly is a term used for a forged application or ballot."[41]

The *Pabey* case also illustrates the difficulty of detecting and investigating election fraud. This fraud occurred right under the noses of local election officials and prosecutors. The only reason it was discovered is because the losing candidate, George Pabey, challenged the outcome, a very expensive and resource-intensive task. The trial judge was "cognizant of the difficulties faced by Pabey in discovering and presenting evidence" of the fraud, stating:

> Given the voluminous, widespread and insidious nature of the misconduct, petitioner Pabey, his legal counsel, and amateur investigators faced a herculean task of locating and interviewing absentee voters, visiting multi-family dwellings and housing projects, gathering and combing through voluminous election documents, and analyzing, comparing, sifting and assembling the information necessary to present their case...In short, the time constraints that govern election contests, primarily designed to serve important interests and needs of election officials and the public interest in finality, simply do not work well in those elections where misconduct is of the dimension and multi-faceted variety present here.[42]

Moreover, the judge noted another problem in any investigation of absentee ballot fraud: the "reluctance [of] voters to candidly discuss the circumstance surrounding their absentee vote." The judge said, "It is wholly natural, of course, that voters would be reluctant to expose themselves to potential criminal liability." Additionally, supporters of the incumbent mayor "were involved in various attempts to influence or prevent witnesses' testimony...including instructing a witness to 'feign a lack of knowledge on the witness stand.'"[43] This even included a local judge who told "prospective witnesses that they did not have to testify unless they had been paid a $20.00 witness fee."[44]

The Indiana State Supreme Court also discussed the difficulty faced by judges and courts in evaluating and quantifying "deliberate conduct committed with the express purpose of obscuring the election outcome based on legal votes cast." This includes "schemes that seek to discourage proper and confidential voting or that endeavor to introduce unintended or illegal votes into the outcome [that] will inevitably produce outcome distortions that defy precise quantification."[45]

The court found that a new election was not only justified, but it was also "compelled" because "a deliberate series of actions occurred making it impossible to determine the candidate who received the highest number of legal votes cast in the election."[46]

### 4. Congressional Election, Ninth District, North Carolina, November 6, 2018

The only challenged congressional race in the 2018 federal election was in the Ninth Congressional District in North Carolina, a district that spans "eight counties along the State's central southern border."[47] The incumbent, Representative Robert Pittenger (R), had been defeated in the Republican primary by Mark Harris. Harris faced his Democratic opponent, Dan McCready, in the November 6 general election.

After the votes were tallied at the end of Election Day, Harris had apparently defeated McCready by 905 votes, a margin of only 0.3 percent of all the ballots cast in the election.[48] The "number of returned absentee ballots [10,500] far exceeded the margin between Harris and McCready."[49]

However, the North Carolina State Board of Elections ("the Board") refused to certify the results of the election when evidence surfaced of "concerted fraudulent activities related to absentee by-mail ballots," including illegal vote trafficking by a political consultant and his associates.[50] In North Carolina, only the voter and "a voter's near relative or the voter's verifiable legal guardian" is allowed to return a completed absentee ballot to election officials.[51]

After an intensive investigation that included 142 voter interviews and "30 subject and witness interviews"[52] as well as public hearings, the Board overturned the results of both the congressional race and two local contests, ordering a new election. The Board concluded that the election "was corrupted by fraud, improprieties, and irregularities so pervasive that its results are tainted as the fruit of an operation manifestly unfair to the voters and corrosive to our system of representative government."[53] The evidence of a "coordinated, unlawful, and substantially resourced absentee ballot scheme" was "overwhelming."[54]

The absentee ballot scheme was "enabled by a well-funded and highly organized criminal operation" run by Leslie McCrae Dowless, Jr., a well-known political gun for hire in North Carolina and convicted felon (for insurance fraud) who had worked for numerous candidates. In this election, he was funded by the Harris campaign (as well as by other candidates, such as Bladen County Sheriff candidate James McVicker) through a consulting firm called Red Dome Group, but he had previously worked for Democratic candidates too.[55]

Among the findings of the Board were the following:[56]

- Absentee ballot "requests were fraudulently submitted under forged signatures, including a deceased voter."

- Dowless paid workers he hired "in cash to collect absentee request forms, to collect absentee ballots, and to falsify absentee ballot witness certifications." Their pay depended on how many forms they collected.
- In addition to using blank absentee ballot request forms, Dowless prefilled the forms using information on voters obtained from prior elections so that his workers could have the voters simply sign the form, which sometimes included Social Security and driver's license numbers and birth dates.
- The absentee ballot request forms were photocopied before being turned into election officials for later use in other elections or for other purposes.
- Because Dowless "maintained photocopies of completed absentee by mail request forms from prior elections—including voters' signatures and other information used to verify the authenticity of a request—Dowless possessed the capability to submit forged absentee by mail request forms without voters' knowledge and without detection by elections officials."
- Dowless withheld the absentee ballot request forms and only submitted them "at times strategically advantageous to his ballot operation," and he tracked when "ballots had been mailed by elections officials using publicly available data."
- One of the Dowless staffers even started forging her mother's name as a witness on absentee ballot envelopes because "she had witnessed too many" such envelopes under her own name and signature.
- During the general elections, "some voters discovered" that absentee ballot request forms "were submitted on their behalf, but without their knowledge, consent, or signature."

- Dowless and his workers went to voters' homes after absentee ballots had been delivered to collect the ballots, often signing as witnesses, even though they had not seen the voter sign the ballots, and they pressured voters by "push[ing] votes for Harris."
- Other absentee ballots were collected uncompleted, and Dowless and his crew "fraudulently voted blank or incomplete" ballots at "Dowless's home or in his office."

Dowless took other steps designed to avoid raising any red flags that provide a practical playbook for avoiding detection by election officials of large-scale absentee ballot fraud involving literally hundreds of ballots.[57] These included the following:

- Delivering small batches of absentee ballots to the post office.
- Ensuring that ballots were mailed from post offices geographically close to where the voter whose ballot had been stolen lived.
- Dating the false witness signatures with the same date as the voter's signature.
- Using the same color ink for witness signatures as the voter's signature, even "tracing over existing signatures to ensure conformity."
- Ensuring that stamps were "not placed in such a way as to raise a red flag for local elections administrators," such as by "affixing the stamp upside-down;"
- Taking some "collected ballots back to the voter for hand delivery to the local Board of Elections," limiting the number of times false witness signatures appeared on ballots.[58]

Dowless would not testify before the Board after it refused to grant him immunity. The Board found that in addition to his election fraud, he engaged in "witness tampering and intimidation" to "obstruct the Board's investigation."[59] Even candidate Mark Harris acknowledged to the Board that the testimony he heard before the Board convinced him that "a new election should be called."[60]

Due to the "coordinated, unlawful, and well-funded absentee ballot scheme" that "perpetrated fraud and corruption upon the election," the Board ordered a new election since it was not possible for the Board to "determine the precise number of ballots" that were affected.[61]

A special election was held on September 10, 2019, and Dan Bishop (R), who replaced Harris as the Republican nominee after a new election was called, beat Dan McCready, the Democratic candidate who had lost to Mark Harris in the original election.[62]

In February 2019, Dowless was indicted by a Wake County grand jury on charges of felony obstruction of justice, conspiracy to obstruct justice, possession of absentee ballots, and perjury in connection to both the 2016 general election and 2018 primary election. A superseding indictment adding perjury and solicitation of perjury to the charges was returned in July 2019. Six other individuals who worked for Dowless also were charged in the absentee ballot scheme.[63] In June 2021, nearly three years after the fraud was committed, Dowless pleaded guilty in federal court to two charges of collecting Social Security disability payments while he was accepting consulting fees. Neither of the two charges dealt directly with the election fraud allegations. Prosecutors agreed to drop the fraud charges despite the mountains of evidence. This proves our point that prosecutors are reluctant to fully press charges of electron fraud and that guilty offenders often get off easy.

## CONCLUSION

All these cases illustrate the vulnerability of absentee or mail-in voting to fraud, forgery, coercion, and intimidation. Many of the elements found in these cases were uncovered in an absentee ballot fraud case in Paterson, New Jersey, involving the city's May 12, 2020, mail-in municipal election. Four individuals, including a city councilman and a candidate, were charged by the state attorney general on a variety of criminal charges involving an absentee ballot trafficking scheme, including submitting fraudulent voter registrations for individuals not eligible to vote in the jurisdiction. A new election was also ordered by Superior Court Judge Ernest M. Caposela, who said the evidence showed that the election was not "the fair, free and full expression of the intent of the voters. It was rife with mail in vote procedural violations constituting nonfeasance and malfeasance."[64]

An astounding 20 percent of the mail ballots in the Paterson election were rejected for everything from signatures not matching (a clear indication of fraud) to the absentee ballots failing to identify the individual other than the voter who "delivered" the completed ballot to election officials. Hundreds of absentee ballots were discovered in an adjacent township outside the voting jurisdiction, another indication of fraud.[65]

Unfortunately, absentee ballot fraud is a persistent problem, and with so many other incidents of fraud, it can make the difference in a close election. The residents of Gordon, Alabama, know that because their mayor was removed from office in 2019 after he was convicted of absentee ballot fraud in an election he won by only sixteen votes.[66]

Uncovering such schemes is resource-intensive, and it requires extensive and in-depth investigations. The admissions made by defendants and other witnesses also indicate that such unlawful actions have often occurred in prior elections without detection, investigation, or prosecution.

As Anthony DeFiglio told state police in Troy, New York, such fraud was "a normal political tactic" used on "both sides of the aisle." Apparently, forging and stealing absentee ballots was commonplace in Troy.[67] DeFiglio's patronizing statement that low-income voters were targeted because "they are a lot less likely to ask questions" about their ballots[68] illustrates why, all too often, other perpetrators of absentee ballot fraud target poor, disabled, and minority voters.

This was demonstrated once again by the arrest of a social worker in Texas shortly before the 2020 general election. She was charged with 134 counts of fraud for submitting fraudulent voter registration forms in the names of dozens of patients who suffered from intellectual and developmental disabilities without their knowledge or consent at the state-supported living center where she worked. In fact, many of them had been declared mentally incompetent by the courts. Fortunately, she was caught before fraudulent ballots were submitted in the names of her victims.[69]

Preventing this type of fraud is necessary to secure the integrity of the election process and ensure public confidence in election outcomes, which is an essential ingredient of a stable democratic republic. Encouraging even more mail-in voting and relaxing security protocols, such as witness or notarization requirements, is a dangerous policy.

As the Miami-Dade grand jury stated in 1997 in the midst of the widespread absentee ballot fraud that corrupted the election process in the Miami mayor's race:

> The right to vote defines the essence of American citizenship. It provides the bedrock upon which our democratic form of government survives. The greatest social struggles in our history, from

the emotional impetus for the American Revolution itself, to the struggle for women's suffrage and the battle for civil rights, have all had at their core the acquisition of the vote for those who were disenfranchised. To a democracy, there can be no greater crime than voter fraud. A single falsely cast vote corrupts the entire electoral process.[70]

## CHAPTER FIVE

# THE MANY WAYS ELECTION FRAUD HAPPENS

I n 2012 when we published *Who's Counting? How Fraudsters and Bureaucrats Put Your Vote at Risk,*[1] we detailed numerous cases of election fraud and outlined the campaign by liberals to deny its very existence. That campaign has only intensified over the past decade. It is as if the fraud deniers live in a fantasy universe in which they can ignore the facts and the evidence and deny the obvious. But denying the existence of fraud is also an intentional effort by many to justify opposing the need for election reforms like voter ID. Since they assert there is no fraud, there is no need to fix the vulnerabilities that exist in our election system.

As we have cited before, the U.S. Supreme Court in 2008 recognized the long history of election fraud in this country when it upheld Indiana's new voter ID law. As the court said, despite the criminal penalties:

> It remains true...that flagrant examples of such fraud...have been documented throughout this Nation's history by respected historians and journalists, that occasional examples have surfaced

in recent years...that...demonstrate that not only is the risk of voter fraud real but that it could affect the outcome of a close election.[2]

Several years ago, The Heritage Foundation started an Election Fraud Database,[3] which is the only one of its kind in the nation. It is a sampling of recent proven instances of fraud from across the country, not a comprehensive or exhaustive list, and it has become the most visited page at The Heritage Foundation's website.

The database is continuously updated with new cases. It only contains proven and documented cases in which an individual was convicted of fraud, a court ordered a new election due to fraud, or there was an official finding by a government agency such as a state board of elections of fraud, as occurred in the Ninth Congressional District race in North Carolina in 2018. As of April 10, 2021, it documented 1,317 cases consisting of 1,134 criminal conviction, 48 civil penalties, 21 judicial findings, 17 official findings, and 97 instances of defendants in a "diversion" program, which usually allows them to have their conviction cleared after they participate in community service or some type of rehabilitation program. The database demonstrates the many different ways that fraud is committed in local, state, and federal elections.

As the introduction to the database explains:

> Each and every one of the cases...represents an instance in which a public official, usually a prosecutor, thought it serious enough to act upon it. And each and every one ended in a finding that the individual had engaged in wrongdoing in connection with an election hoping to affect its outcome—or that the results of an election were sufficiently in question and had to be overturned.

Not all cases of election fraud are as far-reaching as the fraud that changed the outcome of the Ninth Congressional District race. Many are quite small, involving a relative handful of votes, sometimes just a lone voter deciding to commit fraud by, for example, voting twice. But fraud is not nearly as rare as many people (especially in the media) would like to think. The fact is, election fraud is real, and as the many examples in The Heritage Foundation's database show, it can sometimes change the outcome of an election. And when an individual cheats by submitting a fraudulent vote, he is voiding the vote of a legitimate voter.

Yet many in the media would rather look the other way. Worse, some try to dismiss or explain away evidence that does not fit their preapproved "move along, nothing to see here" narrative. They falsely insist that there are no vulnerabilities in the electoral process and are so upset at the existence of the database that they keep attacking it instead of spending their time actually investigating fraud cases.

In October 2020, *USA Today*, PBS *Frontline*, and Columbia Journalism Investigations assigned no fewer than *fourteen reporters* to investigate the database to try to find mistakes and downplay the actions of the individuals who had been found guilty of various election offenses cited in the database. The reporters were unable to find a single error. They did, however, try to excuse and minimize what the database exposes by quoting a well-known (and very partisan) liberal law professor who said that individual acts of election fraud are "not calculated to change election outcomes."

Of course they are. Every person who engages in election fraud, whether it is a single individual or a group of conspirators, is hoping to affect the outcome.

The database lists the many different ways fraud is committed. They include ballot petition fraud, altering the vote count, buying votes, voting more than once, false voter registrations, fraudulent absentee ballots, illegal "assistance" at the polls, impersonation fraud, voting by ineligible individuals such as aliens and felons, and a whole variety of other miscellaneous methods. Unfortunately, those who are willing to cheat are very creative at finding ways to steal votes. In addition to absentee ballot fraud, which we have outlined in detail, the other types of fraud include the following:

## BALLOT PETITION FRAUD

Many states require a candidate to get a certain percentage of registered voters to sign a petition in order to qualify to be on the ballot. Typically, ballot petition fraud is when the petition gatherers forge signatures to meet the qualification requirement. An example of petition fraud that may have altered the course of a presidential election occurred in 2008 in Indiana.

In the spring of 2008, the Democratic primary season was in full swing. Then-Senators Hillary Clinton and Barack Obama were relatively even in the number of delegates each had received. Going into the May 6 primary in Indiana, Sen. Obama had a slight lead over Sen. Clinton.[4] According to a *New York Times* calculation, Sen. Obama had 1,474 delegates to Sen. Clinton's 1,377—a difference of fewer than a hundred delegates.[5] However, Sen. Clinton had an edge in superdelegates,[6] a special category of additional Democratic Party delegates who are automatically designated as delegates by party rules and include elected officials and party committee members. As of May 2, Clinton had 260 pledged superdelegates while Obama had only 241. Thus, Obama was only ahead of Clinton by 78 delegates.

On May 6, Indiana and North Carolina held their primaries. Clinton won Indiana by 50.6 percent to 49.4 percent, while Obama won North Carolina by 56.1 percent to 41.6 percent.[7] The two candidates were fighting over 187 total delegates—72 in Indiana and 117 in North Carolina.

Under Democratic Party rules for these two states, Clinton and Obama split the delegates according to the proportion of their vote totals. As a result, Clinton walked away with 37 delegates from Indiana and 48 delegates from North Carolina. Obama, however, fared better, winning 34 delegates in Indiana and 67 delegates in North Carolina. Obama's thin victory was a disappointment for the Clinton campaign, which hoped to use a big victory in those two states to mount a successful comeback. At the conclusion of the Indiana and North Carolina primaries, Obama had captured a total of 1,575 regular delegates to Clinton's 1,422, increasing his lead to 153 in regular delegates.

With six primaries left totaling 217 delegates, Obama's lead didn't guarantee victory. But on May 10, Obama took the lead in superdelegates with 275 to Clinton's 271[8] and never relinquished it.[9] Soon thereafter, Obama won the Democratic nomination for president and subsequently won the presidency.

But in 2011, a Yale University undergraduate student looking through the ballot petitions that had qualified Barack Obama for the Democratic primary in Indiana noticed that "page after page of signatures" were all in the same handwriting.[10] A forensic specialist confirmed that the signatures on nineteen pages of the ballot petitions were forgeries. However, in an illustration of how prosecutors too often ignore election fraud, David Capp, the U.S. attorney for the Northern District of Indiana who had been appointed by Pres. Barack Obama, refused to take any action.[11]

Instead, state prosecutors went after four Democratic Party and election officials who conspired to commit the fraud. All four were convicted, including the chairman of the St. Joseph County Democratic Party, along with two Democratic members of the local board of elections and a Democratic staffer for the board.[12] The evidence in the case showed that the conspirators had forged signatures on the ballot petitions of both Obama and Clinton. Even with the fraudulent signatures, Clinton still would have had enough legitimate signatures to qualify for the May 2008 primary. However, that was not the case with Obama, who would have fallen short of the minimum number needed to qualify.

The state prosecutor, Stanley Levco, said that had the fraud been discovered in 2008, "Barack Obama wouldn't have been on the ballot for the primary" and Clinton would have won all of Indiana's 72 delegates.[13] The case can be made that this might have changed the outcome of the 2008 primary race.

If Barack Obama had been disqualified from the Indiana ballot, Clinton would have won all 72 of the delegates in Indiana instead of just 34. She would also have had a new total of 1,497 regular delegates compared to Obama's new total of 1,541—a difference of only 44 delegates. And with the addition of the superdelegates, Clinton would have been a mere 25 delegates behind Obama.

The momentum of the campaign might have shifted not only because Clinton would have been almost even with Obama in the total delegate count but also because Obama's campaign would have been enveloped in a major scandal.

Such a scandal could have affected Obama's fundraising and his ability to compete effectively in the remaining primaries as well as the crucial, pending decisions of the on-the-fence super-delegates who had not yet declared which of the two candidates they were supporting. It is impossible to say with certainty what would have happened, but the results of the 2008 election could have been quite different.

For those who would deny the possibility of such events triggering seismic shifts in campaign momentum, look at what happened in the 2012 presidential race in Virginia. Just before the deadline for filing ballot qualification petitions, former Speaker of the House Newt Gingrich submitted petitions with 11,000 voter signatures. However, a review by the Republican Party of Virginia concluded that 1,500 signatures were forgeries, dropping him below the required 10,000 voter signatures for the Virginia primary, dooming his campaign and his ability to win enough delegates to clinch the nomination. The signature gatherer responsible for the forgeries was prosecuted by the state attorney general and eventually pleaded guilty.[14]

## ALTERING THE VOTE COUNT

Altering the vote count is when election officials or others alter ballots, submit fraudulent ballots, or change the actual count of legitimate ballots. For example, Deana Swenson, an election official in Clackamas County, Oregon, pleaded guilty in 2013 to official misconduct and unlawfully altering a cast ballot after she was caught by a coworker.[15] Similarly, in 2013 a Democratic member of the Canton, Mississippi, Municipal Executive Committee was convicted of disorderly conduct, resisting arrest, and providing false information after she tried to steal a ballot box.[16]

Altering the vote count also applies to stuffing the ballot box. In 2020, Domenick Demuro, an election official in Philadelphia, pleaded guilty to accepting bribes to increase the vote totals for certain candidates by adding fraudulent ballots to the voting machines in his jurisdiction. He said that the bribes came from a local political consultant and that the candidates receiving fraudulent votes included candidates for judicial, local, state, and federal offices.[17]

The "local political consultant" who was later indicted for bribing Demuro was Michael "Ozzie" Myers, a former Democratic congressman who was convicted in the 1970s Abscam congressional bribery scandal. Myers was charged with paying Demuro to stuff the ballot box in the 2014, 2015, and 2016 elections. According to the indictment, Myers would "solicit payments from his clients in the form of cash or checks as 'consulting fees,' and then use portions of these funds to pay Demuro *and others* in return for tampering with election results."[18] [Emphasis added.]

As of the time this book is being written, Myers has not yet been convicted, and no further information has been revealed about who the candidates were that paid Myers his "consulting fees" or who the "others" were that also received bribes. Will the new Democratic-controlled Justice Department continue with this prosecution? Or will a Biden administration drop it the same way the incoming Obama-Biden administration dismissed the lawsuit filed by the Justice Department against the New Black Panther Party for intimidating voters in Philadelphia in 2008?[19] Only time will tell.

## BUYING VOTES

Paying for votes has a long, unfortunate history going back to colonial days, and it continues today. In 2019, Brian "Wormy" Hodge and Betty Jane Best were convicted of bribing voters with $20 to $40 each to cast absentee ballots for a candidate for sheriff in a 2014 race in Monroe County, Tennessee. The candidate won his race by only 704 votes. Hodge blamed his actions on the "dirty politics" of Monroe County, which "records more votes by absentee-by-mail ballot as a percentage of population than every county in Tennessee."[20]

This illustrates one of the signs of possible fraud: a higher rate of absentee ballots than in prior races or other similar areas in a state. The prosecutor pointed out that there were over a thousand absentee ballots cast in the 2014 election in Monroe County where voters were bribed, yet Coffee County, with almost the same number of registered voters, "counted only 98 absentee-by-mail ballots." As he said, "these statistics illustrate the serious implications that voter fraud present to the integrity of the election process."[21] A congressional primary in the same election was decided by only 1,474 votes.

Similarly, in 2016 four defendants in Magoffin County, Kentucky, including a county magistrate, Gary "Rooster" Risner, and a deputy county clerk, Larry Shepherd, were convicted of election fraud in a vote-buying scheme for a slate of candidates in a 2014 election. They were paying $50 a vote, and one of the defendants testified that their bribery racket went back to the 2010 election. He also revealed that they had engaged in other fraud, such as adding votes to the total for a candidate while he was serving as a precinct officer with Risner forging the signatures of the voters who had not actually voted in the election.[22]

Can vote buying change the outcome of an election? It certainly did in Turkey Creek, Louisiana, in 2014 when the incumbent mayor, Heather Cloud, lost her reelection by four votes. But the election was overturned by a state court after Cloud sued and it was discovered that a campaign staffer, Stanley Leger, who worked for Cloud's challenger, had paid $15 each to four mentally impaired individuals for their votes. Those four votes were struck, Leger pleaded guilty to election tampering, a new election was held, and Cloud was reelected.[23] Fraud *can* make the difference, particularly in a close election.

## VOTING MORE THAN ONCE

Duplicate voting is when individuals register multiple times in the same or different states and then vote more than once in the same election. Unfortunately, voter registration rolls across the country are so inaccurate and so poorly maintained that this is relatively easy to do.

One of the most notorious cases in recent years was that of Wendy Rosen, who ran for Congress in Maryland in 2012. She won the Democratic nomination to challenge Rep. Andy Harris, the incumbent Republican congressman, after beating her Democratic primary opponent by only 57 votes. But two months before the general election, "state Democrat Party leaders" revealed that Rosen was registered to vote in both Maryland and Florida and had illegally voted in both states in 2006 and 2010. She withdrew, and the opponent she beat by 57 votes became the Democratic congressional candidate.[24]

Rosen pleaded guilty but was only sentenced to five years of probation, community service, and a $5,000 fine. Despite agreeing to plead guilty, in what could only be called political theater, Rosen called what she did an act of "civil disobedience, not arrogance" that would bring to light the supposed efforts of some states to keep the poor and minorities from voting, a completely false allegation.[25]

Keep in mind the most important fact in this particular case. It was not Florida or Maryland election officials who discovered that Rosen was voting in two different states; it was someone inside her own party doing opposition research for the campaign. It seems likely that if Rosen had not run for Congress, she could have continued voting twice with little chance of ever being caught.

There are numerous other cases of duplicate voting in The Heritage Foundation's Election Fraud Database, including that of Spencer McKinnon, a student at the University of New Hampshire who pleaded guilty in 2019 to voting in both New Hampshire and his home state of Massachusetts in the 2016 election.[26] Unfortunately, this type of fraud is relatively easy to commit by college students who are attending school outside their home states.

New Hampshire discovered this through the Interstate Voter Registration Crosscheck Program run by the Kansas secretary of state, in which many states do not participate. This program compares state voter registration lists of participating states. Unfortunately, opposition from liberal organizations like the ACLU and the Lawyers' Committee for Civil Rights that oppose any efforts to clean up voter rolls has reduced membership in the program. These groups lobbied Illinois election officials to withdraw and sued Indiana to force the state out of the program.[27]

## FALSE VOTER REGISTRATION

False voter registration is when someone registers under a phony name or address. That includes claiming to live in a particular jurisdiction where the person does not actually reside and is therefore not entitled to vote. Liberals sometimes try to dismiss this as an unimportant problem, claiming that it is not election fraud when no fraudulent votes are submitted. But it is only if the false registrations are detected that no fraudulent votes occur. That is like claiming that a bank robber who was apprehended while still in the bank didn't actually remove the money and is therefore not really guilty and that we should not worry about attempted robberies.

In 2019 in Bloomingburg, New York, Volvy "Zev" Smilowitz, along with two other conspirators who were real estate developers, falsely registered non-residents of the town and bribed them to vote in the 2014 village election. Their goal was to elect board members who would favor their stalled housing development, which could net them hundreds of millions of dollars. They even created fake leases and decorated apartments to make them look like people lived in them. Fortunately, they were caught before votes were cast. But if these false registrations had not been detected, an election in this town could have been stolen.[28]

A stolen election actually happened in Vernon, California, in 2012 due to false registrations. A city council election decided by only four votes was overturned and a new election held after it was determined that five individuals who did not actually live in Vernon had falsely registered as residents of the city and had voted in the election, including one individual who admitted during his testimony that he lived in Arizona and "just visit[ed]" Vernon.[29]

## ILLEGAL ASSISTANCE

Illegal assistance is when someone provides "assistance" to a voter but then forces, intimidates, coerces, or pressures that individual to vote for particular candidates. Under the federal Voting Rights Act, any "voter who requires assistance to vote by reason of blindness, disability, or inability to read or write" has the right to have someone "of the voter's choice" help them vote "other than the voter's employer or agent of that employer or officer or agent of the voter's union."[30] In the guise of being a helper, someone can steer vulnerable voters to vote for a preferred candidate of the helper, overriding the voter's choice. Illegal assistance can happen in polling places but is much easier to commit when voters are voting absentee with no election officials or poll watchers present to detect and stop the illegal "assistance."

Sometimes this type of fraud may be an isolated case, such as that of Delores "Dee" Handy, who was convicted in Acadia Parish, Louisiana, in 2020 of failing to mark a ballot for an elderly voter as the voter directed. Handy cast a ballot for the candidate she wanted, not the candidate the voter wanted.[31] Like in this case, the targets of illegal assistance are often the elderly, the disabled, the illiterate, and those for whom English is a second language. Instead of helping voters, scammers are stealing their votes.

One would think liberal activists would be concerned about the exploitation of vulnerable voters, but that does not fit with their opposition to any type of election reform. Nor does it fit with their push to give their activists and political consultants access to voters by overriding state laws that ban vote trafficking, which allows strangers to pick up and collect voters' absentee ballots.

Sometimes, however, these are not isolated cases. Facunda Garcia and almost half a dozen other coconspirators were convicted for illegal assistance in a 2012 Democratic primary election in Cameron County, Texas. They were filling out ballots without the permission of voters or their direction in an obvious attempt to throw the election.[32]

In 2005, the U.S. Justice Department filed a federal lawsuit under the Voting Rights Act against the City of Boston in part over illegal assistance to Chinese Americans at polling places. One of the authors (von Spakovsky) was working at the Justice Department at the time and was involved in the case. One of the career lawyers at Justice who spoke Chinese went as an observer and witnessed individuals in polling places who were speaking Chinese and ordering voters to vote for certain candidates under the guise of providing "assistance." The "assistors" were not aware that the lawyer spoke Chinese and that he could tell what they were doing.

The complaint included an allegation that the defendants had abridged the rights of voters by "improperly influencing, coercing or ignoring the ballot choices of limited English proficient Hispanic and Asian American voters."[33] Boston was so embarrassed by the lawsuit that it almost immediately agreed to settle the case. The settlement agreement approved by the court included a requirement that election officers undergo training and agree to "avoid making any statement or allowing any person to make any communication within or near the polls to influence any voter's ballot choice."[34]

## IMPERSONATION FRAUD

Impersonation fraud is when someone votes in the name of another legitimate voter or in the name of a registered voter who is no longer eligible to vote because the voter has died, has moved away, or is a felon who has not had his ability to vote restored. Liberals claim that impersonation fraud is virtually nonexistent, but how would you know whether or not that has happened in states that do not require identification to vote? As the Seventh Circuit U.S. Court of Appeals said in response to that claim when it upheld Indiana's vote ID law:

> But the absence of prosecutions is explained by the endemic underenforcement of minor criminal laws (minor as they appear to the public and prosecutors, at all events) and by the extreme difficulty of apprehending a voter impersonator. He enters the polling place, gives a name that is not his own, votes, and leaves. If later it is discovered that the name he gave is that of a dead person, no one at the polling place will remember the face of the person who gave that name, and if someone did remember it, what would he do with the information? The impersonator and the person impersonated (if living) might show up at the polls at the same time and a confrontation might ensue that might lead to a citizen arrest or a call to the police who would arrive before the impersonator had fled, and arrest him. A more likely sequence would be for the impersonated person to have voted already when the impersonator arrived and tried to vote in his name. But in either case an arrest would be most unlikely (and likewise if the impersonation were discovered or suspected by comparing sig-

natures, when that is done), as the resulting commotion would disrupt the voting.

And anyway the impersonated voter is likely to be dead or in another district or precinct or to be acting in cahoots with the impersonator, rather than to be a neighbor (precincts are small, sometimes a single apartment house). One response, which has a parallel to littering, another crime the perpetrators of which are almost impossible to catch, would be to impose a very severe criminal penalty for voting fraud. Another, however, is to take preventive action, as Indiana has done by requiring a photo ID.[35]

As with other types of fraud, this may be an isolated effort by one or two people, such as Latunia Thomas, a poll worker who pleaded guilty in 2017 to casting a ballot under her daughter's registration with the connivance of another poll official in Harris County, Texas, who was also convicted.[36] The same thing happened in Pennsylvania in 2016 when Robin Trainor, an election official, was convicted for voting under the name of her twenty-three-year-old son with the help of another election official in the polling place.[37]

One of the biggest examples of this type of fraud that has been discovered was revealed in a 1984 New York state grand jury report released by Kings County district attorney and former Democratic congresswoman Elizabeth Holtzman.[38] The report revealed a widespread conspiracy that had operated without detection for fourteen years in Brooklyn involving impersonation fraud at the polls.

Teams were recruited to go from polling place to polling place voting in the names of newly registered voters, voters who had died or moved away but remained registered, and fictitious voters who had been falsely registered by mail by the conspirators. Thousands of fraudulent votes were cast in New York legislative and congressional elections. A key factor in the success of this conspiracy was the fact that New York had no ID requirement. New York still does not have one today despite the grand jury recommendation that the state implement one.

For those who think this is old news and not relevant to elections in New York today, a December 2013 report by the city's watchdog Department of Investigation (DOI) on the mayor's race that year (in which Bill de Blasio was elected) shows how such fraud can still easily be committed without detection.[39] Given the city's long history of election fraud, including under the infamous Boss Tweed, it is not realistic to think that it has suddenly disappeared and that in the intense, contentious political fights that occur in the Big Apple there is no one taking advantage of the insecurity of the current election system.

The report detailed how DOI undercover agents went to sixty-three polling places in the city and pretended to be voters who had died or had moved out of town or who were sitting in jail and thus not eligible to vote. In sixty-one instances, or 97 percent of the time, the testers were allowed to vote. Those who did vote cast only a write-in vote for a "John Test" so as to not affect the outcome of any contest.

Young undercover agents were able to vote using the names of people three times their age, people who in fact were dead. In one example, a twenty-four-year-old female agent gave the name of someone who had died in 2012 at age eighty-seven; the workers at the Manhattan polling site gave her a ballot, no questions asked. A thirty-three-year-old male agent voted under the name of a ninety-four-year-old who had died the previous year.

Even the two cases where poll workers turned away an investigator raise eyebrows. In the first case, a poll worker on Staten Island walked outside with the undercover investigator who had just been refused a ballot; the "voter" was advised to go to the polling place near where he used to live and "play dumb" in order to vote. In the second case, the investigator was stopped from voting only because the felon whose name he was using was the son of the election official at the polling place.

The 2013 report also detailed the incompetence, waste, nepotism, and lax procedures of the city's Board of Elections and the inaccuracy of its voter registration roll. The Board of Elections, which has a $750 million annual budget and a workforce of 350 people, reacted in classic bureaucratic fashion and went after the messenger, which prompted one city paper to deride it as "a 21st-century survivor of Boss Tweed–style politics."[40]

Instead of acknowledging its problems, the board reacted the same way too many election officials do when embarrassed by evidence of incompetence and fraud: it approved a resolution referring the DOI's investigators for prosecution for vote fraud. It also asked the state's attorney general to determine whether DOI had violated the civil rights of voters who had moved or are felons, and it sent a letter of complaint to Mayor Bill de Blasio.

## VOTING BY INELIGIBLE INDIVIDUALS

Forty-eight states do not allow felons in prison to vote and have varying rules on when felons become eligible to vote after they are released. Maine, Vermont, and the District of Columbia allow felons to vote even while they are in prison. In some states where aliens (legal or not) are banned from voting in state elections, a small number of cities and towns—the largest being San Francisco—have authorized them to vote in local elections.[41]

Felons voting before their ability to vote has been restored is a problem in many states that do not do a good job of coordinating state voter registration rolls with Department of Corrections records. Chad Armstrong, a felon on probation, was convicted in 2020 in Wisconsin for voting in the 2018 election despite not yet being eligible to vote.[42]

Can felons voting illegally make a difference in the outcome of an election? If it is close, there is no doubt that can happen. In 2008 in Minnesota, incumbent U.S. Sen. Norm Coleman (R) lost his reelection to Al Franken by 312 votes after a lengthy litigation fight. Yet Minnesota Majority, a conservative watchdog group, came up with compelling evidence that hundreds of felons whose voting rights had not been restored had voted in that election.[43]

Aliens are ineligible to vote in federal and state elections under both state and federal law. Unfortunately, there are almost no safeguards in place in many states to prevent them (whether legal or illegal) from registering and voting because states do not verify citizenship. From Gustavo Araujo Lerma, a Mexican citizen who was convicted in California in 2019 for repeatedly voting in elections for over two decades,[44] to Marcello Villaruz, another alien who (along with his wife) voted in the 2016 presidential election in Illinois,[45] to Michael Nana Baako, a citizen of Ghana who voted illegally in ten federal elections in Maryland,[46] the problem is occurring repeatedly all over the country, although it is rarely caught.

In 2018, the U.S. Attorney for the Eastern District of North Carolina, Robert Higdon, Jr., charged nineteen aliens with voting illegally in North Carolina and then indicted another twenty-four after that.[47] Unfortunately, he was one of the only U.S. attorneys in the nation making a systematic effort to find and charge aliens who were illegally registering and voting. The aliens came from a diverse group of nations, including Mexico, the Dominican Republic, Nigeria, the Philippines, Guyana, Japan, South Korea, and Germany. Many of them told a reporter that they "didn't know that they couldn't vote and that they were urged to do so by campaign workers or election volunteers," pointing out one of the problems in this area: the connivance of those involved in elections to get the votes of aliens.[48]

This is not a new problem. An investigation by the U.S. House of Representatives of the 1996 election contest that incumbent Rep. Bob Dornan (R) lost to challenger Loretta Sanchez (D) by only 979 votes concluded that literally hundreds of ineligible aliens had voted in that election. The election was not overturned because Sanchez squeaked by with just enough legal votes (35) to win.[49]

But California election officials had no clue (or didn't care) that hundreds of registered California voters were aliens. The situation has only gotten worse since then with the state's switch to automatic voter registration. None of the aliens was ever prosecuted for illegally registering and voting, and California never took *any* steps to fix this security hole in its registration system. Not only that, but the House investigation only found registered aliens who were in the Immigration and Naturalization Service records; any illegal aliens who had never been arrested or detained were not in those records and therefore were not detected by the investigation. In its report, the House committee expressed the strong belief that hundreds of other illegal votes had been cast in the race, but Clinton administration immigration officials refused to cooperate further with the House probe.

So how big is the problem of aliens voting? We do not really know because there has been no systematic, in-depth research on this issue, which would only be possible with the full cooperation of state election officials across the country and the U.S. Department of Homeland Security, which seems highly unlikely. But not only are there numerous convictions of aliens illegally registering and voting in The Heritage Foundation Election Fraud Database, other research illustrates the extent of the problem.

The Public Interest Legal Foundation (PILF) is one of the very few conservative nonprofit advocacy organizations dedicated to election integrity. In addition to its research, it counters the dozens of well-funded liberal groups like the ACLU and the Brennan Center that are constantly filing lawsuits to stop states from implementing needed election reforms like voter ID and from trying to clean up and maintain the accuracy of their voter rolls.[50]

PILF undertook a series of projects in various states (and in parts of some states) to research election and registration records on aliens, often having to sue election officials who refused to produce those records as required under applicable state and federal laws. One of the key items PILF looked for were letters from registered voters asking to be removed from voting rolls because they were not citizens, something that is usually prompted by the aliens trying to clean up their records when applying for citizenship. Question 12 on the "Application for Naturalization" specifically asks aliens whether they have "EVER registered to vote" or "EVER voted" in "any Federal, state, or local election," which may bar them from becoming a citizen.[51]

PILF found the following in Michigan, Virginia, New Jersey, and a sampling of sanctuary jurisdictions in places such as Chicago and San Diego:[52]

- 1,444 aliens removed from the rolls in thirty jurisdictions in Michigan
- Over 5,500 aliens removed from the rolls in Virginia, but not before they had cast almost 7,500 ballots, and some of the aliens had been registered since the 1980s
- 1,069 aliens removed from the rolls in eleven counties in New Jersey, 37 percent of whom had cast ballots before their removal
- 3,120 aliens removed in sanctuary jurisdictions in just seven states

PILF concluded from its research that

- Ineligible noncitizens can and do become registered to vote in large numbers across the country
- These noncitizens often remain registered to vote for long periods of time, sometimes for decades
- Noncitizens, in almost all cases, are detected and removed from the voter lists only when they *self-report* and *request to be removed*
- Many noncitizens do vote when they are registered despite being ineligible to do so[53]

One of the recurrent problems that PILF found was election officials registering aliens to vote even when they knew the individual was not a citizen. The standard federal voter registration form promulgated by the U.S. Election Assistance Commission has a question at the very top of the form that asks, "Are you a citizen of the United States?"[54] Yet PILF discovered aliens who were registered to vote despite answering no to that question on the form or leaving the question unanswered.

Outside of PILF research, Pennsylvania state officials were recently forced to admit that a "glitch" in the state's Department of Motor Vehicles driver's license system had registered over eleven thousand aliens to vote without election officials realizing they had a problem until years later.[55] So far, Pennsylvania has refused to reveal how many votes were illegally cast by these aliens.

Of course, the unanswered question is: how many other aliens are on the voter rolls who have not made the effort to ask election officials to remove them? In 2014, three very brave[56] professors at Old Dominion University released a study that analyzed data from the 2008 and 2010 Cooperative Congressional Election Studies, which was based on survey data in each election of a very large sample of individuals (32,800 in 2008 and 55,400 in 2010) selected to mirror the demographic characteristics of the U.S. population.[57]

The surveys "included a question about citizenship status" and asked noncitizens if they voted, "unlike other large surveys which filter out non-citizens before asking about voting."[58]

The study estimated that 6.4 percent of the aliens present in the U.S., or as many at 1.2 million noncitizens, may have voted in the 2008 presidential election. For the 2010 congressional election, the estimate was 2.2 percent.[59] The survey data also showed that a significant majority of noncitizens favored Democratic candidates, including Barack Obama. As a result, the study's authors concluded that the votes of aliens—who were voting illegally—were substantial enough to have potentially given Barack Obama his win in the general election in North Carolina. It may have also "led to Democratic victories in congressional races including a critical 2008 Senate race [in Minnesota] that delivered for Democrats a 60-vote filibuster-proof majority in the Senate."[60]

There are three other important points to note about the problem—and extent—of illegal alien voting. As far as we are aware, not a single election official in *any* of the jurisdictions that PILF issued reports on notified any law enforcement authorities after they removed the registered aliens from the registration list—not one. They simply ignored the potential violation of state and federal law.

Second, despite the fact that the Application for Citizenship asks aliens whether they have ever registered or voted in an election, the Department of Homeland Security does not forward the answers to the Justice Department for investigation and prosecution. Thus, both departments are failing to use this information to enforce federal law that bars aliens from registering and voting.[61]

Finally, the ninety-four federal district courts all over the country use state voter registration lists (sometimes in conjunction with state driver's license lists) to obtain the names of individuals who are called for jury duty in whatever state in which the federal court is located. A 2005 report by the Government Accountability Office that studied federal courts in seven states found hundreds of individuals who had been exempted from jury service in four federal district courts because they were not U.S. citizens.[62]

Yet neither the courts nor Justice Department lawyers take *any* steps to notify election officials from whom they obtained their lists when aliens are excused from jury duty. Not only that, but no steps are taken by Justice Department lawyers to investigate and prosecute any of those aliens. Each U.S. Attorney's Office in each federal district has an assistant U.S. attorney who is the DEO, the designated election officer. They are the lawyers who should be carrying out this duty, yet we are not aware that any DEOs anywhere in the country are doing anything about this.[63]

If proper investigations and prosecutions had been carried out based on the PILF data, federal jury information, and citizenship applications, there is little doubt that the Heritage Election Fraud Database would contain hundreds if not thousands or tens of thousands of more cases.

## HOW BIG IS THE PROBLEM?

We have described the many different types of fraud that occur in our elections. It should be kept in mind that sometimes the election fraud includes not just one type of dishonest behavior but a combination of some or all of these different types of fraud. Take a case in Canton, Mississippi, where five local officials, including an alderman, a city clerk, and the fire chief, were convicted for their efforts to rig the town's 2017 municipal election in a scheme that involved everything from voter registration fraud to intimidating and bribing witnesses.[64]

So how much fraud occurs? Anyone who thinks that the cases that make the news represent the sole extent of fraud must also believe that the drug dealers who are in jail are the only people in the entire country dealing drugs and that there are no other dealers at large. The same is true with election fraud. Not only is it very difficult to detect after it occurs, particularly if there are no measures in place to expose it, candidates who want to contest election results have only a very short window to develop the evidence needed for a challenge.

The PILF reports on alien registration and voting are a strong indication of how much bigger the problem is than the numbers in the Heritage Election Fraud Database. Two other reports are also worth noting.

In 2017, the Government Accountability Institute (GAI) released a report concluding that thousands of votes in the 2016 election were illegal duplicate votes from people who had registered and voted in more than one state.[65]

GAI obtained voter registration and voter history data from twenty-one states. It wanted to gather more data, but many states imposed "exorbitant costs or refuse[d] to comply with voter information requests." These twenty-one states represent "about 17 percent of all possible state-to-state comparison combinations." GAI compared the lists using an "extremely conservative matching approach that sought only to identify two votes cast in the same legal name." It found that 8,471 votes in 2016 were "highly likely" duplicates.

GAI concluded that extrapolating this to all fifty states would likely produce, with "high-confidence," around forty-five thousand duplicate votes. GAI reached this level of confidence by matching not only names and birthdays, which can be the same for different individuals, but also by contracting with companies that have commercial databases to further cross-check these individuals using their Social Security numbers and other information to obtain unique identifiers on each registered voter.

According to GAI, "the probability of correctly matching two records with the same name, birthdate, and social security number is close to 100 percent." In fact, "using these match points will result in virtually zero false positives." A false positive in data comparisons occurs when two different individuals have the same name and birthdate. For example, John James Smith born July 4, 1976, appearing on two state voter registration lists may actually be two different people.

GAI also found more than fifteen thousand voters registered at prohibited addresses "such as post office boxes, UPS stores, federal post offices, and public buildings." In some cases, more than a hundred voters "were registered to the same UPS store locations." It also found voters whose registered addresses were "gas stations, vacant lots, abandoned mill buildings, basketball courts, parks, warehouses, and office buildings."

As with the PILF reports on aliens, not a single election official or law enforcement official in any of the twenty-one states contacted GAI to obtain the names of the voters who had illegally voted twice from two different states or who were registered at nonresidential addresses to investigate and possibly remove them from their voter rolls and prosecute them.

PILF carried out similar research, creating what is probably the most accurate database of voter registrations and voting history in the nation, SAVE (Safeguarding America's Votes and Elections). This is the database former Pres. Trump's Presidential Advisory Committee on Election Integrity wanted to create but was prevented from doing so. In September 2020, PILF released a report, "Critical Condition," that highlights the severity of the problem: inaccurate voter rolls, duplicate registrations, dead voters, and incomplete registrations, all of which allow fraud by those willing to exploit vulnerabilities in the system.[66]

The foundation discovered more than 144,000 instances of

potential election fraud in the 2016 and 2018 elections, ranging from individuals illegally voting in multiple states to someone voting in the name of a deceased person.

To create the SAVE database, PILF obtained voter registration and voter history data for the 2016 and 2018 elections from forty-two states. It had to sue three states—Illinois, Maine, and Maryland—to get what is supposed to be public information after they refused to comply with their own laws. Just like the Government Accountability Institute, PILF supplemented the state voter registration information with commercial and government data sources, such as credit agencies, obituaries, and the Social Security Death Index to sift out as many "false positives" as possible.

PILF found 349,773 deceased registrants on the voter rolls in forty-one states. The worst states were Michigan, Florida, New York, Texas, and California. Even worse, state records showed that 7,890 of these deceased voters were credited by state officials with casting ballots from the grave in the 2016 presidential election and that 6,718 did so in the 2018 congressional elections.

PILF also found

- 8,360 individuals who registered and voted in two different states during the 2018 election
- 43,760 individuals who registered more than once at the same address and who cast second votes in the 2016 election
- 37,889 individuals who registered more than once at the same address and who voted twice in 2018 (thousands of these apparent double votes were exclusively mail-in ballots)
- 5,500 individuals who voted twice in the same state from two different registration addresses in 2018

- 34,000 voters who registered at nonresidential, commercial addresses—such as gas stations, casinos, and restaurants—and who voted in the 2018 election

That last problem, registering at a commercial address, is a serious issue. In fact, former Rep. Steve Watkins (R-Kan.) agreed to a plea deal to enter a diversion program in 2021 after he was charged with election fraud for claiming a UPS store as his residence when he registered to vote, then voting in a 2019 municipal election in Topeka, Kansas.[67] PILF found that seventeen ballots were cast from a self-storage facility in Compton, California, and four ballots were cast from the NPR headquarters in Culver City, California (which is clearly not a residence), including by one of its reporters, Carrie Jane Kahn, and a producer, Anjuli Sastry.[68] This was particularly ironic given that NPR falls within the media-election-fraud-denial camp. NPR never responded to this story, and California officials just ignored this potential violation of the law.

PILF even produced a video in which it sent a crew to Nevada to visit the registered addresses of "voters" who had cast ballots in the 2018 election from commercial addresses like liquor stores, post offices, and vacant lots where the supposed voters obviously do not live—if they even exist.[69]

As with the GAI report, not a single state election or law enforcement official contacted PILF to request the names of the thousands of voters who may have committed fraud in their states. Neither did the Election Crimes Unit of the Public Integrity Section of the U.S. Justice Department, which is supposed to supervise the prosecution of federal election crimes by the department. In fact, J. Christian Adams, the president and general counsel of PILF, says his lawyers "spent hours upon hours explaining the data, methodology and conclusions to assistant U.S. Attorneys and FBI special agents" trying to get them interested in using PILF's data to investigate violations of federal election laws.

But Adams says "they didn't lift a finger to validate any of it. They were more concerned with finding a reason not to do something than finding potential crimes. They worked harder to develop reasons not to act—such as there being no way to be sure it was actually the person voting in their own name—than they did to talk to one single potential double voter."[70]

So 144,117 potential cases of election fraud through double voting, voting from the grave, and voting from false residential addresses, as well as thousands of registrations and voting by aliens, remain uninvestigated and unprosecuted, and the fraud-sters remain on the rolls, free to cheat again. And why not? Their chances of being caught or punished are virtually nil.

# LIBERALS' DREAM LEGISLATION: H.R.1 AND THE THREAT TO ELECTION INTEGRITY AND THE FIRST AMENDMENT

W hen Democrats took over the House of Representatives in 2019 and elected Nancy Pelosi as the speaker, the very first bill they introduced was H.R.1, the deceptively named For the People Act. It represented every change that liberals, especially left-wing advocacy groups, have wanted to make in both the nation's election laws and federal campaign laws.

The first goal of H.R.1 was a complete federal takeover from the states of the rules governing the administration of elections. The states have been administering our elections since the founding of the country. H.R.1 was written in a way that destroys all security and safety protocols and rules that states have implemented to protect the franchise and the integrity of the voting and election process. The effect would be to make it easy to cheat and easy to manipulate election results in order to ensure the victory of the left side of the political aisle.

The second goal of H.R.1 was to change the federal rules that govern presidential and congressional campaigns to silence opposition to liberal policies and candidates and to put the enforcement machinery of the federal government to work in a partisan manner to go after the Democratic Party's opponents. Sen. Sheldon Whitehouse (D-R.I.), one of the chief supporters of H.R.1 and its equivalent in the Senate, S.1, proudly admitted as much in a Zoom meeting for liberal activists.[1] Whitehouse apparently believes that nonprofit organizations and other groups that voice their opinions on public policy issues that do not disclose all of their members and donors use "dark money" and have no right to participate in the American political and policy-making process despites the protections of the First Amendment. The federal campaign finance changes being pushed by Whitehouse include changing the Federal Election Commission, the federal agency that enforces the Federal Election Campaign Act, from a bipartisan commission to a commission controlled by one political party.[2]

One of this book's authors, Hans von Spakovsky, testified against H.R.1 in the first hearing of the House Judiciary Committee held under its new chairman, Rep. Jerrold Nadler (D-N.Y.) on Jan. 29, 2019. As he told a very hostile audience on the Committee,

> In summary, many of the provisions of H.R.1 are clearly unconstitutional. Others are redundant and unnecessary, covering areas and issues where existing federal law is more than sufficient to protect voters. Many of the provisions are just bad policy that will neither help voters nor election officials in administering a fair and secure voter registration and election process.
>
> H.R.1 interferes with the ability of states to determine the qualifications of their voters, to secure the integrity of the election process, and to determine the districts and boundary lines of their representatives. Overall, H.R.1 is an attempt to federalize and micromanage the election process and impose unnecessary, unwise and in some cases unconstitutional mandates on the states, reversing the decentralization of the American election process that our Founders believed was essential to preserving liberty and freedom.[3]

H.R.1 passed the House on a party-line vote on March 8, 2019, but then, fortunately for the public, the bill came to a complete stop in the Senate. Sen. Mitch McConnell (R-Ky.) declared it dead on arrival, saying it would "not get any floor time."[4] The misleading propaganda about the bill engendered by the left and amplified by its allies in the media was, however, pervasive. A bill that was anti-democratic, anti–First Amendment, and anti-integrity was instead falsely portrayed as an "anti-corruption and pro-democracy reform bill."[5]

After the 2020 presidential and congressional elections, H.R.1 (with very few changes) was reintroduced in the House, and it passed almost immediately on March 3, 2021, with no hearings and again on a party-line vote with the sole exception of Rep. Bennie Thompson (D-Miss.). He told Fox News that he voted against the bill (even though he was a cosponsor) because his constituents did not like the "redistricting portion of the bill as well as the section on public financ[ing]" of congressional campaigns.[6]

Fortunately, H.R.1 was stopped in the Senate when Republicans successfully filibustered the bill and Democrats were unable, on June 22, 2021, to get enough votes to end the filibuster. Its passage would have been a massive setback for American voters and our democratic process. Halting it was imperative to protecting the integrity of our elections and the ability of citizens to freely speak and act in the public sphere. Even though Republicans managed to stop H.R.1 in 2021, there is no doubt it will rear its head again in future congressional sessions, either in its entirety or with the bill broken up into many separate bills.

So what would the 2021 version of H.R.1 do? In essence, H.R.1 would implement nationwide the worst changes in election rules that came about during the 2020 election, many of them masquerading as emergency provisions needed due to the pandemic. It would then go even further in making other changes that would increase, not decrease, the security weaknesses inherent in the current "honor" voter registration and voting system that exists in states across the country. All the changes in H.R.1 represent the long-term goals of liberals to completely change the way elections (and political campaigns) are administered in this country, changes that will inevitably corrupt the system and make it completely untrustworthy.

To start with, H.R.1 would force every state to implement same-day voter registration.[7] This would mandate that states allow individuals to register at polling places on Election Day and then immediately vote. This would give election officials no opportunity and no time to verify the accuracy of the voter registration information and the eligibility of the individual to vote, which is the reason most states require individuals to register prior to Election Day. States that want individuals to provide proof that they are citizens and therefore entitled to vote would be out of luck; H.R.1 prohibits a state from requiring more than a signature to verify their eligibility to vote.[8]

What makes this same-day registration requirement especially pernicious is that H.R.1 guts all state voter ID laws. Under H.R.1, states can only require individuals to sign a form in which they "attest" that they are who they claim they are and that they are eligible to vote.[9] This makes photo ID laws unenforceable and opens the door to fraud. When combined with same-day registration, it means that anyone willing to cheat or steal an election could walk into any polling place anywhere in the country, register under a fake name and address, immediately vote, then walk out of the polling place scot-free—and election officials could do absolutely nothing to stop it.

Moreover, same-day registration could lead to chaos at polling places. Election officials decide how many ballots and how many personnel are needed at polling places based on the number of registered voters. This helps ensure that there are enough ballots for all the voters who may show up on Election Day. However, if hundreds of unregistered voters show up on Election Day, election officials may not have enough ballots or staff, leading to the disenfranchisement of voters.

Another H.R.1 mandate would lead to similar problems. It requires states to count the ballots of individuals who vote outside their assigned precinct, overriding the precinct system traditionally used by almost all states.[10] A voter is assigned to a precinct based on his or her address, and precincts get different ballots based on the various districts in which the precinct is located to account for those running for local, state, and federal offices. So each precinct might have its own unique slate of races that is not interchangeable with other precincts. This provision of H.R.1 would encourage voters to vote outside their assigned precincts, resulting in voter disenfranchisement not only because polling places may be understaffed or may run out of ballots but because voters will not be able to vote for the local, state, or federal races from their assigned precinct that are not the same as those in the precinct where they end up voting.

Automatic voter registration is another requirement in H.R.1. The bill requires all states to implement automatic registration of individuals without their permission from state and federal databases.[11] Among the state agencies included in the mandate are state Departments of Motor Vehicles, corrections and welfare offices, agencies that administer certain provisions of the Social Security Act and the Affordable Care Act (i.e., Obamacare), and "institutions of higher learning." The federal agencies include the Social Security Administration, the Department of Veterans Affairs, the Department of Defense, the Department of Labor, the Center for Medicare & Medicaid Services of the Department of Health and Human Services, the Federal Bureau of Prisons, and the Bureau of

Citizenship and Immigration Service at the Department of Homeland Security.[12]

We explain in more detail in another chapter the drawbacks and problems with automatic voter registration, but there is one main problem worth highlighting here. Not only will automatic registration lead to multiple and duplicate registrations in the same state and in different states, but it is also highly likely to lead to the registration of ineligible individuals such as felons and noncitizens. States do not even have to notify individuals for up to four months that they have been registered. This mandate will also put federal agencies in the dubious position of trying to determine the domiciles of individuals in their databases for voting purposes, which could affect their tax status.

Supporters of H.R.1 claim that it will not lead to the registration of aliens since agencies are only supposed to forward information on individuals for whom they have citizenship status. But they cannot know if that will happen given the long, extensive list of state and federal agencies subject to the mandate in H.R.1, which includes public schools that make a point not to learn the citizenship status of their students. Databases are inaccurate, and bureaucrats make mistakes and may send in information even when they are not sure if it qualifies.

Government bureaucrats at both the state and federal levels greatly fear accusations of denying people their civil rights, and if they are in doubt, they will submit the registration information rather than rock the boat and risk an accusation of having engaged in discriminatory behavior, particularly when they know it is a violation of federal law for any such official to "make any statement . . . or take any action the purpose or effect of which is to discourage" anyone from "registering to vote."[13]

It is quite clear that the sponsors of H.R.1 fully expect that the automatic voter registration mandate will result in aliens being registered. Why else would they include a provision saying that an alien who is automatically registered as a result of this mandate cannot be "prosecuted under any Federal or State law, adversely affected in any civil adjudication concerning immigration status or naturalization, or subject to an allegation in any legal proceeding that the individual is not a citizens of the United States"?[14]

As if same-day and automatic voter registration were not enough, H.R.1 additionally would force states to implement online voter registration, an invitation for massive voter registration fraud by hackers and cyber criminals.[15] The bill includes forcing states to accept electronic signatures, which many experts say are easily forged.[16] While some states have implemented online voter registration, they have done so for individuals for whom they already have an existing state record, such as a driver's license, limiting the risk of false registrations. H.R.1 would force states to allow online registration to anyone, which is very risky given how unreliable and unverifiable so much activity is on the Internet.

At the same time that H.R.1 compels states to put in same-day, automatic, and online voter registration, which will add ineligible individuals and duplicates to registration rolls, it severely restricts the ability of election officials to verify the accuracy of those same rolls, fix errors, and challenge or remove individuals who should not be on the rolls. For example, it bans states from removing any registrants within six months of an election as part of any general program to find voters who have moved or otherwise become ineligible.[17] So even if election officials obtain absolute proof a week before an election that a voter has moved to another state, they cannot remove him from the voter roll to prevent him from voting.

Some states participate in crosscheck programs, where states compare one state's voter registration list to different states in order to identify multiple registrations or people who have moved. The bill mandates that states cannot use information from a crosscheck unless it provides the full name, including the middle name, of the voter along with his birthdate and the last four digits of his Social Security number.

The result is that if any of that specific information is missing, election officials are barred from removing voters even if they have irrefutable proof that the same voter is registered in two different states. An example would be if a report shows that John A. Smith is registered in state A and that John Aaron Smith is registered in State B, with both Smiths having the same birthdate and the same last four digits of their Social Security number, H.R.1 would not allow Mr. Smith (who is obviously the same person) to be removed even if the state has other evidence such as affidavits from family members swearing that both Smiths are the same person.[18]

The only exception to this is if a state has "documentation" from the ERIC program showing an individual is registered in another state. ERIC is the Electronic Registration Information Center program started by Pew Charitable Trusts. Favoring the ERIC program is an attempt through H.R.1 to discourage states from using any other crosscheck program, particularly the Interstate Cross-Check Program started by Kansas and Missouri.

Why would federal law favor one program over another? Because former Kansas Secretary of State Kris Kobach is hated by liberals for his work on election integrity. Unlike the Kansas program that has no fees, ERIC charges participating states and requires states to send out yearly notices to individuals who are not registered to vote, enticing them to register.

States routinely use the National Change of Address (NCOA) system of the U.S. Postal Service to find individuals who have moved. The NCOA system was expressly sanctioned for states to use in the National Voter Registration Act and was upheld (to the consternation of liberals) by the U.S. Supreme Court in *Husted v. A. Phillip Randolph Institute* in 2018.[19] H.R.1 reverses this result by designating a list derived from this information as an "unverified list" that cannot be used to delete voters without additional evidence of ineligibility.[20] It even creates a criminal offense called "vote caging" for using undeliverable mail as the basis to remove or challenge the eligibility of a registered voter.

In fact, states are prohibited from ever removing any registered voter for the "failure of the registrant to vote in any election" or "to respond to any notice" sent by election officials even if the notices are undeliverable and the voter cannot be located.[21] In other words, if a registered voter doesn't vote for a hundred years and doesn't respond to notice after notice after notice from election officials trying to find out if he is alive, has moved, or has otherwise become ineligible to vote, a state still can't remove him from the registration roll.

Moreover, H.R.1 makes it a criminal offense punishable by a fine of up to $100,000 and five years in prison for anyone, "whether acting under color of law or otherwise," to "hinder, interfere with, or prevent another person from registering to vote."[22] Notice that this provision applies to "persons," not eligible citizens. Thus, this provision could be used to prosecute someone, including an election official "acting under color of law," who rejects a voter registration application or challenges the eligibility of an alien or felon or someone who lives out of state to register to vote.[23] The fear of criminal prosecution will no doubt prevent election officials and ordinary citizens from challenging voter registrations even when they have evidence that a particular "person" is not eligible to be registered.

Not only that, but ordinary citizens are prohibited from challenging a person's eligibility to vote on Election Day or challenging an individual's eligibility to register to vote fewer than ten days before Election Day unless that individual registered to vote fewer than twenty days before Election Day.[24] This means that if you are in a polling place on Election Day and you see someone impersonating your neighbor who died before Election Day, not only can you not challenge the impersonator's right to vote, you could be criminally charged for doing so.

The same provision of H.R.1 bars challenges based on the age of the voter. Using the same example, if you are in a polling place on Election Day and you see the son of your neighbor, who is only sixteen, come in to vote, you could be criminally prosecuted if you challenge his right to vote. What is particularly troublesome about this is that H.R.1 makes it a violation of federal law for states to *refuse* to preregister sixteen- and seventeen-year-olds.[25] Since the voter registration lists provided to precinct officials do not usually contain the age of a registered voter, this will make it very easy for underaged minors to vote.

H.R.1 also severely restricts the public disclosure of voter registration information, limiting the ability of nonpartisan organizations to review voter rolls to find voters who are deceased, have moved, or have otherwise become ineligible to vote. This provision is clearly aimed at preventing the work of conservative organizations like the Public Interest Legal Foundation, which has raised the ire of the left with its reports on the thousands of aliens, dead voters, and individuals registered multiple times in the same and different states on state registration rolls.[26] As we have explained, absentee or mail-in ballots are the tool of choice for vote thieves. Therefore, it should come as no surprise that H.R.1 does everything it can to swamp the election process with absentee ballots. Not only does it require states to implement "no-fault" absentee ballots, which allow anyone to vote using an absentee ballot without needing an excuse, but it also forces states to[27]

- Give American Indians special privileges by compelling states to send all Native Americans living on tribal lands mail-in ballots without requiring them to even request a ballot, treating them differently than other voters
- Mail absentee ballot request forms to all registered voters
- Accept absentee ballots for ten days after Election Day as long as they are postmarked by Election Day
- Pay for return postage on all absentee and mail-in ballots
- Allow one request for an absentee ballot from a voter to serve as a permanent request for absentee ballots to be sent to the voter in all future elections
- Accept absentee ballots delivered by anyone, including candidates, party activists, campaign staffers, and political operatives

States are banned from implementing the most basic security protocols to prevent fraud in the absentee balloting process. H.R.1 prohibits states from requiring "identification as a condition of obtaining an absentee ballot." Further, states cannot enforce any "notarization or witness signature" requirement for absentee ballots.[28] And H.R.1 restricts the ability of states to do signature comparisons on absentee ballots except under certain limited conditions and requirements.

All of these mandates of H.R.1 degrade the security of the election system. For example, given the notorious inaccuracy of voter rolls (which will get worse under H.R.1), sending out absentee ballot request forms to all registered voters means that envelopes will be arriving all over the state at the residential addresses of registered voters who are deceased or have moved. Those envelopes will have the exact, official registration name and address of the voter, making it even easier for fraudsters to obtain absentee ballots in the names of those voters.

Requiring prepaid postage on the return envelopes sent to voters will make it easy for individuals to wait until after Election Day to vote. Election officials are obviously not going to put stamps on tens of thousands of envelopes; instead, they will use their own postmarking machines to postmark the envelopes. Those envelopes may thus have the date they were postmarked prior to Election Day before they were sent to voters. The U.S. Postal Service will in all likelihood not re-postmark those envelopes when they collect them.

So the H.R.1 provision requiring states to accept absentee ballots for ten days as long as they are postmarked by Election Day may not serve as an obstacle to voters waiting until after Election Day to vote, after they see the early returns. Or more dangerously, it will serve as an incentive to vote traffickers working for candidates and political parties to spread out in neighborhoods after Election Day to find absentee ballots that have not yet been completed or sent in.

The desire of the sponsors of H.R.1 to ensure that they obtain the votes of rapists, child molesters, and other criminals is exposed in H.R.1, as is their contempt for the Constitution. Section 2 of the Fourteenth Amendment specifically gives states the authority to abridge the right to vote of citizens "for participation in rebellion, or other crime." So it is entirely up to states to decide if felons will lose their right to vote and, if they do, when and how that right will be restored. Forty-eight states do not allow felons to vote and have differing rules on when that right to vote is restored, while Maine, Vermont, and the District of Columbia allow felons to vote even while in prison.[29] Felon voting is an issue that is entirely up to the people of each state to decide.

Yet Section 1403 of H.R.1 requires states to restore the ability of felons to vote the moment they are out of prison even if they have not completed all the requirements of their sentences, such as probation or the payments of court costs and restitution to their victims. This violates the Fourteenth Amendment, and it is obvious to anyone—except, it seems, the sponsors of this bill—that you cannot use a congressional act to override a constitutional amendment.

Aside from the constitutional issue, the argument that felons have paid their debts to society and are entitled to the full rights of citizenship upon their release is not persuasive. While serving a sentence discharges a felon's "debt to society" in the sense that his basic right to live in society is restored, serving a sentence does not require society to forget what he did. It does not bar society from making reasonable judgments based on his past crimes and possible future behavior (or misbehavior, given the extremely high rates of recidivism of felons) or to require a felon to complete *all* the terms of his sentence, including restitution to the victims of his crimes, before this ability to vote is restored.

Despite all the noble-sounding sentiment contained in this provision about how restoring the right to vote "reintegrates individuals with criminal convictions into free society," if the sponsors really thought that was true, why does this provision not restore all the other civil rights felons lose, such as the right to own a gun or serve on a jury? The fact it does not shows that the sponsors want felons in the ballot booth for their votes but do not trust them in the community at large.

While we are concerned with the destruction of election integrity caused by H.R.1's changes to state election laws, it is worth mentioning two other dangerous changes made in this monstrosity of a bill, one affecting redistricting and another making major changes to federal campaign laws.

H.R.1 would force state legislatures to hand over the redistricting process to unaccountable, appointed bureaucrats, implement both racial and gender quotas, and impose what amounts to a religious test on the people chosen to participate in redistricting that violates the associational and religious rights of the public.

People often complain about gerrymandering by state legislatures when they draw the political lines after every decennial census. But legislators at least are accountable to voters, who can vote them out of office if they are not satisfied with the job the legislators do.

That is certainly not true with the appointed members of government commissions.

Yet that is exactly what H.R.1 creates.[30] It would abrogate the authority of state legislators to draw the boundary lines of congressional districts and transfer it to so-called "independent" redistricting commissions, which in states like Arizona and California have not, in fact, proven to be very independent.

The detailed requirements for eligibility to serve on these commissions, hidden deep inside the bill, are shocking and offensive.

Are you an American who has recently changed his mind about which political party best supports your values, views, and principles? If you have done so within the past three years, you cannot serve on a commission because you are only eligible if you have "been continuously registered to vote with the same political party" for the three years prior to your appointment.

If you want to be considered for appointment, you have to disclose your "household income for the most recent taxable year." Apparently, your income somehow determines whether you are qualified to determine the political boundaries of congressional districts.

But it gets worse.

You cannot even be considered for the commission unless you disclose your "involvement with, or financial support of, professional, social, political, religious, or community organizations or causes."

In other words, not only do you have to disclose which church, mosque, or synagogue you attend, but you also must disclose your support for nonprofit organizations like the NAACP or the NRA, NARAL, or Citizens for Life.

That's exactly the kind of information the U.S. Supreme Court in 1958 told Alabama that it could not require to be publicly disclosed because it violated the constitutional rights of citizens to associate for the advancement of their beliefs and ideas.[31]

In today's "woke" cancel culture, forcing such disclosure would likely subject anyone who wants to be in the "selection pool" to harassment and intimidation—exactly what the NAACP feared would happen to its members when it went to court in 1958.

Furthermore, religious tests are strictly outlawed by Article VI of the Constitution for federal offices, and the Supreme Court extended that prohibition to all state offices in 1961.[32] Forcing individuals to disclose their religious affiliation puts them in the position of not being chosen due to their religious beliefs, which is essentially a prohibited religious test.

What possible explanation is there for the sponsors of H.R.1 to put this into their bill other than to allow that to happen?

But H.R.1 is even more insidious. The Civil Rights Act of 1964 bans discrimination based on race, color, religion, sex, or national origin. So why does H.R.1 require anyone who wants to be in the "selection pool" to disclose their "race, ethnicity, [and] gender"? It is because H.R.1 sets up what amount to discriminatory quotas for membership, that is why.

H.R.1 requires that membership on the redistricting commission be "representative of the demographic groups (including, racial, ethnic, economic, and gender)...of the State." In other words, the membership of the commission has to match the racial, ethnic, and gender proportions of the state's population. In short, that is a racial- and gender-quota system.

To be a considered for appointment, you also have to disclose your "employment and educational history." That history is not relevant to whether you are entitled to vote, and we would all be highly offended and incensed if Congress said there should be "employment and educational" requirements before you are allowed to vote.

So where is the outrage over your job and education history being a consideration with respect to whether you, as a citizen, are allowed to be selected to draw the lines of the congressional district in which you are qualified to vote or run as a candidate?

Moreover, this provision discriminates against spouses and family members of those who are active in politics. You cannot be on a commission if your spouse or other "immediate" family member holds public office, even if that is a local or state office that has nothing whatsoever to do with Congress or congressional districts. And an "immediate family member" is broadly defined as someone's "father, stepfather, mother, stepmother, son, stepson, daughter, stepdaughter, brother, stepbrother, sister, stepsister, husband, wife, father-in-law, or mother-in-law."[33] So huge swaths of the public will be excluded from the redistricting process because of their family's political involvement or their race, ethnicity, gender, income, employment, religious beliefs, or education.

The redistricting portion of H.R.1 also requires states to count aliens, both legal and illegal, in the population used to draw new congressional districts, which critics claim violates the "one person, one vote" principle.[34] Noncitizens, particularly illegal aliens, are not entitled to any representation or constituent services. Forcing aliens to be counted distorts the redistricting process and shifts political power in a way that is fundamentally unfair to citizens. It dilutes the votes of citizens who live in districts with a high percentage of citizens in comparison to voters who live in districts with large numbers of noncitizens, including illegal aliens who are not eligible to vote.

Forcing the inclusion of aliens is pure power politics. Democratic-controlled legislative seats tend to have larger numbers of noncitizens than do Republican seats. Sean Trend, the senior elections analyst at RealClearPolitics, points out that in the heavily Democratic areas of Queens and Kings County, New York, only 78 percent of the residents are citizens. Compare this to Republican Nassau County, where 91 percent of the residents are citizens. Similarly, in the 2012 election, "counties with high citizen populations were more likely to vote for Mitt Romney" than Barack Obama.[35] If states started using citizen population for redistricting, congressional and state legislative districts would be redrawn in numerous parts of the country with large noncitizen populations, with a noticeable shift away from Democrats and toward Republicans. H.R. 1 wants to make sure no states have the option to use citizen population in redistricting.

Finally, H.R.1 makes numerous changes to federal campaign finance law that will infringe on the First Amendment rights of Americans to speak and act in the political life of the country. As Bradley Smith, former chairman of the Federal Election Commission, said in testimony before the Senate Committee on Rules and Administration on March 24, 2021:

> Labelling this bill the 'For the People Act' is Orwellian. In reality, [H.R.1] would subsidize the speech of politicians while suppressing the speech of the people...Significant portions of the bill would violate the privacy of advocacy groups and their supporters—including those groups who do nothing more than speak about policy issues before Congress or federal judicial nominees. Other key provisions would limit political speech on the Internet and compel speakers to recite lengthy government-mandated messages in their communications, instead of their own speech.

[H.R.1] would impose onerous and unworkable standards on the ability of Americans and groups of Americans to discuss the policy issues of the day with elected officials and the public... The proposal would coerce Americans into funding the campaigns of candidates with which they disagree...

Among the legislation's biggest violations of First Amendment rights are provisions requiring nonprofit groups to publicly expose their supporters when speaking about government. These requirements will subject Americans to harassment for their beliefs and allow politicians to build enemies lists of contributors to causes they dislike.[36]

Included among the disastrous changes would be a reduction of the number of commissioners on the Federal Election Commission from six to five.[37] This would break the bipartisan structure of the FEC, which has always had three Republican and three Democratic commissioners. Because it takes the votes of four commissioners for the FEC to take an enforcement action, it has acted in a bipartisan manner during its entire history. However, if three members of the FEC are members of the same political party and it only takes three votes to initiate an enforcement action, they will always be able to out-vote the two members of the opposing political party, in which case H.R.1 will, as Smith said in his testimony, "allow for partisan control of the regulation of campaigns and enable partisan control of enforcement."

The provisions of H.R.1 are so concerning that nine former commissioners with over six decades of service on the FEC wrote a letter in February of 2021 to Senate and House leaders voicing their objections to the bill. They focused particularly on its "harmful impact on First Amendment speech and association rights" that would "stifle constitutionally protected political speech."[38] The change in control of the FEC, said the commissioners, was "designed for partisan control" of a federal law enforcement agency and, in fact, makes dangerous changes designed to bias "the judicial review process" in enforcement actions "in favor of findings of guilt against candidates, campaigns, and other defendants." As the former commissioners said, this turns on its head the "American justice system [that] has traditionally erred in favor of the accused, so as to protect the innocent and unjustly convicted."

H.R.1 is without doubt the most dangerous bill to election integrity, free speech, and associational rights we have seen in all our years in the political arena. Moreover, its provisions are almost uniformly supported by Democrats and well-funded, radical left-wing advocacy groups and foundations. They are intent on winning elections, silencing those who disagree with them, and retaining and consolidating their political power, and they see H.R.1 as their tool to do that. Unfortunately, they are willing to damage the fundamental structure and integrity of our democratic process and to limit free speech and political activity by those they perceive as opposing the utopia they envision to replace the "old" America they want to cancel.

## CHAPTER SEVEN

# MARC E. ELIAS, INC., THE LEGAL GENERAL FOR THE LEFT

The legal mastermind probably most responsible for the leftist push to subvert our democracy, overturn elections, and destroy election integrity is Marc E. Elias, a partner at Perkins Coie, a Washington, D.C., legal powerhouse for the Democratic Party. Elias is the head of the law firm's political law practice, and he has grown astoundingly wealthy representing Democratic candidates, political action committees, and party organizations, earning "tens of millions of dollars in legal fees."[1] In fact, Perkins Coie has "billed over $170 million to Democratic campaigns, committees and candidates" since 2009, and that does not include the legal fees paid by nonprofit advocacy organizations that use his firm for lawsuits attacking election requirements like voter ID laws.[2]

Elias is probably best known to the public as the lawyer who (along with the DNC, his other client) retained Fusion GPS and paid for the infamous Steele Dossier when he was the general counsel for the Hillary Clinton presidential campaign in 2016.[3] Fusion GPS hired former British spy Christopher Steele, who created the now entirely discredited opposition research that claimed there was collusion between the Trump campaign and the Russian government to fix the 2016 presidential campaign. This hoax consumed the time and resources of the Trump administration for years while it fought false charges and a special counsel investigation, and it was used by the FBI to obtain four Foreign Intelligence Surveillance Act warrants.[4]

Elias took over Perkins Coie's political law practice from Bob Bauer, candidate Barack Obama's 2008 campaign lawyer who became President Obama's White House counsel. No one should forget that it was Bauer, as the general counsel for the Obama presidential campaign, who wrote a letter to the Justice Department on October 17, 2008, asking that a special prosecutor investigate Republicans like John McCain for talking publicly about voter fraud. According to Bauer, such talk was not only evidence of a "partisan political agenda," but it also supposedly intended to "suppress voting" by harassing voters and impeding "their exercise of their rights."[5] So just engaging in speech about election fraud—in the eyes of one of the Democratic Party's key lawyers—should be criminally prosecuted.

Unlike Republicans who are represented by many different lawyers and law firms, Elias seems to have a monopoly on the Democratic political machine. Democrats go to him and his law firm for representation, and the media treat him like a hero, in sharp contrast to their attacks on those who support election integrity. Even the *New York Times* acknowledges him as the "Democrats' lead lawyer" and the "most influential of unelected Democrats in Washington."[6]

As Elias brags in his biography on the law firm's website, he represents "dozens of U.S. senators, governors, representatives and their campaigns as well as the Democratic National Committee, Democratic Senatorial Campaign Committee, Democratic Congressional Campaign Committee, National Democratic Redistricting Committee, Priorities USA, Senate Majority PAC and the House Majority PAC."[7] He represents the Democratic Governors Association and has managed multiple recounts in United States Senate elections, such as Washington Senator Maria Cantwell's defeat of Slade Gorton. In other words, he represents every major Democratic Party organization. He has used that representation to reshape "the law and regulations governing American politics, from voting access to redistricting to campaign fund-raising and spending."[8]

Elias was also "accused of rigging the 2016 Democratic presidential primaries to thwart Bernie Sanders and facilitating a deluge of big money into politics."[9] He apparently engineered a memorandum of understanding in 2015 in which the Democratic National Committee essentially handed over its operation to the Clinton campaign for the 2016 election. Being the lawyer for both the party and the campaign raises serious legal and ethical concerns and is generally not allowed. Donna Brazile, who served as the interim chair of the DNC during the fall 2016 campaign, defended the arrangement as "not illegal," but that was far from clear.[10] At a minimum, the parties would have to execute what are called conflicts waivers acknowledging that they are aware that the lawyer is representing parties with conflicting interests and agreeing to the representation, though some conflicts can never be waived. This cozy arrangement may have been just one of the many reasons that candidate Kamala Harris hired Elias to be her presidential campaign's general counsel in 2019.[11]

Elias has been on the scene for years, and he was the lawyer who engineered the debut of former *Saturday Night Live* comedian Al Franken to the U.S. Senate in 2008. It was Elias, through litigation, who overturned one of the closest senate races in U.S. history. Norm Coleman, the incumbent Republican senator, won the race on Election Day by 725 votes out of 2.9 million cast, including approximately 300,000 absentee ballots. With the help of Democratic Secretary of State Mark Ritchie, who changed the rules regarding absentee ballots after the election, Elias managed to turn a loss for Franken into a 312-vote victory. Elias developed tactics now familiar to everyone, such as convincing election officials and courts in Minnesota to count absentee ballots that had already been rejected as legally defective and to ignore the problem that some ballots were actually double counted.[12]

Former Sen. Norm Coleman admitted in 2018 that he had been "out-lawyered" in his recount fight when he urged then U.S. Senator–elect Rick Scott of Florida to aggressively oppose the tactics of Elias, who represented losing candidate Bill Nelson in the recount of that race.[13] As the *Wall Street Journal* editorialized after Franken was seated as a Senator: "Modern elections don't end when voters cast their ballots. They only end after the lawyers count them."[14] Elias also helped overturn Republican Mark Obenshain's Election Day victory in the 2013 attorney general's race in Virginia, giving the initial loser, Democrat Mark Herring, a 164-vote victory out of 2.2 million cast. He has been involved in so many recounts to overturn Democratic losses that he has been dubbed the "Democrat's Recount King," and the 2018 Scott-Nelson battle in Florida was one of his few losses.[15]

It was Elias who engineered the legal campaign that plagued the 2020 elections. He filed the majority of the lawsuits that resulted in rules enacted by state legislatures and signed by governors being suspended by courts and election bureaucrats.

His anti-democratic strategy to suspend laws was nothing new. He has been active for years in misusing federal law such as the Voting Rights Act to obtain partisan political objectives that have nothing whatsoever to do with preventing racial discrimination in voting. For example, he filed a meritless lawsuit in 2017 claiming that a recall effort against three state

Democratic senators in Nevada violated the Voting Rights Act[16] even though the ability to mount recalls of state legislators and other elected officials has been a standard part of our election laws for decades.

The claim that trying to recall a state senator for misbehavior in office is somehow a discriminatory denial of voting rights is absurd. Elias actually made the laughable but patronizingly racist argument in his complaint that it would be too much of a "burden" on minority voters to have "to educate [themselves] about the logistical details of a recall election" and that they "would be burdened by the time it takes to vote."[17] In the complaint, Elias also actually alleged that blacks and Hispanics were not suited to follow public issues closely enough to vote in a recall election because they are not "politically astute."[18] This lawsuit shows the infamous lengths to which Elias will go to twist the law to help his political party. If a Republican lawyer or candidate made such a specious and insulting argument about minority voters, they would be justly condemned as racist.

J. Christian Adams, who opposed Elias in the Nevada recall case, told us, "His business model is to make outlandish arguments to judges who are inclined to agree with him but make sure the public never hears the preposterous legal theories he pushes. Otherwise, he'd be run out of town on a rail. He makes patronizing, demeaning, ridiculous arguments about how incapable blacks are at functioning in modern America and forum shops for courts where someone might just believe it. That's how he nullifies state election laws."[19]

His model is similar to the claim constantly made against voter ID laws: that showing an ID is just too burdensome for minority voters, another patronizingly racist argument. On April 22, 2021, North Carolina Lt. Governor Mark Robinson (R), the first black lieutenant governor in the history of the state, testified before the Judiciary Committee of the U.S. House of Representatives. He told the committee that he keeps hearing election reforms

> compared to Jim Crow, that black voices are being silenced and that black voices are being kept out. How? By bullets? By bombs? By nooses? No, by requiring a free ID to secure the vote. Let me say that again: by requiring a free ID to secure the vote. How absolutely preposterous.
>
> Am I to believe that black Americans who have overcome the atrocities of slavery, who were victorious in the civil rights movement, and now sit in the highest levels of this government could not figure out how to get a free ID to secure their votes? That they don't think we can figure out how to make our voices heard?
>
> Are you kidding me? The notion that people must be protected from a free ID to secure their votes is not just insane—it is insulting.[20]

As the premier investigative Capital Research Center think tank has reported, Elias "has led the charge" in lawsuits "against voter ID laws" and changes in "early voting in a number of red states," convincing leftist judges of the false claim "that measures intended to strengthen voting integrity actually created disparate impact on minority voters."[21] Elias often works in conjunction with leftist Democratic allies like the supposedly nonpartisan American Civil Liberties Union and the NAACP Legal Defense and Educational Fund. But as the CRC notes, "Perkins Coie isn't a *pro bono* defense fund. When the firm filed [voting rights] cases independently, the suits were paid for by a trust. But who funded this trust? None other than Georgia Soros,"[22] who put up $5 million to sue states like North Carolina over its voter ID law.[23]

There is no constitutional right to either early voting or same-day registration. Indeed, many states have neither. Failure to offer these options does not constitute racial discrimination, nor is it discriminatory to shorten an early-voting period. That reducing it or not implementing same-day registration is *de facto* racially motivated is the bizarre claim pushed by Elias and other leftist groups, including in the lawsuit they filed against North Carolina during the Obama administration with the help of Eric Holder's Justice Department.

At a hearing in 2014 before Judge Thomas D. Schroeder in the U.S. District Court for the Middle District of North Carolina, the Justice Department produced Prof. Charles Stewart of MIT's political science department. According to the transcript of that proceeding, when Stewart was asked why he believed that eliminating same-day registration was discriminatory, he said that same-day registration provides "a mechanism and a time that's well situated for *less sophisticated voters*, and therefore, it's less likely to imagine that these voters would—*can figure out or would avail themselves of other forms of registering and voting.*" [Emphasis added.]

And who are those "less sophisticated voters" who can't "figure out" how to register to vote? They "tend to be African Americans," according to Stewart. He added that "people who register to vote the closer and closer one gets to Election Day tend to be . . . less-educated voters, tend to be voters who are less attuned to public affairs." Stewart said that these voters "tend to be African Americans." Of course, the voter registration data in North Carolina directly contradicted this since Stewart was forced to admit that blacks in North Carolina actually "were registered at a higher rate than whites" before Election Day in the 2012 election.

Professor Stewart leveled the same type of criticism at a measure to reduce the number of early voting days in North Carolina from seventeen to ten. African Americans would be deterred from voting, he said again, because they are "less sophisticated voters." He denied that he was racially stereotyping blacks even when he said they have a harder time figuring out how "to navigate the rules of the game."

Stewart is the same expert the DOJ used in its unsuccessful 2012 challenge to South Carolina's voter ID law. There, he testified that the law would have a "disparate impact" on black voters. But a federal court was not persuaded by his "expert" testimony, and the law was subsequently implemented without any of the problems predicted by Stewart.

Back in North Carolina, Stewart was further embarrassed when he was forced to admit during cross-examination that, in testimony in a lawsuit challenging Florida's reduction in early voting days, he had predicted a "disparate impact" on black voters and that his prediction there was also that turnout would go down. Reality intruded on Dr. Stewart's theory, and black voter turnout actually increased.

The NAACP's expert was another professor, Barry Burden, of the University of Wisconsin. Burden claimed that blacks and Hispanics are less able "to pay the costs of voting" because of the "stark differences between whites, on the one hand, in North Carolina and those of blacks and Latinos in North Carolina." By costs, Burden was referring to "the time and effort that a voter has to put in in order to participate." That includes "locating the polling place, getting the right paperwork, understanding who the candidates are, becoming informed." From his testimony, it was clear that Burden did not think that blacks and Hispanics have the same ability as whites to accomplish basic tasks such as locating a polling place, filling out a one-page voter-registration form, and learning what issues candidates support or oppose.[24]

The patronizing and dismissive attitude toward black Americans and other minority voters is not much different from the attitudes one heard in the South during the Jim Crow era, when blacks were falsely stereotyped—then as now usually by Democratic elitists—as lazy and unable to competently function in society. Unfortunately, in *North Carolina State Conference of the NAACP v. McCrory*, a three-judge panel of the Fourth Circuit with two judges appointed by Barack Obama and one by Bill Clinton overruled the federal district court conclusion that none of these reforms were discriminatory in either purpose or effect.[25] Instead, it issued an almost insulting opinion that read more like a policy brief for the NAACP, ignoring the detailed analysis by the trial judge of the factual evidence and the expert's opinion that demonstrated that the various reforms were not enacted with any discriminatory intent and would not have a discriminatory effect on any voters.[26]

There seems little doubt that this partisan opinion by the three leftist judges of the Fourth Circuit would have been over-turned if the Supreme Court had actually reviewed the case. But in a graphic example of how important it is to elect the right people, the Supreme Court refused to take the appeal. Why? The appeal to the Supreme Court was filed by the state on behalf of its Republican governor prior to the 2016 election. But voters in 2016 elected a Democratic state attorney general, Josh Stein, and a new Democratic governor.

Stein immediately moved to dismiss the appeal. The North Carolina legislature, controlled by Republicans, objected, claiming that the attorney general had no authority under state law to dismiss the petition on behalf of the state. But because of this dispute, the Supreme Court decided not to take the case. According to Chief Justice John Roberts, "Given the blizzard of filings over who is and who is not authorized to seek review in this Court under North Carolina law, it is important to recall our frequent admonition that 'The denial of a writ of certiorari imports no expression of opinion upon the merits of the case.'"[27]

Elias has made it clear that he has no interest whatsoever in bipartisanship when it comes to changing voting laws. As an example, he told the *Washington Post* in 2016 that the way to reauthorize Section 5 of the Voting Rights Act of 1965 was "to make Nancy Pelosi the speaker of the House and Chuck Schumer the majority leader and put Hilary Clinton in the White House."[28] He got two of those three in 2020, and really three out of three with a Democratic president. President Biden urged Congress to reauthorize Section 5 by passing the John Lewis Voting Rights Advancement Act in his speech to Congress on April 28, 2021.

Section 5 was originally an emergency five-year provision that required certain covered states, like Alabama and Georgia, to get the preapproval of any changes in their voting laws from the very partisan, leftist career lawyers inside the Voting Section of the Civil Rights Division of the U.S. Justice Department or a three-judge panel in federal court in Washington, D.C. It kept getting renewed by Congress until the U.S. Supreme Court stuck it down in 2013 in the *Shelby County* decision, saying the discriminatory conditions that justified it no longer existed: "history did not end in 1965...yet the coverage formula that Congress reauthorized in 2006...[kept] the focus on decades-old data relevant to decades-old problems, rather than current data reflecting current needs."[29]

The *Shelby County* decision did not in any way affect Section 2 of the Voting Rights Act, which is a national, permanent provision that prohibits discrimination on a racial basis in the voting context. But what has angered leftist like Elias is that under Section 2, they have to file a lawsuit and go to court and *actually prove* that a voting requirement like voter ID or a witness signature on absentee ballots is racially discriminatory.

Under Section 5, they could simply call their friends in the Voting Section of the Civil Rights Division at the Department of Justice and get them to object to any new voting law or regulation they did not like. Almost all the career lawyers who worked there used to work at ultra-leftist civil rights organizations that are allied with the Democratic Party. In fact, a 2013 report by the Justice Department's inspector general faulted the Voting Section for hiring almost all its lawyers from just five organizations: the ACLU, La Raza, the Lawyers' Committee for Civil Rights Under Law, the NAACP, and the Mexican American Legal Defense and Education Fund.[30]

Elias wants Section 5 reinstated so that Democrats can use the Justice Department to stop any voting changes they do not like for partisan and political reasons having nothing to do with what the Voting Rights Act is intended to stop: racial discrimination.

Just how bad is this abuse of the law enforcement power of the Justice Department that Elias wants to reinvigorate? The Justice Department had to pay Georgia almost $600,000 in attorney fees in 1997 for its misfeasance in a redistricting case under the Voting Rights Act. A federal court was shocked at the collusion between the career lawyers inside the Voting Section and the ACLU, calling it "disturbing" and saying the "professed amnesia" exhibited by the lawyers about their communications with the ACLU lawyers were "less than credible."[31] The court found that "the considerable influence of ACLU advocacy on the voting rights decisions of the United States Attorney General is an embarrassment." The partisanship of the lawyers inside the Justice Department has only gotten worse since then, which is why Elias and other leftists want to bring back Section 5 of the Voting Rights Act.

Elias and his lawyers were actually sanctioned in 2021 in one of the voting rights cases he filed. The Fifth U.S. Circuit Court of Appeals issued an order sanctioning lawyers at Perkins Coie for filing a "redundant and misleading" motion in the court in an election case out of Texas.[32] The court said they "violated their duty of candor to the court."

In 2020, Elias filed a lawsuit against Texas, representing the Democratic Senatorial Campaign Committee, the Democratic Congressional Campaign Committee, and Sylvia Bruni, the chairwoman of the Webb County Democratic Party.

In 2017, the Texas Legislature had eliminated straight-ticket voting, in which a voter can simply mark one of the political parties on his ballot and a vote is automatically cast for every candidate of that political party.

The bill was signed into law on June 1, 2017, and was set to take effect on Sept. 1, 2020. Yet Elias and the Democratic Party waited nearly three years—until March 5, 2020—to file a lawsuit claiming that eliminating straight-ticket voting was somehow unconstitutional and discriminatory under the Voting Rights Act.

That claim is just as absurd as so many of his other claims. The Constitution says nothing about straight-ticket voting, and that voting option has nothing whatsoever to do with race. The first lawsuit was dismissed June 24, 2020, when a federal court said the original plaintiffs had no standing to sue.

Elias waited until Aug. 12 to file a new lawsuit, adding the Texas Alliance for Retired Americans as a plaintiff. This time, they lucked out and got an injunction from U.S. District Court Judge Marina Garcia Marmolejo, an Obama appointee, ordering Texas to reinstate straight-ticket voting for the impending election.

In the judge's view, having to mark each candidate that you want to vote for on a ballot is an "undue burden" on voters and their "right to associate" under the First and Fourteenth Amendments.

No, really, that was her rationale.

Texas filed an emergency appeal, and fortunately a panel of the Fifth Circuit unanimously stayed (voided) her injunction. As the panel said in its Sept. 30, 2020, decision, the U.S. Supreme Court has "time and time again over the past several years...stayed lower court orders that change election rules on the eve of an election."

Here, Marmolejo's injunction would have changed "election laws eighteen days before early voting begins." It would have done so, according to the Fifth Circuit, based on "shaky factual and legal ground[s]."

The court added that Marmolejo displayed a "fundamental misunderstanding of the way straight-ticket voting worked in Texas" and apparently thought that forcing voters "to make individual selections" would increase "the amount of time it will take to complete a ballot" and that this somehow rendered the law unconstitutional.

Furthermore, the district court judge accused the Texas Legislature of altering the status quo. But as the Fifth Circuit panel said, it was Marmolejo's "eleventh-hour injunction that alters the status quo."

She "ignores the fact that in June 2017, a majority of the Texas legislature—composed of officials elected by Texas voters to represent them—passed a law that ended the long practice of straight-ticket voting."

That "law became the new 'status quo,' and Plaintiffs had plenty of time over the past three years to challenge it," the appeals court held.

Texas had already mailed out thousands of ballots without straight-ticket voting, and suddenly voiding the law would have caused huge problems, something Elias obviously didn't care about. The stay was issued to "minimize confusion among voters and trained election officials."

So why did Elias and his fellow lawyers get sanctioned?

On Feb. 10, 2021, they filed a motion attempting to supplement the record in the case. But as the Fifth Circuit panel said, the new motion was "nearly identical" to a motion to supplement the record filed by the same lawyers in September.

Elias "failed to notify the court that their previous and nearly identical motion was denied."

This "inexplicable failure" violated "their duty of candor to the court. Moreover, their motion, "without directly saying so, sought reconsideration of their already denied motion," yet they filed it far beyond the fourteen-day deadline under the rules to seek reconsideration and "did not seek permission to file out of time."

The panel dismissed Perkins Coie's attempt to excuse their misbehavior, saying that if they were confused, "they could have and should have disclosed the previously denied motion in their new motion."

Moreover, Perkins Coie could have withdrawn its motion after Texas said it intended to seek sanctions against the firm "based on this lack of candor and violation of local rules."

Instead, Elias and his team of lawyers "stood by a motion that multiplied the proceedings unreasonably and vexatiously."

The March 11 order directed the individual lawyers (not Perkins Coie as a firm), including Elias, to pay the attorneys' fees and costs incurred by Texas for having to respond to their "vexatious" motion as well as "double costs."

And while the court did not order the lawyers to do it, the court "encourage[d]" them to review the Model Rule of Professional Conduct on "Candor Toward the Tribunal" and to "complete one hour of Continuing Legal Education in the area of Ethics and Professionalism."

In March 2020, at the same time Elias filed his losing Texas case, he set out what he intended to force states to do through litigation in a post at the *Democracy Docket*, his "progressive platform" dedicated to "opinion, advocacy and information about voting rights, elections, redistricting and democracy."[33] He listed four "minimum" requirements that he demanded states put in place in addition to "no-excuse absentee and vote by mail":

1. Postage must be free or prepaid by the government.
2. Ballots postmarked on or before Election Day must count.
3. Signature matching laws need to be reformed to protect voters.
4. Community organizations should be permitted to help collect and deliver completed, sealed ballots.

We have explained why all of these provisions threaten election integrity. Elias clearly wanted to make it as difficult as possible for states to actually conduct signature comparison on absentee ballots, and he boasted that he had already been successful in Florida, Georgia, and Iowa and that he was in the midst of suing Michigan. He also wanted to override state laws barring vote trafficking so that party activists and campaign staffers could get their hands on absentee ballots, with all the risks that entails, although he was careful to try to hide that by referring to the importance of "community organizations" being able to collect those ballots.

When you combine the first two pillars—providing prepaid postage on absentee ballots with a deadline that allows absentee ballots to come in after Election Day as long as long as they are postmarked by Election Day—it means that voters may be receiving return envelopes with pre–Election Day postmarks, allowing them to vote after Election Day when they have seen early returns. When that is combined with the other two pillars—ineffective signature matching with vote trafficking by political guns-for-hire—you have the perfect environment for election fraud and the ability to pressure and coerce voters in their homes.

The four pillars described the strategic plan for how leftists intended to weaken election integrity in the 2020 election, and it describes that continued plan as laid out in H.R.1.

What is ironic about this is that Elias tries to paint himself as "protecting civil rights, [which] ought to be something that we all strive to do." Yet a spokesman for George Soros, Michael Vachon, admitted that when Elias approached Soros for funding with proposals for challenging state election laws, they agreed with Elias that his work would be helpful "up and down the ballot" and that while other groups had to be nonpartisan, "there was a need to look at this from a partisan viewpoint."[34]

So no matter how noble Elias tries to sound, his attacks on election integrity have one purpose: to help the Democrats that he represents get elected. The fact that he and his allies believe the best way to do that is to destroy basic security protocols that states have in place to try to prevent fraud is more revealing than anything else they say or tell the fawning media.

# CHAPTER EIGHT

# ZUCKERBUCKS AND THE CENTER FOR TECH AND CIVIC LIFE

A sleepy Chicago-based nonprofit foundation, the Center for Tech and Civic Life (CTCL), had made nothing but small grants until 2019, when it grew explosively in the run-up to the 2020 election backed by a $350 million donation from Mark Zuckerberg, the chief executive of Facebook, and his wife, Priscilla Chan.

The money was then regranted to thousands of local government election offices across America to ostensibly "preserve the integrity of our elections."

You would think it would make a huge news story. Instead it was largely left to think tanks to notice what Hayden Ludwig of the Capital Research Center calls "perhaps the biggest underreported story" of the 2020 election.[1]

CTCL used its newfound fortune to send grants to government officials responsible for administering the 2020 election.

The CTCL money went to 2,500 jurisdictions to pay for additional polling places, ballot drop boxes, "voter education," and extra efforts to turn out non–English speaking voters. Strings were clearly attached to the grants, and the result was that elections in key swing states were effectively "privatized" with hardly anyone noticing.

That is not an exaggeration. When county election officials in New York begged the State Board of Elections for more money after a chaotic primary in which they were overwhelmed by absentee ballots, the *New York Times* reported that the board told the county officials they should "apply for grants—not from the state, but from a nonprofit foundation, the Center for Tech and Civic Life" backed by Zuckerberg.[2]

The Facebook angle should have seemed odd to media observers. It was Facebook's admitted lack of oversight of supposed disinformation in the 2016 election that led to accusations of electoral meddling and strong condemnations from Democrats and Republicans. And its founder clearly dominated CTCL's funding. It was nothing more than a subsidiary of Zuckerberg, Inc. during the 2020 campaign. In 2018, CTCL had only $1.4 million in revenue and only $560,000 of that from grants. Zuckerberg's bucks allowed it to increase its revenue by an astounding 25,000 percent.

Details about what CTCL did with its 2020 revenue windfall aren't easy to come by because it has refused to answer media questions. Despite CTCL declaring that its grants were meant to offset unforeseen expenses due to COVID-19, reports show that only a tiny fraction of the monies typically went to things like personal protective equipment. CTCL spent much more on financing the placement of drop boxes for mail-in votes and foreign-language get-out-the-vote ads in liberal enclaves.

In September 2020, the Philadelphia City Council held an emergency five-minute Zoom meeting in order to approve a $10 million grant from CTCL to the city's election office. The contract specified in great detail where and how the money would be spent. The city's entire election administration budget before the grant was $15 million.

CTCL's $10 million grant to Philadelphia stipulated that the city use its funds to provide printing and postage for mail-in ballots and to scatter ballot drop boxes. CTCL's intervention effectively greased the wheels for an unprecedented flood of largely untraceable, potentially fraudulent mail-in ballots submitted via private drop boxes throughout an urban stronghold for the Democratic Party with no official oversight or accountability after the fact.

Besides turning Election Day into Election Month, the flood of millions of mail-in ballots opened the system to unprecedented confusion and largely untraceable fraud. There's a reason that a bipartisan commission cochaired by former President Jimmy Carter in 2005 called mail-in absentee ballots the "largest source of potential voter fraud" and that most countries in the European Union have banned "postal voting" over the same concerns.[3]

As *The New Yorker* magazine laconically noted about the CTCL grant: "Turnout by Philadelphia's Black voters is vital to the Democrats' hopes to retake Pennsylvania from Trump, who won the state by just 44,000 votes in 2016."[4] The $10 million grant from CTCL represented a whopping $13.60 for every voter who cast a ballot in Philadelphia.[5] In essence, Democrats were using local government as their get-out-the-vote program for the presidential election.

The thought of liberal billionaire donors using nonprofits to manipulate elections through gifts to government offices should have rung alarm bells. For years, we've heard left-leaning election officials and campaign finance reform advocates rail against political donations by billionaires. Indeed, New York Rep. Alexandria Ocasio-Cortez has used her Twitter account to tell her millions of followers that she objects to the very existence of billionaires.[6]

Perhaps that explains why the Center for Tech and Civic Life took great pains to fly under the radar in the 2020 election. "Liberals often complain about 'dark money' that isn't fully transparent," says Scott Walter of the Capital Research Center. "Well, CTCL's money is as 'dark' as it comes."[7]

Indeed, CTCL refused to disclose the hundreds of millions of dollars it received from Zuckerberg. The revelation came from Zuckerberg himself, many weeks after the donation was made. CTCL declines to provide its full donor list, and it's organized as a 501(c)(3) nonprofit, which allows it to avoid revealing any donors.

CTCL also refuses to reveal where its hundreds of millions went in the last election. It has admitted that thousands of local election offices in dozens of states received grants, and it has posted a "preliminary" list of local government offices that received funds.

But of course the critical question is how much money went to which election offices. CTCL refuses to make public that information even though federal law requires CTCL to report every grant of $5,000 or more to any government agency on its IRS Form 990, a public document.[8] Conveniently, CTCL can delay filing that document until November 2021. It has refused to answer questions from the Associated Press, NPR, *The New Yorker*, and others about who specifically funded its large grants to major cities in battleground states.

Luckily, we do know something about CTCL's footprint. The Capital Research Center has examined CTCL's sketchy disclosure list as well as news databases and local government reports, and it assembled a data report on its activity in key states. It found that CTCL money was directed to heavily Democratic areas, including $26 million in grants spread across twelve cities in Michigan, Pennsylvania, Minnesota, and Wisconsin that together cast more than 75 percent of their 2 million votes for Hillary Clinton in 2016.

For every state the center examined, it became clear that Zuckerberg's funding via CTCL produced a highly partisan pattern. J. Christian Adams, the head of the Public Interest Legal Foundation, an organization dedicated to election integrity, concludes that the Zuckerberg largesse "converted election offices in key jurisdictions with deep reservoirs of Biden voters into Formula One turnout machines."[9]

## WHERE CTCL CAME FROM

CTCL's founders all came from another now-defunct group, the New Organizing Institute. Unlike CTCL, which is a so-called 501(c)(3) charitable nonprofit that's legally required to be non-partisan, the New Organizing Institute (NOI) was a 501(c)(4) nonprofit, which allowed it more flexibility to meddle in politics. And meddle it did. The *Washington Post* bluntly called it, "the Democratic Party's Hogwarts for digital wizardry" because it spread that party's state-of-the-art voter turnout techniques.[10]

The NOI was funded by liberal donors that included George Soros's Open Society Foundation, the Ford Foundation, and Atlantic Philanthropies. CTCL director and cofounder Tiana Epps-Johnson worked for NOI and is a former Obama Foundation fellow. Former Obama campaign manager David Plouffe, author of *A Citizen's Guide to Beating Donald Trump*, worked for the Zuckerberg foundation that financed CTCL's activities.

How similar are CTCL and the New Organizing Institute? They're so similar that the Capital Research Center posted a quiz with text from both groups' websites to see if readers could tell one from the other.

The following quotes were taken from training courses for activists and elections officials offered on both websites. Try to guess which is the old (c)(4) political nonprofit and which is the new (c)(3) "nonpartisan" nonprofit:

- Learn how to reach "displaced" and "hard-to-reach voters" with "language barriers."
- "Hispanics are the future of progressive growth."

- "In jail or have a conviction? The only time you cannot register and vote is when you are serving a sentence in jail or prison."
- "Fight voter suppression in your campaign by talking with voters about IDs."
- "Identify different forms of misinformation, malinformation, and disinformation and how to respond."
- "Build momentum for real civic participation, and an infrastructure that creates power for the long term."
- Hire a "disinformation expert to report and correct disinformation, particularly from foreign actors."
- "Protect voters rights across the country" from the "voter suppression tactics threatening our most vulnerable voters."

The first, third, fifth, and sixth statements are from CTCL. The rest are from NOI.

It's a hard test because the groups' missions are essentially the same: turn out voters that will favor their preferred, liberal, progressive (i.e., Democratic) candidates.[11]

Did that happen in November 2020? Yes. CTCL's cash went disproportionately to big cities rich with Democratic votes.

## CTCL IN ARIZONA

The near-universal effect of CTCL's grants was disproportionately greater turnout for one political party. Let's look at Arizona and compare the votes for president in 2020 versus 2016. All fifteen counties increased their votes for both parties, but not at all equally. And both parties saw their votes increase even more in the nine counties CTCL funded than in the six counties it did not. Here especially the results were unequal.

For the Republicans, the funded counties' votes increased by 46 percent more than the rate at which votes in the unfunded counties increased. For the Democrats, the funded counties' votes skyrocketed upward 81 percent more than they rose in the unfunded counties.

That inequality in turnout translated into a lot of votes. Again, both parties had more 2020 votes in those nine CTCL-funded counties. But the additional votes Democrats received in Arizona gave them a margin over their opponents of 129,000 votes, or more than ten times the Democrats' statewide margin of victory.

CTCL funded four of the five counties Biden won. Only one county in the state flipped in 2020: Maricopa County (Phoenix and its suburbs), which narrowly broke for Biden by 50.3 percent to 48.1 percent. Maricopa County gave Biden 1,040,774 votes (62 percent of his statewide total), doubling Clinton's 2016 figures.

In 2016, Trump won Maricopa 49.1 percent to 45.7 percent with 590,465 votes. Yet he lost the county in 2020 despite winning an additional 405,000 votes, bringing his total to 995,665 votes (59.9 percent of his statewide total).

CTCL gave Maricopa County election officials close to $3 million, or $1.80 for every Biden vote in the jurisdiction. "Mark Zuckerberg was, in effect, able to tilt the outcome of the vote in Arizona to favor Biden using the wrong vehicle, while receiving a tax break in the process," concludes Hayden Ludwig.[12]

No wonder that in April 2021, Arizona's legislature joined Georgia and Florida in banning the private funding of county election offices. "CTCL's involvement in 2020 raises the question of whether Arizona's elections were fair and if they were controlled by billionaires instead of the people's elected representatives," says Rep. Shawnna Bolick, the Republican chair of the state house Ways and Means Committee.[13]

## A PATTERN EMERGES

The pattern repeats in state after state: First, CTCL was far more likely to fund election jurisdictions that are rich with Democratic votes. Second, it funded those jurisdictions much more heavily per capita than majority Republican jurisdictions. Third, jurisdictions it funded boosted Democratic turnout far beyond the statewide margin of victory.

It is hard to square these facts with the federal requirement that 501(c)(3) nonprofits like CTCL must be nonpartisan at all times and that they may not conduct "voter education or registration activities" that "have the effect of favoring a candidate," as the IRS puts it.[14]

Unfortunately, left-wing nonprofits have for years been ignoring federal law by conducting registration and get-out-the-vote-efforts that favor one party.

Liberal journalist Sasha Issenberg, in his 2012 book, *The Victory Lab: The Secret Science of Winning Campaigns*, wrote of one such nonprofit, the Voter Participation Center, that remains prominent in elections: "Even though the group was officially nonpartisan, for tax purposes, there was no secret that the goal of all its efforts was to generate new votes for Democrats."[15]

Molly Ball, the author of a new biography of House Speaker Nancy Pelosi, has written a fascinating report on just how much the operations of nonprofits tried to tilt the 2020 election and smother questions about how it was conducted. In a column in *Time* magazine titled "The Secret History of the Shadow Campaign That Saved the 2020 Election,"[16] Ball set up her thesis this way:

> "It was all very, very strange," Donald Trump said on December 2. "Within days after the election, we witnessed an orchestrated effort to anoint the winner, even while many key states were still

being counted." In a way, Trump was right. There was a conspiracy unfolding behind the scenes, one that both curtailed the protests and coordinated the resistance from CEOs.

This is the inside story of the conspiracy to save the 2020 election, based on access to the group's inner workings, never-before-seen documents and interviews with dozens of those involved from across the political spectrum.... The participants want the secret history of the 2020 election told, even though it sounds like a paranoid fever dream—a well-funded cabal of powerful people, ranging across industries and ideologies, working together behind the scenes to influence perceptions, change rules and laws, steer media coverage and control the flow of information."

Of course, Ball frames all this hyperactivity as virtuous and justified. She notes that the work of pro-Biden groups

"touched every aspect of the election. They got states to change voting systems and laws and helped secure hundreds of millions in public and private funding. They fended off voter-suppression lawsuits, recruited armies of poll workers and got millions of people to vote by mail for the first time. They successfully pressured social media companies to take a harder line against disinformation and used data-driven strategies to fight viral smears. They executed national public-awareness campaigns.... After Election Day, they monitored every pressure point to ensure that Trump could not overturn the result. They were not rigging the election; they were fortifying it."

## TELLING OFFICIALS WHAT TO DO

A particularly egregious example of how CTLC's grant-making corrupted the election process comes from Green Bay, Wisconsin.

The Badger State is known for very close presidential elections. Between 2000 and 2020, the winner in three out of five presidential elections in the state was decided by less than eight-tenths of a single percentage point.

Nor is Wisconsin a stranger to voter fraud. In 2008, the Milwaukee Police Department's Special Investigation Unit released a stunning report after an eighteen-month probe. It found an "illegal organized attempt to influence the outcome of an election in the state of Wisconsin," namely the 2004 presidential election that was won by John Kerry by fewer than twelve thousand votes. Among the problems it cited were ineligible voters casting ballots, felons not only voting but *working* at the polls, transient college students casting improper votes, and homeless voters possibly voting more than once. Between 4,600 and 5,300 more ballots were cast than voters who were recorded as having shown up at the polls in Milwaukee. More than 1,300 registration cards filled out at the polls by people registering on Election Day were declared "un-enterable" or invalid by election officials.

Sadly, the Milwaukee police report concluded that manifest incompetence and poor record keeping by Milwaukee's election bureaucracy made holding fraudsters accountable impossible. "The Milwaukee Election Commission, through their ineptitude, raised enough reasonable doubt to prevent any further criminal prosecution" of voting violators.[17]

Flash forward to 2020. What happened in Green Bay in that year's election was a different story, one in which the incompetence of election officials directly facilitated the manipulation of the election more than outright fraud as extensively described by intrepid reporter Matt Kittle.[18]

Green Bay's handling of the 2020 election clearly violated at least five state statutes, and its mayor, Eric Genrich, may have personally engaged in official misconduct.[19]

Emails obtained by the Wisconsin Assembly's Committee on Campaigns and Elections[20] show that Genrich usurped the lawful authority of Green Bay City Clerk Kris Teske to run the election, thereby running afoul of Wisconsin Statute § 7.15(1), which requires that "each municipal clerk has charge and supervision of elections and registration in the municipality."

Teske did not. Genrich used $1.6 million in grant money from the Center for Tech and Civic Life to essentially replace Teske with Michael Spitzer-Rubenstein, the Wisconsin lead of the liberal National Vote at Home Institute.[21]

"I am being left out of the discussions and not listened to at the meetings," a frustrated Teske wrote on July 9, 2020, as Genrich made it clear that he and what he referred to as "the grant team" were now overseeing election preparations, not her.

"I just don't know where the Clerk's Office fits in anymore," she added in another email the same day.

Her frustrations would only grow over the next month.

Genrich had no legal authority to run Green Bay's election, yet he did so anyway. He had no legal authority to replace Teske with Spitzer-Rubenstein, yet he did so anyway.

"I am very frustrated, along with the Clerk's Office," she wrote on August 28. "I don't know what to do anymore. I am trying to explain the process, but it isn't heard. I don't feel I can talk to the Mayor. . . . I don't understand how people who don't have the knowledge of the process can tell us how to manage the election."

Legally, they couldn't. Wisconsin Statute § 7.30(2)(a) mandates that "only election officials appointed under state law may conduct an election." Mayors cannot legally run elections. Nor can they subcontract them out to left-wing special-interest groups.

On October 7, Spitzer-Rubenstein offered to "help with curing absentee ballots that are missing a signature or witness signature address." Teske declined, but Genrich's Chief of Staff Celestine

Jeffreys stepped in to let her know that the "grant mentors would like to meet with you to discuss, further, the ballot curing process. Please let them know when you're available."

Under Wisconsin Statute § 6.87(9), "if a municipal clerk receives an absentee ballot with an improperly completed certificate or with no certificate, the clerk may return the ballot to the elector, inside the sealed envelope when an envelope is received, together with a new envelope if necessary, whenever time permits the elector to correct the defect and return the ballot."

Brown County Clerk Sandy Juno was so alarmed by what was going on in Green Bay that she contacted the Wisconsin Elections Commission.

"In reviewing many of the emails received through open records request and shared with me, it's apparent that the election duties and responsibilities of the municipal clerk were thwarted by the Mayor's office during the 2020 election cycle," she said in written testimony before a Wisconsin Assembly Committee. "An appointed municipal clerk doesn't have the same independence and freedom in running elections as that of an elected official. The City of Green Bay Mayor's Office demonstrates how to effectively remove the city clerk from election responsibilities and confiscate the clerk duties protected under Wisconsin election laws."

Teske was so frustrated that she decided to take leave just days before the election and eventually left her position early in 2021.

"I want you to be aware about the Clerk Staff that stated if they had the money, they would walk out the door now, another said I don't want to work here anymore, and the third is actively looking for a new job," Teske wrote in an email on October 22. "All because the Mayors staff... is bossing the Clerk Staff around. They call me crying or say they went home crying."

After Teske left her position, Genrich and Spitzer-Rubenstein totally took over the last-minute preparations for Election Day voting.

Spitzer-Rubenstein, who was not Green Bay's clerk or employed by the city at all, had unfettered access to thousands of absentee ballots before they were cast.

"Are the ballots going to be in trays/boxes within the bin?" Spitzer-Rubenstein asked Genrich and several other people in an email on November 1. "I'm at (the Central Counting site) now, trying to figure out whether we'll need to move the bins around throughout the day or if we can just stick them along the wall and use trays or something similar to move the ballots between stations."

Amazingly, several days before the election, Spitzer-Rubenstein was given four of the five keys to the room where the absentee ballots were stored. A Hyatt Regency checklist ordered staff members to not "unlock the grand ballroom until Michael Spitzer-Rubenstein is with security when unlocking the grand ballroom doors."

On Election Day, multiple election observers witnessed him giving orders to poll workers and presenting himself as running the show—and he did so unlawfully.

"First of all there was no consistency how the various tables were processing absentee ballots," Juno testified. "Opened ballots were face up exposing votes, and poll workers were observed reviewing how the ballots were marked."

This constitutes election fraud under Wisconsin Statute § 12.13 (2)(b), which provides that no election official may "observe how an elector has marked a ballot unless the official is requested to assist the elector" or "intentionally permit anyone not authorized to assist in the marking of a ballot to observe how a person is voting or has voted." Doing so is a Class I felony punishable by up to three and a half years in prison.

To shield all this from election observers, Genrich and Spitzer-Rubenstein likely violated state law in shutting them out altogether.

"Election observers were located far away from poll workers, so [there was] no opportunity to see or hear the absentee ballot process," Juno said. "Green Bay provided access to the central count location but prevented observers from participating in the observation process.

"The physical location where they were placed does not meet state statutes. This was in direct violation of election laws. Observers had no opportunity to hear absentee electors' names announced by election officials, observe within legal distance to see ballots being processed, rejected or remade, or challenge questionable electors' ballots."

Wisconsin Statute § 7.41(2) requires that "observation areas shall be not less than 3 feet from nor more than 8 feet from the table at which electors announce their name and address to be issued a voter number at the polling place, office, or alternate site and not less than 3 feet from nor more than 8 feet from the table at which a person may register to vote at the polling place, office, or alternate site. The observation areas shall be so positioned to permit any election observer to readily observe all public aspects of the voting process."

This obviously did not happen. When Mayor Genrich essentially replaced Teske with himself and delegated some of her duties to Spitzer-Rubenstein, Genrich may have committed misconduct in public office, which is defined by Wisconsin Statute § 946.12(2) as performing an act "which the officer or employee knows is in excess of the officer's or employee's lawful authority."

If Genrich did so to help a preferred candidate or candidates, he very well may have violated Wisconsin Statute § 946.12(3), which prohibits the exercise of "a discretionary power in a manner inconsistent with the duties of the officer's or employee's office or employment or the rights of others and with intent to obtain a dishonest advantage for the officer or employee or another."

After the Wisconsin Assembly hearing on how Mayor Genrich let what he called "the grant team" essentially run the 2020 election, city officials scrambled to obfuscate the issue.

City Attorney Vanessa Chavez released a report in April 2021 that was intended to absolve Mayor Eric Genrich of any blame. But the MacIver Institute notes that "it made several key admissions that underscore just how corrupt the city's mishandling really was."[22]

"No allegations of fraud have been made with respect to the City's conduct of the November 3, 2020, election," Chavez concluded, "and no issues affecting the integrity of the election have been found." But her own report concedes that this wasn't the case in Green Bay last November.

Chavez's report admits that, against City Clerk Kris Teske's wishes, Spitzer-Rubenstein was allowed to "provide assistance on-site to assist with setting up Central Count in a way that was safe and efficient for the Clerk's staff and observers, and to assist with election tasks that the City chose to assign." However, she claims that "Mr. Spitzer-Rubenstein had no decision-making authority" and only "made recommendations." But his recommendations were amazingly all adopted.

There is clear evidence that Spitzer-Rubenstein was giving orders and presenting himself as running operations there, and Chavez's report notes that "he was provided with a 'City Employee' tag at that time," although he was most certainly not a city employee. Instead, he was working for a private organization whose national policy director, Audrey Kline, is the former political director for Colorado's AFL-CIO Denver central labor council.

One of the last lines of Chavez's report is also one of the most intriguing: "There were some challenges at Central Count, such as the DS450 rejecting a large number of ballots that had to be reconstructed as a result."

Who oversaw that ballot reconstruction? And what is the DS450? It just happened to be the "high-speed tabulator" purchased with…CTCL grant money. Did Spitzer-Rubenstein or anyone else who had no lawful authority to run Green Bay's election have any role whatsoever in reconstructing or overseeing the reconstruction of those ballots? And what, exactly, is that "large number" that had to be reconstructed?

The Green Bay horror story just shows how corrupting the injection of private grants into the administration of elections can be. Wisconsin legislators are calling for a criminal probe of Green Bay's elections, and it's clear that there is abundant evidence to justify one.

## WILL ZUCKERBUCKS MAKE A REAPPEARANCE IN 2022 ELECTIONS?

Even if Zuckerberg decides to reduce his involvement in the 2024 election, either because he develops other priorities or due to new state-level prohibitions on election offices accepting his largesse, there is still plenty of mischief that could occur. Some states explicitly tilted some of their taxpayer-funded voter "education" efforts in a partisan direction in 2020.

In 2020, the state of California signed a $35 million "emergency" contract with a political consulting firm run by a top adviser to the Joe Biden campaign. The money was for a PR blitz explaining California's new expansive vote-by-mail system. The contract was signed by Secretary of State Alex Padilla, who was later appointed to replace Kamala Harris in the U.S. Senate.

But State Controller Betty Yee, a fellow Democrat, refused to okay the outlay, arguing that Padilla's office lacked the authority to spend that money on behalf of county election boards. There were other unspoken objections from her office. Such contracts are supposed to be nonpartisan, but the SKDKnickerbocker firm proudly listed the Biden presidential campaign at the top of the client list on its website.

The firm also bragged that it had "developed the Biden campaign's vote-by-mail program in Pennsylvania, Michigan, Wisconsin and Arizona." What a coincidence.[23]

Rep. James Comer (R-Ky.), the ranking member of the U.S. House Committee on Oversight and Reform; Rep. Rodney Davis (R-Ill.), the ranking member of the House Administration Committee; and Rep. Jody Hice (R-Ga.), ranking member of the Government Operations Subcommittee, have demanded that the inspector general of the U.S. Election Assistance Commission, Patricia Layfield, investigate this contract. They want to know if any of the $825 million in grant funding that Congress provided to the EAC in 2020 to distribute to the states to help fund unexpected election expenses arising from COVID-19 went to this Biden political consultant. Comer says this is "a highly questionable contract awarded to a pro-Biden firm to contact voters."[24]

No matter the level of Mark Zuckerberg's involvement in future election grants, millions of his 2020 dollars will likely carry over to the 2022 election when Florida Governor Ron DeSantis and other possible GOP presidential nominees will be on the ballot.

According to an analysis by the Public Interest Legal Foundation, Florida's Miami-Dade County got a grant for $2.4 million on Oct. 15 and didn't spend any of it for the 2020 election. In February 2021, the CTCL approved a six-month extension to the grant.

Palm Beach County got one of the largest grants in that state, $6.8 million. Wendy Sartory Link, the Palm Beach County supervisor of elections, says she got permission from CTCL to spend money left over from 2020 in the next election cycle. So even though Florida has a new law barring private grants to election offices, old Zuckerbucks will live on in Florida's upcoming elections.

"Some counties didn't spend effectively any of their funds in 2020. These Zuckerbucks will be targeted to try to defeat DeSantis in 2022," J. Christian Adams of the Public Interest Legal Foundation told Fox News.[25]

The CTCL blithely insists in a tone that P. T. Barnum would love that there is no partisan motive behind any of its activities.

"All local election offices responsible for administering election activities covered by the CTCL COVID-19 Response grant program were eligible to apply for grant funds," CTCL told Fox News.

## WHAT IS AT STAKE

The CTCL grants built structural bias into the election where structural bias matters most: in densely populated cities that are easily organized for maximum turnout. The grants built systems, hired employees from activist groups, and provided both equipment and PR campaigns. They did everything street activists could ever dream up to turn out Biden voters if only they had unlimited funding, and they had the machinery and official imprimatur of local governments to help them do it.

"In 2020, they had unlimited funding because billionaires made cash payments to non-profit groups that in turn made cash payments to government election offices," notes J. Christian Adams of PILF.[26]

"The sanctity of our electoral process is being violated by the unprecedented infusion of private money," warns Phillip D. Kline, a former Kansas attorney general who has sued over some of the CTCL grants. "Instead of being distributed equally, as the law requires, election funding is now being doled out by private interests seeking to influence the process for partisan advantage."[27]

The ethical problems involved with such grants should be obvious. Private interests are leveraging the election administration powers of the state to pursue their political agenda, while in some cases government officials are letting private interests appear to influence or even dictate how elections are run. None of this is reassuring about the fair administration of our election system.

CHAPTER NINE

# VOTE TRAFFICKING, AUTOMATIC VOTER REGISTRATION, AND RANKED CHOICE VOTING: A RECIPE FOR COERCION, FRAUD, AND CONFUSION

The combination of vote trafficking, automatic voter registration, and ranked choice voting—election procedures that liberals are recklessly promoting nationwide—is a recipe for intimidation and coercion, voter registration and election fraud, and confusion and disenfranchisement of voters.

## WHAT IS VOTE TRAFFICKING?

Vote or ballot trafficking (what liberals euphemistically call "harvesting") is the collection of absentee ballots from voters by a third party who then delivers them to election officials. The term was essentially unknown to the general public until the North Carolina State Board of Elections overturned the results of the 2018 election for the Ninth Congressional District due to illegal vote trafficking, what the board called a "coordinated, unlawful and substantially resourced absentee ballot scheme."[1]

Vote trafficking was also raised as a concern that year in California, which had legalized it in 2016. In 2018, seven Republican-held congressional seats, including in Orange County, a traditional Republican stronghold, were unexpectedly lost. The Orange County registrar of voters told reporters that individuals were "dropping off maybe 100 or 200 ballots" at a time.[2] A 2020 report issued by U.S. Rep. Rodney Davis (R-Ill.), the ranking minority member of the Committee on House Administration, said vote trafficking provided political operatives the opportunity to engage in "undue influence in the voting process" by "pressuring voters" and "destroy[ing] the secret ballot."[3] Those political operatives "are the new Tammany Hall ward bosses, controlling the votes of their harvested area."[4]

States have allowed individuals to vote through an absentee ballot, sometimes referred to as a mail-in ballot, since the Civil War.[5] Absentee ballots are usually mailed back to election officials by the voter, although every state allows voters to personally deliver their ballots to local election officials. Nine states allow a member of the voter's family to hand deliver the absentee ballot, one state (Alabama) only allows the voter to return the ballot, and thirteen states do not specify whether someone other than the voter can hand deliver the ballot on the voter's behalf.[6]

Twenty-seven states (plus the District of Columbia)[7] have legalized vote trafficking by allowing anyone to return an absentee ballot. Those states are handing party activists, campaign managers, consultants, and other political guns for hire, all with a vested political or monetary interest in winning an election, the ability to manipulate the outcome through intimidation and coercion of voters or the outright theft, forgery, or discarding of their ballots. It is a dangerous and reckless public policy that threatens the integrity of elections. It should not be implemented by state legislatures, and it should be prohibited in the states that currently allow it.

In fact, such fraud occurred in 1864 when mail-in ballots were first legalized for Union troops from New York in a plot intended to prevent the reelection of Abraham Lincoln. A ballot trafficker named Moses Ferry, who was working for New York Gov. Horatio Seymour, set up an operation to collect mail-in ballots from New York regiments, including sick and wounded soldiers under treatment in hospitals, that were then altered and forged to provide votes for Lincoln's challenger, George McClellan. So vote trafficking has a long and corrupt history.[8]

## A RECIPE FOR INTIMIDATION, COERCION, AND FRAUD

Allowing individuals other than the voter or his immediate family to handle absentee ballots is a recipe for mischief and wrongdoing. Neither voters nor election officials have the means to verify that the secrecy of the ballot has not been compromised or that the ballot was not fraudulently altered by the vote trafficker.

It also gives campaign and party intermediaries the opportunity to interact with voters while they are casting a ballot out of sight of and without any supervision by election officials. Thus, there is no one present to ensure that voters are not being coerced, intimidated, or paid for a vote. As a report about illegal vote trafficking in Texas says, "Away from on-site monitors and electioneering restrictions at traditional polling places," the law that prohibits anyone from telling voters how to vote or marking their ballot without consent "is often honored in the breach."[9]

This coercion problem is illustrated by the conviction in 2017 of the former mayor of Eatonville, Florida, Anthony Grant. He won his election based on absentee ballots but was later found to have coerced absentee voters to cast ballots for him.[10] Another case involved the former mayor of Martin, Kentucky, Ruth Robinson, who (along with her husband and son) was convicted of election fraud in 2014 for, among other things, threatening and intimidating poor and disabled citizens (like the wounded soldiers in 1864) into casting absentee ballots for Robinson, including ballots that the Robinsons had already filled out.[11]

Given the very sophisticated campaign data available on the voting history and campaign contributions of registered voters, it is not difficult to send traffickers into neighborhoods, apartment buildings, or condominium complexes in which voters are known to be highly likely to vote for certain candidates. Supporters of the opposition candidate could collect those absentee ballots and make sure they are *not* delivered to election officials.[12]

Unless a voter checks with election officials after the election to verify that her ballot was received, the voter will never know what happened. It seems highly unlikely that the vast majority of absentee voters, particularly the elderly, the infirm, or the disabled, will verify that the ballot was received. Even if they do, they may not be able to identify which campaign operative picked up their ballot or what happened to it or whether the ballot was altered or changed.

Kara Sands, clerk of Nueces County, Texas, says this type of absentee ballot fraud targets the vulnerable and often "involves older voters and the homebound." Those voters "don't even realize their votes are being stolen," she says. The vote harvesters "have these neighborhoods mapped out and they can go door to door . . . Elderly people are being victimized and they don't even know it."[13]

This was confirmed by a top Democratic campaign operative who explained in 2020 to Jon Levine of the *New York Post* how he had been stealing local, state, and federal elections through fraudulent absentee ballots in New Jersey for decades without ever being caught. As the campaign operative said, "An election is swayed by 500 votes, 1,000 votes—it can make a difference."[14] He had "led teams of fraudsters and mentioned at least 20 operatives" he had trained in New Jersey, New York, and Pennsylvania. A Bernie Sanders supporter, he came forward because he predicted—accurately, it turned out—that "there is going to be a f-king war coming November 3rd over this stuff.... If they knew how the sausage was made, they could fix it."

The political operative described how straightforward it was to commit fraud with absentee ballots. He would start by photocopying a blank absentee ballot, which had no security feature such as a stamp or watermark, so the photocopy was indistinguishable from the official ballot. He would mark the fake ballots for his candidates. His operatives would then fan out into neighborhoods, "going house to house, convincing voters to let them mail completed ballots on their behalf as a public service."

With the completed ballots in hand, the team of fraudsters would steam open the envelopes, remove the completed ballot, and replace it with a photocopied fake ballot. Along with the certificate *already signed by the voter*, they would reseal the envelope with glue. It took them "Five minutes per ballot tops."[15] They then dropped the resealed envelopes in post office mail collection boxes all over the particular jurisdiction where the election was being held, being careful to ensure that no suspicions were raised by large numbers of ballots being found in just a few postal boxes.

In fact, the political operative called the absentee ballot fraud scheme that had been uncovered in Paterson, New Jersey, in 2020 "sloppy" because hundreds of absentee ballot envelopes were discovered in just three mailboxes: "If they had spread them in all different mailboxes, nothing would have happened."[16] It seems obvious that this difficulty for harvesters would go away if the proliferation of official absentee ballot drop boxes in the 2020 election using the COVID-19 pandemic as an excuse becomes a regular feature in future elections. All these security vulnerabilities are why a 1998 report by the Florida Department of Law Enforcement examining multiple cases of absentee ballot fraud called absentee ballots the "tool of choice" for those who are willing to commit voter fraud to win elections.[17] Similarly, a Miami-Dade County grand jury issued a public report in 2012 recommending that the Florida legislature change its law to prohibit anyone from being "in possession of more than two absentee ballots at one time" unless the ballots are "those of the voter and members of the voter's immediate family."[18]

The Miami grand jury summarized all the problems associated with vote trafficking and allowing an unsupervised third party (other than a member of the voter's immediate family), commonly called "boleteros," access to absentee ballots:

> Once that ballot is out of the hands of the elector, we have no idea what happens to it. The possibilities are numerous and scary....
>
> If the ballot is complete and the return envelope is *signed and not sealed*, the boleteros/ballot brokers can remove the ballot from the secrecy envelope and see the private, confidential selections the elector made on the ballot. Similarly, if the ballot is not completely voted and the return envelope is signed and not sealed, the boletero/ballot broker can remove the ballot from the secrecy envelope... and then vote the rest of the ballot in lieu of the elector. If the boletero does not like the selections made by the elector, the boleteros can simply throw the ballot away and no one would ever know. All of these possibilities are present if an elector relinquishes, to a boletero, control of a fully or partially marked ballot contained in a signed but unsealed return mailing envelope.
>
> The more unsettling issue for us is each of the above illegal actions can also take place with a boletero picking up a fully or partially marked ballot contained in a *signed and sealed* return mailing envelope. The boletero can either stealthily or surgically open the envelope, view the choices of the voter and then decide whether the un-voted portions of a partially completed ballot will be filled out by the boleteros or whether, depending on the elector's choices, the ballot will simply be discarded.[19]

## ILLEGAL VOTE HARVESTING IN NORTH CAROLINA

Even though vote trafficking is illegal in North Carolina, what happened in the 9th Congressional District race provides an object lesson in what can happen when campaign operatives have access to the absentee ballots of voters, just as predicted by the Miami-Dade grand jury.

In that race, Mark Harris (R) was running against Dan McCready (D) for a congressional seat. Despite the nine-hundred-vote lead that Harris had over McCready at the end of the election, the North Carolina State Board of Elections refused to certify the race because of accusations against Leslie McCrae Dowless, who was working for the Harris campaign, of fraud and vote harvesting.

After holding hearings that produced evidence of absentee ballot fraud, the election board overturned the results and ordered a new congressional election in that district (as well as in two local contests in Bladen County).[20] Dowless and seven other individuals were indicted on charges of obstructing justice and unlawfully possessing absentee ballots for the purpose of "scheming to illegally collect, fill in, forge and submit mail-in ballots" from voters as well as committing perjury by lying to the state election board in sworn testimony.[21]

Dowless's stepdaughter testified before the board, admitting that she filled out blank or incomplete ballots for Republican candidates.[22] Additional evidence collected by the board indicated that Dowless and his coconspirators submitted absentee ballot request forms on behalf of voters and then gathered unsealed and unwitnessed (and blank or incomplete) ballots directly from voters. Those ballots were then filled out in Dowless's office before being mailed in small batches at post offices geographically close to where the voter lived to avoid any warning signs that this was a vote harvesting operation.[23] Dowless collected several hundred ballots, paying his workers for their criminal activity: "$150.00 per 50 absentee ballot request forms and $125.00 per 50 absentee ballots collected."[24]

These actions that resulted in forged, fraudulent, and improperly completed absentee ballots being submitted as votes would have been even harder to detect had vote trafficking been legal in North Carolina, as it is California. In fact, there might have been no basis on which to even open an investigation.

It should also be noted that the state board had referred Dowless to prosecutors for similar alleged misdeeds in the 2016 election, but no action was taken then, demonstrating a continuing problem with election fraud: the refusal of prosecutors to pursue these cases.[25] If the 2016 election had been properly investigated and prosecuted, the 2018 election might never have been compromised.

## ILLEGAL VOTE HARVESTING IN TEXAS

Texas law allows an absentee ballot to be personally delivered to election officials by the voter; someone "related to the voter within the second degree by affinity or the third degree by consanguinity"; someone registered to vote at the same address as, or physically living with, the voter; or someone "lawfully assisting a voter who was eligible for assistance." The "official carrier envelope" (containing the completed absentee ballot) cannot be "collected and stored at another location for subsequent delivery" to election officials.[26]

Texas has had a series of prosecutions and convictions for illegal vote trafficking.[27] One of those convicted traffickers, Zaida Bueno, described not only how she requested absentee ballots for voters but made sure that the ballots were cast for the candidate who was paying her. She said that when the requested ballots arrived, she would go to those homes and would vote the ballots "for the one I want, the one I'm helping." She had engaged in this illegal election fraud for candidates in the "whole county and the whole courthouse—city council, school board, any election you name I've done."[28]

In 2016, a former city commissioner in Weslaco, Texas, Guadalupe Rivera, was convicted of illegal "assistance" for filling out absentee ballots for voters in an election she won by only sixteen votes. A new election was ordered, and Rivera lost.[29] Four vote traffickers—or politiqueras, as they are known in Texas—were prosecuted in Tarrant County for fraudulently obtaining absentee ballots from older voters using intimidation, false pretenses, and forged signatures and of subsequently marking those ballots "without the voter's consent or knowledge."[30]

This scheme came to light only because of an "unlikely alliance" between a former Democratic state representative (who was defeated in a March 2014 primary by 111 votes), several Democratic consultants, and Direct Action Texas, a Tea Party–backed organization.[31] They went through the time-consuming task of reviewing applications for absentee ballots and discovered that "the applications were filled out in a machine-like fashion, each address and name of the requestor scrawled in identical handwriting on scores of ballots."[32]

And how do the vote traffickers find the absentee ballot voters they want to target? One example is demonstrated by the 2017 federal bribery conviction in McAllen, Texas, of a postal carrier. Noe Olvera was paid $1,000 by a campaign worker for a list of the names and addresses of absentee ballot recipients on his postal route.[33]

These cases, as well as others in Texas, demonstrate the vulnerabilities of the absentee ballot process. This type of abuse of voters who are "elderly" and "infirm" is so pervasive, says Omar

Escobar (D), district attorney of Starr County, Texas, that "the time has come to consider an alternative to mail-in voting." Escobar says it needs to be replaced with "something that can't be hijacked."[34] Much of that "fraud in Texas happens in down-ballot contests that can be decided by a couple dozen votes or less."[35]

## PERMANENT ABSENTEE BALLOT LISTS

A growing number of states allow voters to make a single request to be placed on a permanent absentee ballot list.[36] Election officials will then send those voters absentee ballots for *every* election without the voter having to make any further requests. While convenient for some voters, a permanent absentee list creates too many chances for fraud.

Election officials are notoriously slow in cleaning up voter registration lists and removing voters who have moved, died, or otherwise become ineligible to vote. They have also gotten remarkably averse to conducting list maintenance because they are invariably sued by liberal advocacy organizations when they try to conduct such routine maintenance. That is one reason why a 2012 study by the Pew Foundation on the inaccuracies of state voter registration lists found that "approximately 24 million—one of every eight—registrations in the United States are no longer valid or are significantly inaccurate."[37] That included registrations for more than 1.8 million deceased voters and 2.75 million registered in more than one state.[38]

Thus, with a permanent absentee ballot list, it is highly likely that ballots will continue to be sent to registered voters even after they have died or have moved before election officials receive notice that the voter should be removed from the list. This puts the ballots in the hands of other individuals who reside at those addresses or to vote traffickers who are there to collect them. It also provides vote traffickers with a list of voters to target. As the Miami-Dade County grand jury said, "Maintaining such a list is an invitation to target those voters for fraud and undue influence."[39]

The grand jury recommended that Florida eliminate the permanent absentee ballot list and "require voters who desire to vote by absentee ballot for a specific election to request an absentee ballot for such election."[40] Other states should follow that lead.

Obviously, there needs to be a way for individuals to vote who cannot vote in person on Election Day due to illness or other valid reasons. Absentee ballots are the easiest way to make that possible, but the rules and regulations governing them should not make them susceptible to theft, forgery, and coercion. The handling of absentee ballots should be restricted to voters and their most immediate family members or an individual residing in their household, such as a designated caregiver, to prevent campaigns, political parties, and other third parties from mishandling absentee ballots.

All of these vulnerabilities also illustrate why states should extend voter ID requirements to absentee ballots as well as in-person voting and require either witness signatures or notarization of absentee ballots. Signature comparison, where election officials compare the signature of a voter on the absentee ballot certificate with the signature of the voter in his or her registration file, should also be a state requirement.

However, signature comparison is more of an art than a science and takes substantial training, something election officials do not have. Nor do they have sufficient time to conduct a detailed analysis since the average election worker is literally processing thousands of absentee ballots very quickly.

Just how inadequate this security measure is to detect fraud was demonstrated in 2020 in Nevada when a columnist for the *Las*

*Vegas Review-Journal*, Victor Joecks, conducted an experiment to test just how good election officials would be at detecting a forged signature on absentee ballots. Clark County officials accepted his forged signature on eight out of nine absentee ballots without detection, an 89 percent failure rate.[41]

While illegal vote trafficking still occurs even in states in which it is outlawed, banning it not only acts as deterrence, but it also gives authorities a basis for investigating potential wrongdoing that is otherwise difficult to detect, namely when it is evident that third parties are collecting and delivering ballots to election officials.

Under both state and federal law, voters who are blind, disabled, or illiterate are entitled to assistance when they need it, both in the polling place and when voting absentee.[42] But if that occurs in the absentee ballot setting, both the voter and the assistor should be required to sign a declaration form on which the voter certifies that he or she requested assistance and that provides the name and address of the assistor. This would help authorities when they are investigating claims of coercion, intimidation, and illegal assistance.

Also, voters should be required to request an absentee ballot each time they need one for a specific election. No state should allow a permanent absentee ballot voter list that automatically sends an absentee ballot to a registered voter for each election.

When it comes to absentee ballots, giving third parties who have a stake in the outcome of an election access to voters and their absentee ballots in an unsupervised setting is a reckless policy and a proven threat to the integrity of the election process.

## AUTOMATIC VOTER REGISTRATION

Automatic voter registration is a proposal of the left that will significantly damage the integrity of our current voter registration system, which is already in notoriously bad condition. The argument for automatic registration, that it will increase voter participation, is refuted by study after study. The administrative errors and burdens it will raise outweigh any benefit it might bring. All in all, automatic registration will increase fraud and mistakes.

Our current system, based on the National Voter Registration Act (NVRA), asks individuals interacting with state agencies whether they would like to vote. In contrast, automatic voter registration registers the person automatically without asking, effectively without their consent. It also would register people using information in various existing state and federal government databases, which predictably will lead to the registration of large numbers of ineligible individuals, such as aliens and felons, as well as multiple or duplicate registrations of the same individual, both in the same and different states.

Think about what happens when a state has both automatic registration and same-day registration. Same-day registration allows individuals to register and vote on Election Day. Together, they create the perfect storm for registration and voter fraud. People could go to multiple voting sites, register, and vote without being detected. People can vote multiple times because they are registered multiple times. Bad actors can find the ineligible or duplicate voters and vote their ballots.

Automatically registering individuals to vote without their permission also violates their basic right to choose whether or not they wish to participate in our political and election process. One of the most cherished liberties of Americans is the right to be left alone by the government.

The push for mandatory voter registration accelerated a month after 2012 presidential election, when the leaders of more than three dozen liberal advocacy groups met in Washington, D.C., to plan strategy over election-related issues at an off-the-record meeting (though covered by *Mother Jones* in some detail). One of the top three goals was expanding voting rolls by mandating "voter registration modernization" (a code phrase for automatic voter registration) and same-day voter registration. At the very same time, one of the other agreed-upon goals was to oppose any efforts to improve election integrity through voter ID and proof-of-citizenship requirements.[43]

The head of the Justice Department's Civil Rights Division at the time, Thomas Perez, who later became labor secretary and subsequently led the Democratic National Committee, said in a speech on November 16, 2012, that "all eligible citizens can and should be automatically registered to vote" by compiling information "from databases that already exist." Perez also claimed that one of the "biggest barriers to voting in the country today is our antiquated registration system."[44] At a speech in Boston on December 11, 2012, Attorney General Eric Holder voiced the support of the Obama administration for automatic registration.[45] Multiple bills have been introduced in the U.S. Congress to make automatic registration (among other election procedures) a federal mandate on the states.

The proposal for automatic registration is based on the false premise that large numbers of Americans do not vote "for no other reason than they are not registered to vote."[46] But the evidence does not support that contention.

The U.S. Census Bureau publishes reports on the levels of registration and voting after federal elections, including surveys of individuals who do not vote. Those reports *disprove* the claims that the major reason individuals do not vote is because of a lack of registration opportunities.[47]

Of the 146 million people who the Census Bureau reported were registered to vote in 2008, 15 million, or approximately 10 percent, did not vote. Of those who did not vote, only 6 percent (or about half a percent of the total) said it was because of registration problems. The vast majority of these registered nonvoters said they did not vote for reasons ranging from forgetting to vote, not liking the candidates or the campaign issues, or not being interested.

The Census Bureau report also analyzed people who were not registered. The report shows that the major reason individuals did not register was because they were not "interested in the election/not involved in politics." That represented *46 percent* of the individuals in the Census Bureau's survey. Another 35 percent of individuals did not register for a variety of reasons, such as not being eligible to vote, thinking their vote would not make a difference, not meeting residency requirements, or difficulty with English. Only 4 percent of individuals reported not registering to vote because they did "not know where or how to register."

The Census Bureau's 2010 and 2016 reports have similar results.[48] Only 3.3 percent of individuals in 2010 and 4.4 percent in 2016 reported not voting because of supposed registration difficulties. The overwhelming majority of registered voters who did not vote in 2010 and 2016 said they were not interested (16 percent and 15.4 percent), were too busy (27 percent and 14.3 percent), forgot to vote (8 percent and 3 percent), did not like the candidates or the campaign issues (9 percent and 24.8 percent), or had other various reasons.[49]

Moreover, of the tiny percentage of voters who said they did not vote because of "registration problems," there was almost no racial differential. The percentage of whites who claimed they did not vote because of a registration problem in 2010 was 3.2 percent compared to 3.3 percent of blacks and only 2.8 percent of Hispanics. In 2016, the difference was 4.5 percent of whites compared to 4 percent of blacks and 5.4 percent of Hispanics. It is apparent then that registration problems do not disproportionately affect minorities as is often claimed by liberal advocates.

The oft-repeated assertion that "voter-initiated registration" (e.g., having to say "yes" when you are asked whether you want to register at a DMV or welfare office) has a "disproportionate impact on low-income citizens and those who are less educated" also is contradicted by the census surveys.[50] For example, in 2008, the percentage of registered voters who did not vote because of "registration problems" was 6 percent. Of those voters with a bachelor's degree or more, the percentage was 7.4 percent compared to only 3.2 percent for those with an educational attainment of "less than high school graduate," while those attaining "high school graduate or GED" had a rate of 5.8 percent. The data in the census survey actually showed that less educated voters had fewer registration problems. The 2010 and 2016 surveys had similar results for those who did not vote due to registration problems: less than high school, 2.5 percent and 3 percent; high school graduate, 2.6 percent and 4 percent; bachelor's degree or more, 4.3 percent and 5.7 percent.

On income, the 2010 and 2016 census surveys showed no discernible "disproportionate impact." For example, the percentage of voters with a family income of $100,000 to $149,000 who did not vote because of purported registration problems was 3.5 percent in 2010 and 4.2 percent in 2016, the percentage of those with an income of $15,000 to $19,999 who claimed registration problems was 1.9 percent in 2010 and 6.6 percent in 2016, the percentage of voters with an income of $10,000 to $14,999 who supposedly had registration problems was 2.8 percent and 2.4 percent in the 2010 and 2016 elections, respectively, and the percentages for individuals making more than $150,000 was 2.6 percent in 2010 and 4.4 percent in 2016.

Thus, according to the federal government's own surveys, the claim that "the single greatest cause of voting problems in the United States"[51] is the voter registration system is patently false. The greatest causes of individuals not registering and not voting is their lack of interest in politics or the candidates or other reasons having nothing whatsoever to do with the registration process.

Multiple studies have found that because of the motivations of nonvoters, making registration "easier" does not affect voter participation. Registration today is easier than it has ever been, but higher turnout is not an inevitable outcome. As one study accurately said, "Research has shown that the motivation to vote is especially internal: people register because they *plan* to vote. Therefore, people who are registered are very *likely* to vote. However, people who have no interest in voting do not register to vote."[52]

Another detailed study of nonvoters concluded that it is "another misconception about nonvoters . . . that they would vote if only the [registration] process was easier." The study concluded that the reason people do not vote is because for many of them "voting is neither duty nor ritual." They are not interested in politics, or are cynical about its outcomes, or don't believe their votes will make a difference.

In other words, there are "competing strains of alienation and complacency" among the ranks of nonvoters. That is why electoral "reforms" such as "easing voter registration through motor-voter legislation, same-day registration, or uncoupling registration from jury duty have had at best a negligible net effect on voter participation." Implementing automatic voter registration would have the same "negligible" effect but would ensure multiple registrations of eligible voters and registering large numbers of ineligible individuals.

There are numerous practical issues with automatic registration. In addition to automatic registration by the DMV, social services, and income tax agencies, proponents want automatic registration of individuals from state agencies that provide benefits under the Social Security Act, that maintain records on students enrolled at secondary schools, that are responsible for administering criminal convictions, and that determine mental competence as well as from numerous federal agencies and offices such as the U.S. Immigration and Customs Enforcement Bureau, the Social Security Administration, the Federal Bureau of Prisons, the U.S. Probation Service, the Department of Veterans Affairs, the Defense Manpower Data Center of the Department of Defense, and the Indian Health Services and Center for Medicare and Medicaid Services of the Department of Health and Human Services.[53] Beyond the technical issues of reconciling data in different formats from so many sources, using all these databases will create numerous other problems.

First, ineligible voters will be registered. Using government databases such as "motor vehicle departments, income tax authorities, and social service agencies," as recommended by the liberal advocacy group the Brennan Center, would fail to differentiate citizens from noncitizens. All states provide driver's licenses to aliens who are legally in the United States, for example, and many states are now providing driver's licenses to illegal aliens. Many individuals who reside in the United States but are not citizens also file tax returns, which would allow individuals who filed with "income tax authorities" the ability to become registered to vote.

Second, it does not ensure that a signature will be on file. There are many government databases that lack a signature, which is essential for verifying petitions for candidates and ballot initiatives and requests for absentee ballots and voted absentee ballots.

Third, it would lead to multiple, duplicate registrations. For example, some people might be listed in different government databases, such as individuals who own property or pay taxes in more than one state. Or their names may not be identical in the different databases, so the same person will be registered with various versions of their name.

Automatic voting has now been implemented in a number of states, including California and Illinois, and many of these problems have surfaced.[54] California has already been forced to acknowledge making 105,000 "processing errors" since it implemented automatic voter registration on April 23, 2018.[55] That includes registering aliens who are banned from registering and voting. And California apparently designed its system to prevent federal authorities from using it to discover aliens who are illegally in the sanctuary state. Election officials in California have been unable to say, for example, "whether non-citizens voted in the June 2018 primary because a confusing government questionnaire about eligibility was created in a way that prevents a direct answer on citizenship."[56]

In fact, California election officials had mistakenly automatically registered 1,500 aliens to vote but were apparently unaware of the error until a Canadian citizen who had been registered, Randal Marquis, went to the *Los Angeles Times*.[57] An audit discovered that the state's automatic registration system had created nearly 84,000 duplicate registrations in its first five months, introduced inaccuracies into the registration records of 23,000 voters, and failed to correctly register the political party affiliation for 171,000 voters.[58]

Illinois has experienced similar problems. In 2020, it was reported that an error in the state's new automatic voter registration system "led to a possible 545 non-U.S. citizens being registered to vote, 15 of whom cast ballots."[59] The aliens had "self-identified" as noncitizens when they applied for a driver's license yet were registered anyway. What this statistic does not reveal—because Illinois election officials have no idea—is how many aliens either have been registered from state databases that do not inquire into citizenship status or who did not identify themselves as noncitizens.

What is particularly ironic about the proposal to automatically register individuals using government databases is that many of the same organizations supporting this concept have questioned the accuracy of government databases in the past. Many groups have been involved in lawsuits contesting the use of government databases to verify the citizenship and identities of individuals registering to vote and the accuracy of the information they provide.[60] For example, the Brennan Center, the NAACP, and the Advancement Project sued Florida in 2007 for comparing registered voters' information with the state driver's license database and the Social Security Administration's database.[61] It complained in a press release about "common database errors" and opposed matching as "an error-laden practice."[62]

The Brennan Center and other so-called civil rights organizations sued the state of Washington in 2006, claiming that data matching voter registration information with other government databases violated the Voting Rights Act and the U.S. Constitution and would disenfranchise voters.[63] In fact, the Brennan Center issued a report in 2006 complaining about the supposed "wide variety of common database matching errors" caused by "data entry" mistakes.[64] Yet now the Brennan Center wants to use those same supposedly inaccurate databases to automatically register voters.

Using federal databases would be no better. There is no question that there are inaccuracies in state databases, including voter registration rolls. Federal databases are also riddled with errors and may, in many instances, be worse than state databases. We have transparency with state registration lists because they are available to candidates, political parties, and the public. But there is no transparency with most federal databases, so election officials and the public have no clear idea how accurate they are.

Supporters of a federal mandate for automatic and same-day registration rarely, if ever, mention that Canada has had such a system since 1997. This registration system is administered by Elections Canada, which is responsible for conducting all federal elections and referendums. Canadians are automatically registered from a host of government databases.[65] But they can also register and vote on Election Day.

Yet Canada's automatic registration system has had no effect in increasing turnout. Before the implementation of Canada's new system in 1997, Canadians turned out in larger numbers than Americans. But Canada has seen *declines* in turnout since the 1970s.[66] In its 2008 election, Canada's turnout of 58.8 percent was lower than the 62.2 percent turnout of the voting-age population of the U.S. In its 2011 election, Canada's turnout of 61.6 percent was only slightly higher than the turnout of 58 percent of the voting-age population in our 2012 election.[67]

Canadian voters who have been automatically registered by the government give various reasons for not voting that are similar to those identified in the U.S. According to a census survey, 28 percent were not interested, 23 percent were too busy, and the rest said that "they were out of town, ill or didn't like any of the candidates."[68] The Canadian experience demonstrates that automatic voter registration is no panacea for declining turnout or the unwillingness of individuals to participate in the voting process. Thus, there are many reasons to think Canada's approach would risk much mischief in our state-administered election system while providing no benefit regarding voter turnout.

Pouring huge amounts of data, much of it full of errors and mistakes, from federal and state databases into state voter registration databases would only make the current problems with the databases exponentially worse. Requiring automatic registration from government databases risks the integrity of the election process.

## RANKED CHOICE VOTING

The latest proposal from liberal "reformers" is ranked-choice voting (or "instant runoff voting"). It is a scheme to disconnect elections from issues and allow candidates with marginal support to win elections. Some jurisdictions in the U.S. have already replaced traditional elections with the ranked-choice scheme, including Maine (but only for federal elections) and Alaska.[69]

Rep. Jamie Raskin (D-Md.), one of the most left-wing members of Congress, introduced a bill in 2019 that would require all states to adopt ranked-choice voting for congressional races.[70] H.R.1, the radical bill introduced in 2021 to federalize the election process, requires a federal study on ranked-choice voting.

Here is how it works: In 2008, instead of choosing to cast your ballot for John McCain, Barack Obama, Ralph Nader, Bob Barr, or Cynthia McKinney, all of whom were running for president, you would vote for all of them and rank your choice. In other words, you would list all five candidates on your ballot from one to five, with one being your first choice for president and five being your last choice.

If none of the candidates were chosen as the number-one pick by a majority of voters in round one, the candidate with the smallest number of votes would be eliminated from the ballot. People who selected that candidate as their top pick—let us say it was McKinney—would automatically have their votes changed to their second choice. Then the scores would be recalculated, over and over again, until one of the candidates finally wins a majority as the second, third, or even fourth choice of voters.

In the end, a voter's ballot might wind up being cast for the candidate he ranked well below his first choice—a candidate to whom he may have strong political objections and for whom he would not vote in a traditional voting system.

Former California Governor Jerry Brown, Jr. was right in 2016 when he vetoed a bill to expand ranked-choice voting in his state, saying it was "overly complicated and confusing" and "deprives voters of genuinely informed choice."[71] Such a system would present many opportunities to rig the electoral system.

Ranked-choice voting effectively disenfranchises large numbers of voters because of a phenomenon known as ballot exhaustion. A study published in 2015 that reviewed six hundred thousand votes cast using ranked-choice voting in four local elections in Washington state and California found that "the winner in all four elections receive[d] less than a majority of the total votes cast."[72]

Going back to our original example of the 2008 presidential election, not all voters are going to rank all five presidential candidates on their ballot. Many voters may only list their top two or three candidates, particularly when there are candidates on the ballot for whom they would never even consider voting.

Thus, if a voter only ranks two of the five candidates and those two are eliminated in the first and second rounds of tabulation, their choices will not be considered in the remaining rounds of tabulation. This ballot exhaustion leads to candidates being elected who were not the first choice of a majority of voters but only a majority of *"all valid votes in the final round of tallying."* Thus, "it is possible that the winning candidate will fall short of an actual majority," eliminating the "influence [of many voters] over the final outcome."[73] As Jeff Jacoby, a columnist for the *Boston Globe*, said over a 2020 ranked-choice voting ballot referendum, ranked-choice voting "effectively disenfranchises" voters "who don't rank enough candidates for their ballot to last through multiple rounds of tabulations."[74]

An example of this problem is demonstrated by what happened in Australia (which uses ranked-choice voting) in the 2010 election. The left-wing Labor Party won the Australian House despite receiving only "38 percent of first-place votes on the initial ballot, while the second-place Liberal-National coalition [the center-right choice] captured 43 percent" of first-place votes.[75] In other words, more voters wanted a center-right government than a left-wing government, but ranked choice made sure that did not happen.

Or consider the mayor's race in Oakland, California, in 2010, in which the candidate that received the most first-place votes lost the election to "a candidate on the strength of nearly 25,000 second- and third-place votes" after *nine rounds* of redistribution of the votes.[76]

This also happened in Maine in 2018, the first-ever general election for federal office in our nation's history decided by ranked-choice voting. In the Second Congressional District election, Jared Golden (D) was declared the eventual winner even though incumbent Bruce Poliquin (R) received more votes than Golden in the first round. There were two additional candidates in the race, Tiffany Bond and William Hoar. However, Maine's Secretary of State Matt Dunlop "exhausted" or threw out a total of 14,076 ballots of voters who had not ranked all the candidates.[77]

You never really know who will be running against whom in the final vote count with ranked choice. Your votes are thrown into a fictional fantasy in which no one knows which candidate is really a substitute for another candidate who may not survive the initial rounds. It is all a numbers gimmick. You, as a voter, are not given the opportunity to make the final decision between competing substitutes.

As Professor James G. Gimpel, an expert on voter behavior, testified in the case challenging Maine's ranked-choice voting law that "unlike ordinary elections and ordinary runoffs, voters are required to make predictions about who will be left standing following an initial tabulation of the votes."[78] Gimpel believes that "a portion of the voting public has insufficient interest and information to make a meaningful assessment about likely outcomes."[79]

Ranked choice destroys clarity of political debate and forces voters to cast ballots in hypothetical future runoff elections. When we have Republicans versus Democrats versus Greens and Libertarians, we know who is running against whom and what the actual distinctions are between the candidates on issues. Second- or third-choice votes should not matter in America; they do not provide the mandate that ensures that the representatives in a republic have the confidence and support of a majority of the public in the legitimacy of their decisions.

Not only is ranked-choice voting too complicated, but it also disenfranchises voters because ballots that do not include the two ultimate finalists are cast aside to manufacture a faux majority for the winner. But it is only a majority of the voters remaining in the final round, not a majority of all of the voters, who actually cast votes in the elections.

Ballot exhaustion is not just a minor problem with ranked-choice voting. According to a 2015 study, "a substantial number of voters either cannot or choose not to rank multiple candidates, even when they have the ability to do so."[80] Instead, many voters "opt to cast a vote for their top choice, neglecting to rank anyone else."[81]

Additionally, some jurisdictions limit the number of candidates that can be ranked. All the localities in the Burnett/Kogan study limited voters to ranking three candidates even when there were more candidates in the race. Thus, "if each of a voter's top three candidates is eliminated, his or her ballot becomes exhausted and, as a result, is excluded from the final total."[82]

In other words, a ranked-choice election will, in the end, boil down to only two opposing candidates, but many voters (not knowing how the roulette wheel will spin) will not cast ballots between those two choices. That voter ends up with no say in the contest between the final two candidates in the black-box elections governed by ranked-choice voting.

Of course, had that election been between just those two candidates in the first place, that same voter would have heard debates, listened to the issues discussed, and made an informed choice between those two. With ranked-choice voting, a candidate whose support was too marginal to get into public debates may end up winning, avoiding the process that informs the electorate and forcing average American voters into trying to predict the chances that particular candidates will survive multiple rounds of vote tabulation.

Ranked-choice voting also provides political operatives and voters with an incentive to tactically game the system and falsify their preferences for candidates.

For example, if our presidential elections used ranked-choice voting and enough Ross Perot voters listed George H. W. Bush as their second choice over Bill Clinton in 1992, Bush might have won that presidential election in the second round of vote tabulation instead of Clinton.

If you could convince enough other voters to do something like that, you could potentially eliminate a viable candidate from the next rounds of ballot tabulations even though he is one of the two candidates in a multiple-member field with the largest plurality of support. As one analyst says, the tactic is to "'up-vote your lesser-evil candidate and 'bury' your lesser-evil candidate's most viable opponent."[83]

While this might sound farfetched, in today's social media world, it would not be that difficult to implement and coordinate such a strategy, particularly in local elections where there is a much smaller electorate. It is easy to imagine sophisticated insiders and campaign consultants creating and employing this kind of strategy to reach their candidate's supporters and voters for second-, third-, or fourth-round recalculations of voting results.

The answer to this gimmickry is to stick with what we have had in place for a very long time: runoff elections. In the normal electoral process, there is usually a runoff election several weeks after an election in which no candidate won a majority of the vote.

It is true that some voters might not turn out for a runoff election because their preferred candidate did not gather enough votes to be in the runoff. However, the added time window gives potential voters the opportunity to reexamine and reeducate themselves about the character and views on issues of the two final candidates as occurred in the Georgia U.S. Senate races in 2020. Voters have a greater opportunity to make an informed choice than with instant runoffs (i.e., ranked-choice voting). Runoff elections guarantee that the winner of that election has a genuine mandate from a majority of the voters, a crucial factor in a democratic system.

Consent of the governed is what fosters domestic tranquility. When people believe that elections produce clear results between known opposing ideas, people learn to live with results even if they do not like the outcome. The vast number of Americans who are perfectly comfortable with how elections have been run for centuries will likely see ranked choice as a gimmick. When a body politic comes to believe elections outcomes are a gimmick, beware.

Ranked-choice voting is not about reforming the election process to make it better. Liberals look at what happened in Maine, how a Democratic candidate won even though the candidate got fewer votes than the incumbent Republican congressman, and see ranked-choice voting as a way of winning elections even when they are not the choice of the majority of voters.

Vote harvesting, automatic voter registration, and ranked-choice voting are all examples of so-called reforms that will not achieve the goal of increasing voter engagement. Instead, these changes to administrative election rules will create bureaucratic burdens, complicate registration and voting, compromise security, and allow inside operators to manipulate election outcomes to obtain power.

# NOTHING WAS PEACHY IN GEORGIA DURING THE 2020 ELECTIONS

The great Japanese filmmaker Akira Kurosowa's classic 1950 film, *Rashomon*, deals with the idea of truth from different perspectives centering on the murder of a samurai warrior.

The film has a lot of relevance in today's America where institutional truths are constructed and could very well be unreliable because of ideological and media bias.

The 2020 election was full of *Rashomon* moments, where the same events were given contradictory interpretations by different individuals and different media organizations. Each side seemed to inhabit different universes and accused the other of living in an "alternate reality."

Nowhere was this more evident than on the issue of election fraud. And nowhere as much as in Georgia, a key battleground state where the final result showed Joe Biden defeating Donald Trump by a mere twelve thousand votes. Two months later, Georgia delivered control of the Senate to Democrats by narrowly defeating two incumbent GOP senators in runoffs.

Mark Niesse, an *Atlanta Journal-Constitution* reporter, wrote a story a month before the 2020 general election about an investigation by Georgia Secretary of State Brad Raffensperger revealing that some Georgia voters had voted twice in the state's June primary. Niesse wrote a story entitled "Inquiry shows 1,000 Georgians may have voted twice, but no conspiracy."[1]

Niesse found that double voters could have made a difference. Bobby Smith, a probate judge in Long County, said he was shocked to learn that seven people may have voted twice in his close election and that others may have cast improper absentee ballots.

"I was like, there's no way you can vote twice," said Smith, who unsuccessfully asked a judge for a new election after he appeared to lose reelection by only nine votes. "There should have been no way. There should have been safeguards."

What struck Niesse during his reporting was how many people he met who gravitate to one extreme or the other on the issue. They believe fraud is either rampant or nonexistent and that someone who holds the opposing view is either trying to steal elections or engaging in voter suppression. Niesse blames this in part on "messaging from political organizations trying to drum up enthusiasm" for their side.[2]

Certainly, President Trump was guilty of frequent exaggeration and bombast in his claims that the 2020 election would be fatally flawed and illegitimate if mail-in votes were counted. Trump also undermined his own cause after the election when he ignored his campaign lawyers who told him that any lawsuits challenging the results had to be carefully documented and rely on solid evidence.

New lawyers representing Trump held a news conference at the Republican National Committee on November 18 to make their case. Rudy Giuliani and Sidney Powell alleged that they had convincing evidence that the presidential election was rigged and that in addition to "low tech" election fraud, hundreds of thousands of votes had been added to Joe Biden's totals through electronic manipulation.[3]

Powell claimed that the Dominion Voting Systems and Smartmatic software used in the alleged manipulation were created in Venezuela at the direction of Hugo Chavez to corrupt elections there. "President Trump won by a landslide," Powell concluded. "We are going to prove it." Giuliani echoed her by saying, "I can prove to you that Trump won Pennsylvania by 300,000 votes. I can prove to you that he won Michigan by probably 50,000 votes."

Powell and Giuliani never submitted any evidence to support their claims, and their court cases were thrown out largely for lack of standing. Powell went on to attend rallies in Georgia with eccentric former Democratic donor Lin Wood[4], at which they told Republicans not to vote in the Georgia Senate runoffs because the system was rigged.[5] Former Trump National Security Adviser Michael Flynn endorsed a call for "limited martial law" and a "revote" of the presidential election.

These kind of antics gave mainstream media outlets an excuse to ignore or disparage any real problems with the 2020 election. Reporters who spent countless resources on the dry hole that Trump had colluded with the Russians in the 2016 election showed a complete lack of curiosity over election fraud even in places that have had a long history of problems, including Georgia, where Jimmy Carter himself had to sue after his first race for the state legislature was stolen by voter fraud.

Local residents said the voter fraud in Carter's home county "had been going on on election days as long as most people could remember." Fortunately for Carter, he was successful in his litigation and went on to serve in the state senate, the governor's office, and the presidency.[6]

Trump ally Elizabeth Harrington took CNN anchor Christiane Amanpour to task, saying the media wasn't doing its job pursuing both the Hunter Biden story and election irregularities: "I would love if you guys would start doing that digging and start doing that verification."

She was promptly shot down. "No, we're not going to do your work for you," Amanpour snapped.

"That's a journalist's job!" Harrington said. "It's a journalist's job to find out if this is verified."

The media had a responsibility to dig into the issues swirling around the 2020 election. They knew that much of the public didn't believe that the 2020 election was fair. A Quinnipiac poll released on December 9 found that 38 percent of Americans believed that the election was marred by widespread fraud. That included 35 percent of independents and 77 percent of Republicans.

While many of the lawsuits challenging the election results lacked specific allegations or were rejected for lack of standing, one filed in Georgia's photo-finish presidential race presented a volume of circumstantial evidence raising serious questions about the election that deserved a hearing and full investigation. Instead, it never went before a judge.

The Trump campaign and David Shafer, the chairman of the Georgia's Republican Party, filed a lawsuit on December 4 (*Trump v. Raffensperger*) in state court[7] alleging violations of state election law and the counting of enough specific ineligible votes in the November election to create "systemic failure" in the election.

The suit argued that these ineligible votes, combined with the reduced scrutiny applied to mail-in ballots and difficulties contesting ballots during tabulation, created "substantial doubt regarding the results of the election" and required a completely new election.

"Our lawsuit does not rely on theories about the voting machines," Shafer said when the suit was filed.[8] "Instead, using official government data and licensed sources, we painstakingly show thousands of examples of 'low tech' voting irregularities and fraud sufficient in scale to place the election result in doubt."

The suit accused Secretary of State Brad Raffensperger of failing to maintain and update an accurate list of registered voters. It alleged that the chaos this created resulted in fraudulent votes.

It cited plenty of examples that called the accuracy of the vote count into question.

It noted the utter chaos in Fulton County on Election Night, where outside election monitors were prevented from observing the vote count. Fulton County elections officials also falsely denied for weeks that they shut down counting for the night, packed everything up, and proceeded to restart the count after monitors had left.[9]

Poll workers who reported irregularities were fired in retaliation, prompting an angry letter of complaint from Fulton County Commissioners Liz Hausmann, Bob Ellis, and Lee Morris.[10]

The errors and obfuscations of Fulton County Elections Director Richard Barron were so manifest that county government bodies were tied up for months during early 2021 debating whether he should be fired.[11]

The lawsuit pointed out that DeKalb County officials, who did allow monitors, were informed by one of them of a 9,626-vote error in the DeKalb County hand count. One batch of votes was labeled 10,707 for Biden and 13 for Trump. The actual count for the batch was 1,081 for Biden and 13 for Trump. DeKalb County fired an elections manager after a series of errors were made in a state-ordered audit of ballots cast in the presidential race.[12]

The Coffee County Elections Board had been unable to replicate its electronic recount results. The discrepancy was large enough to put the winner of that county in doubt, and the glitch could have affected other counties. But Secretary Raffensperger had forced an arbitrary December 4 deadline on Coffee to certify the election results despite the county warning him that the results "should not be used."

The lawsuit then laid out the extensive set of research conducted by the lawyers who represented a potential nightmare of illegal or improper votes.

- 2,560 felons voted before their rights were restored.
- 66,247 underage people registered.
- 2,423 people voted who were not on the state's voter rolls.
- 4,926 voters registered in another state after they registered in Georgia, making them ineligible.
- 395 people cast votes in another state for the same election.
- 15,700 voters filed a national change of address form without reregistering.
- 40,279 people moved counties without reregistering.
- 1,043 people claimed the physical impossibility of a post office box as their residential address.
- 98 people registered after the deadline.
- 10,315 deceased people voted on election day (8,718 of whom had been registered as dead before their votes were accepted).
- 305,701 people applied for an absentee ballot past the deadline (more than 180 days before the election), according to state records.
- 92 voters cast absentee ballots before they even requested one.
- 13 people who weren't registered voted with absentee ballots.
- 2,664 absentee ballots were mailed from elections offices before the earliest date permitted by law.
- 50 absentee ballots were counted despite being returned and accepted before the earliest allowed date.

- 2 people whose ballot applications were rejected voted anyway.
- 217 people voted by absentee ballots that were "applied for, issued, and received all on the same day."

Some of these numbers, the complaint alleged, might be higher, but they couldn't be verified by the plaintiffs because the election officials responding to the lawsuit "have the exclusive capability and access to data to determine the true number of Double Voters." The lawsuit included sworn affidavits from dozens of witnesses supporting the claims of election incompetence by officials, especially in Fulton County, which includes metropolitan Atlanta, a Democratic urban stronghold.

The complaint also shows comparisons of data from 2016 demonstrating the state's extremely low rate of rejected absentee ballots in 2020 of .034 percent compared to the 2.90 percent rejection rate in 2016 and the 3.46 percent rejection rate in 2018. The complaint alleged that this was a direct result of the misguided "Compromise Settlement Agreement" between the secretary of state and Democrats in March 2020. It changed the absentee ballot process set by state law and made election officials' jobs more difficult by tripling the number of people required to reject an absentee ballot due to problems like a signature not matching.

"A stunning 48 out of Georgia's 159 counties did not reject a single mail-in ballot in the 2020 presidential election," says Matt Braynard, a statistician and former Trump campaign staffer who compiled the data. "Had Georgia's historical rejection rate stayed consistent in 2020, there would have been 33,719 to 41,155 more ballots rejected than the 4,471 that were actually rejected. Again, Biden's final margin in Georgia was 11,769 votes."[13]

After presenting Braynard's data, the lawsuit concludes: "There will be irreparable damage to the Citizens of Georgia through their loss of confidence in the integrity of the election process by virtue of the illegal votes included in the tabulations of the Contested Election, which outweighs any potential harm to Respondents."

According to Shafer, the number of likely illegitimate votes the lawsuit identified without the benefit of the extra information held by the Peach State's election officials still largely outnumbers Joe Biden's final 11,779 vote lead in the state. The plaintiffs in the lawsuit demanded an audit of ballot signatures to ensure they matched those on record with the secretary of state's office.

"Under Georgia law, we must show that the number of unlawful votes exceeds the purported margin of victory," the suit said. "It does not require us to show for which candidate the unlawful votes were cast."

The lawsuit was clearly a hot potato, and it became evident that no one wanted to deal with it. It was electronically filed with the Fulton County Superior Court on Friday, December 4, but its accompanying 1,500 pages of exhibits crashed the system and prevented the filers from paying the filing fee. The news media immediately and erroneously reported that the suit had been rejected for lack of a filing fee.

Because the Fulton County Board of Registration and Elections was a defendant in the suit, the case had to be assigned to a judge outside the county in a nearby jurisdiction. Despite this, the court assigned the case to Fulton County Judge Constance Russell, the same liberal judge who struck down Georgia's 2004 ballot measure to constitutionally prohibit recognition of same-sex marriages.

Ignoring the vital urgency of the issues raised by the lawsuit, she ordered that the case be considered "in due course." In the Fulton County docket, that means an average wait of six months.

"It was as if she were handling a divorce case or debt collection," Trump lawyer Ray Smith said in an interview with the authors.[14]

The Georgia lawyers then filed an emergency appeal to the state's supreme court. They were entitled to a hearing within twenty days of filing. The presidential electors of the Electoral College would be meeting on December 13 to cast their votes for president, with January 6 being the day they would be counted and certified in the U.S. Senate. So time was of the essence.

The Supreme Court nonetheless rejected the appeal, saying it should be directed to the Fulton County courts. Shafer and the GOP's lawyers went back to Fulton County Chief Judge Christopher Brasher with an appeal. The judge took three days to respond and then said they should wait for a Supreme Court ruling they had already received!

"No one wanted to touch this case with a 10-foot pole," Shafer recalls. "They were running the clock out on us."

The case was finally reassigned to Superior Court Judge Adele Grubbs in neighboring Cobb County, who finally set a hearing date of January 8, two days *after* the U.S. Senate would certify the Electoral College's votes and the case would be moot. In the face of this judicial intransigence, partisanship, and political cowardice, the frustrated Trump lawyers gave up and withdrew the case.

The only scrutiny the Braynard research received was in a House Government Affairs Committee hearing before the state legislature in early December. The hearing was strongly opposed by Secretary of State Raffensperger.

"Giving oxygen to this continued disinformation is leading to a continuing erosion of people's belief in our elections and our processes," said Gabriel Sterling, Georgia's voting information systems manager, at a news conference. But if what was being presented was "disinformation," why did the secretary of state and his aides invoke their right to remain silent when invited by the House Government Affairs Committee to testify about election problems?[15]

As the hearing got underway, State Rep. Bee Nguyen, an Atlanta Democrat who holds the state House seat once occupied by Stacey Abrams, pounced. She said she had visited constituents and had confirmed that they were not out-of-state voters as they were listed in Braynard's report. She said some of the voters accused of using post office boxes as addresses lived in apartment buildings with mail centers on the ground floor.

Braynard responded and said that his data had used public records to raise legitimate questions about "potentially illegal ballots" and that only the secretary of state could verify whether they were legitimate voters. He noted that in trying to determine if dead people had "voted," they only had names and birth years to go by. When he requested the actual birth dates from Secretary Raffensperger's office, he was refused based on supposed privacy concerns.

"The Secretary of State a few days later came to us and said we could get that birth date information but only if we dropped our suit first," Shafer recalls. "This was the same Secretary of State who had responded to our case in court filings by listing dead people with their full birth dates. Complete hypocrisy and negligence."

Braynard says he has since refined his data and has concluded that by very conservative estimates there were 12,547 illegitimate ballots cast in Georgia, a number that exceeds the margin of victory in the presidential race, which was 11,779. "The outcome is unknowable," he concluded.

As for the audit of mail-in ballot signatures by professional handwriting experts that the Trump lawyers requested, the secretary of state finally conducted an audit of only one county out of 159. It is not known what professional training, if any, the signature reviewers had.

In one welcome development, a Georgia court did agree in May 2021, six months after the November election, to unseal more than 145,000 absentee ballots to allow for an audit of results in Fulton County, Georgia's most populous.

Superior Court Judge Brian Amero's ruling stemmed from a lawsuit against Fulton County alleging that ballots had been fraudulently cast and improperly counted. The judge ordered county officials to scan the ballots and produce high-resolution images. The plaintiffs plan to use those images to determine whether the ballots were completed by hand or machine to determine their legitimacy.

The audit can't change any election results. But in a bit of a surprise, it was endorsed by Secretary of State Brad Raffensperger.

"From day one I have encouraged Georgians with concerns about the election in their counties to pursue those claims through legal avenues," Raffensperger said in a statement. "Fulton County has a long-standing history of election mismanagement that has understandably weakened voters' faith in its system. Allowing this audit provides another layer of transparency and citizen engagement."

Although they were not highlighted in the media, the many problems found with Georgia's 2020 elections were noted by the state legislature, which in March 2021 passed an extensive election reform bill to address many of the concerns. In future elections, there will be no awkward signature verification issue. Voters who want to mail in a ballot will provide a driver's license or state ID number when they apply or a copy of other forms of easily obtainable ID. It's a simple measure that is hugely popular.[16]

The challenge for the future is to convince the media, state election officials, and the general public that election integrity cannot depend on a kind of honor system. Human nature is too fallible, and the temptation to acquire power is too great for that.

Election fraud has a long history in this country, and it has not suddenly disappeared in the modern era.

The "investigations" by Georgia's secretary of state are particularly risible. At first, he declared the election "the most secure election in Georgia history." When that proved to be untrue, he reluctantly opened several probes, none of which were in the kind of in-depth, intensive investigations needed to verify the accuracy of the claims raised by the lawsuits and legislative hearings.

But when Raffensperger investigated Fulton County officials for their bizarre and secretive behavior on Election Night, his staffers simply accepted the explanations of Fulton County election bureaucrats at face value. We are reminded of Cindy Lou Who, the little girl in the Dr. Seuss story who discovered the Grinch stealing the family Christmas tree. With a sweet smile, Cindy Lou accepted the Grinch's explanation that he was taking the tree back to the North Pole for repairs.

As Ronald Reagan said many years ago when asked how he conducted diplomatic negotiations: "The proper attitude is trust, but verify."

## CHAPTER ELEVEN

# A BRIEF HISTORY OF ELECTION FRAUD

W e are constantly told by liberals and the media that voter fraud isn't a problem.

Glenn Thrush of the *New York Times* claimed in 2018 that "there is essentially no voter fraud in this country."

Marie Strinden, a Democratic state legislator from North Dakota, insisted last year that "There is no voter fraud problem."

"The Myth of Voter Fraud" was a headline in the *New Yorker* magazine in 2012.

FactChecker.org ran out of adjectives describing claims of fraud as "thin allegations," "misleading claims," "faulty," "baseless," "fabricated," and "bogus," and that was all on the opening page.

Lorraine Minnite, a political scientist at Rutgers University–Camden who claims she is an "expert" on the issue despite her lack of experience as an election official, is a top voter fraud denier. "Voter fraud remains rare because it is irrational behavior," she claims. "You're not likely to change the outcome of an election with your illegal fraudulent vote, and the chances of being caught are there and we have rules to prevent against it."[1]

Tim Alberta, writing in *Politico*, claimed in 2020 there was "a daily deluge of dishonest allegations and out-of-context insinuations" coming from "conservative media's wall-to-wall coverage of exotic conspiracy theories."[2]

We certainly agree that in 2020 there were too many conspiracy theories about election fraud that didn't pan out, that some were hyped by grifters and exaggerators who knew better, and that their proliferation did damage to those who were trying to report and uncover legitimate concerns about election fraud and incompetence by election officials.

But as for those liberals who claim it isn't a problem and hasn't been one for many years, we would refer them to the statement of one of Shakespeare's characters who said they "doth protest too much."

Christopher Coates, former chief of the Voting Section in the U.S. Department of Justice and a former ACLU voting rights lawyer, says election fraud remains a real problem. "The claim by the liberal left that there is no voter fraud that is going on is completely false," he told News21. "Anytime that there are people voting that are not legally entitled to vote that's a big issue. It carries with it the potential for deciding elections a way that is contrary to the voting majority of people."

In *Crawford v. Marion County Election Board*, the seminal 2008 case upholding Indiana's voter ID law, the Supreme Court noted that, despite criminal penalties, election fraud was both real and enduring.

"It remains true...that flagrant examples of such fraud in other parts of the country have been documented throughout this Nation's history by respected historians and journalists, that occasional examples have surfaced in recent years...that...demonstrate that not only is the risk of voter fraud real but that it could affect the outcome of a close election."[3]

The majority opinion in *Crawford* was written by Justice John Paul Stevens, a stalwart liberal, rather than one of the conservative justices. But the cries of activist groups that voter fraud is a myth did not resonate with a justice who had practiced law in Chicago, a city that both historically and currently has one of the worst records of electoral malfeasance in American history.

The relative rarity of prosecutions for, say, voter-impersonation fraud, as the Seventh Circuit Court of Appeals pointed out in the Indiana case, is not evidence that it doesn't happen. The court ruled that the low incidence can be "explained by the endemic underenforcement" of voter-fraud cases and "the extreme difficulty of apprehending a voter impersonator" in many states without the tool, a voter ID, needed to detect such fraud.[4] This nation should not tolerate even one election being stolen, but without the tools to detect these illegal schemes, it is hard to know just how many close elections are being affected.

The 2020 election debacle led many Americans to worry about the integrity of our election system. With so many Americans now believing that the election system doesn't count their votes accurately, it's worth taking a look back at the nation's long tradition of electoral shenanigans. It's comic—until you start to wonder just how much of it is still going on.

## FRAUD IN THE NINETEENTH CENTURY

Nowhere has election fraud had a more notorious record than in Tammany-era New York. Tammany Hall's ruthless efficiency in manufacturing votes, especially at the zenith of its power in the second half of the nineteenth century, is legendary. At the time, America didn't yet have privacy-protecting voting machines, a secret ballot, or even official government ballots, so Tammany fixers could ensure that voters would cast ballots as promised or bought. Vote riggers would simply give people pre-marked ballots and watch as they deposited them into the voting box.

Practical Tammany pols preferred to deal with "strikers," wholesale operatives who would guarantee thick bundles of votes for a price. One New York candidate who hadn't yet paid his strikers made the mistake of visiting the polls on Election Day. The angry operatives swiftly surrounded him, demanding their cash. Historian Mark Summers recounts that "the politician was nearly torn to pieces...and as he fled the pack cursed him for 'a mean cuss' and emptied out the ballot-boxes, tearing up every ticket bearing his name."

The immigrants flooding into New York were easy prey for the Tammany pols. Each state then set its own standards for naturalizing new citizens, and New York's were lax. In 1868, *The Nation* reported that Tammany Hall had set up a "naturalization mill," instantly certifying folks right off the boat as citizens—and Tammany voters. (In 1996, the Clinton administration similarly sped up the naturalization of up to 1 million new citizens so they could vote in time for that year's election.)

Tammany was so efficient at election fixing that between 1868 and 1871, the votes cast in the city totaled 8 percent more than the entire voting population—"the dead filling in for the sick," as one contemporary wag put it. Historian Denis Tilden Lynch describes how thugs would go from one polling place to the next, impersonating citizens who hadn't yet voted. One such "repeater" posed as the dignified pastor of a Dutch Reformed church. The election clerks asked him his name.

"Jones," shouted the repeater, startling the poll workers with his scraggly beard, unclean face, and whiskey breath.

"What is the first name, Mr. Jones?" asked the election clerk.

"John," snarled the repeater.

"The Reverend Dr. John Jones, pastor of the Dutch Reformed church around the corner?" asked a clerk.

"Yes, you dirty, lousy @$#%%^^!" said the repeater. "Who'n else did you thick I was, eh?"

The officials let "Reverend Jones" vote.

After his fall from power, the infamous Tammany Hall leader William Marcy Tweed (Boss Tweed) candidly assessed the conduct of elections in his city. His 1877 testimony before the New York Board of Aldermen remains fascinating for its matter-of-fact explication of how to corrupt democracy:

Q: "When you were in office, did the Tweed Ring control the elections in the city at that time?"

A: "They did sir. Absolutely."

Q: "Please tell me what the modus operandi of that was. How did you control the elections?"

A: "Well, each ward had a representative man, who would control matters in his own ward, and whom the various members of the general committee were to look up to for advice how to control the elections."

Q: "What were they to do, in case you wanted a particular man elected over another?"

A: "Count the ballots in bulk, or without counting them announce the result in bulk, or change from one to the other, as the case may have been."

Q: "Then these elections really were no elections at all? The ballots were made to bring about any result that you determined upon beforehand?"

A: "The ballots made no result; the counters made the result.... That was generally done to every ward by the gentleman who had charge of the ward."

Q: "Mr. Tweed, did you ever give any directions to any persons, to falsify or change the result of the actual bona fide ballots cast in any election?"

A. "More in the nature of a request than a directive."

Later in Tweed's testimony, this exchange occurred:

Q: "Can you state now, at this time, whether the election which
   took place in the City of New York at that time 1868 was a fair
   and honest election?"
A: "I have not the details in my memory."
Q: "What is your best impression?"
A: "I don't think there was ever a fair or honest election in the
   City of New York."

Tammany's fraud was so all-encompassing, says historian
Mark Summers, that "even men who have passed through history
with clean reputations thought little of raising a majority that
way." Henry Raymond, cofounder and first editor of the *New York
Times*, railed against corruption. But when he ran for speaker of
the New York State Assembly in 1851, he asked Senator Hamilton
Fish for $1,000 so that he could buy the election. "Truly a pretty
suggestion," Fish confided to his diary, "but corruption in connection with these primary elections has become so prevalent
that one loses astonishment at its evidence in any quarter."

## FRAUD IN THE TWENTIETH CENTURY

Boss Tweed died in disgrace, but Tammany Hall flourished into
the twentieth century. In 1905, William Randolph Hearst, owner
of the *New York Morning Journal*, decided to take Tammany on
and run for New York mayor on the ticket of his own third party,
the Municipal Ownership League. Hearst had already beaten a
Tammany-backed candidate in 1902, winning a New York congressional seat with a lavish campaign that would have put former
New York Mayor and presidential candidate Michael Bloomberg
to shame. Hearst spent the equivalent of $100,000 for fireworks

in Madison Square Park and offered free trips to Coney Island for every man, woman, and child in his district.

But Hearst bit off more than he could buy in running for mayor, a key position in the Tammany empire. On Election Day, notes Hearst biographer David Nasaw, "there were instances of voter fraud, of poll watchers being chased away, of delays in reporting returns, of unopened and uncounted ballot boxes mysteriously turning up in the East River." The *New York Independent* declared it "the most extraordinary election ever witnessed in New York City"—and that's saying something. The *New York Times* reported that the challenger's poll watchers, having been beaten up and driven off by Tammany goons, "came into the Hearst headquarters last night with bandaged hands. Some carried their arms in slings. At about ten o'clock in the evening a report was received that the returns were being held back from these districts," presumably as Tammany stuffed the ballot boxes to achieve the desired count. One poll watcher, an R. Little, "had a finger chewed off and his face cut."

While the newspapers deplored the violence, they also expressed relief that incumbent Tammany mayor George Brinton McClellan beat Hearst by a margin of 3,472 votes out of more than 600,000 "cast." The *New York Times* congratulated city voters for having "spared the city the humiliation, the trials, and the dangers of a four years' mismanagement of its affairs by a peculiarly reckless, unschooled, and unsteady group of experimenters and adventurers."

Hearst believed that he had won the election as ballots went into the boxes but lost it as they came out. After organizing a blue-ribbon committee to protest the fraud and demand a recount, he held massive demonstrations throughout the city and went to court. But the courts and the state legislature ignored him, and no recount took place.

New York City's corruption, severe as it was, was far from unique. In Baltimore, for instance, vote fixing could get even uglier: a notorious Whig Party organization, the "Fourth Ward Club," hired thugs to seize innocent strangers and foreigners, drug them with bad whiskey and opiates, and send them out to cast multiple votes. (James Harrison, a biographer of Edgar Allan Poe, speculates that when Poe died in 1849, he was a victim of ruthless vote-fraud toughs who kidnapped him and left him drunk and near death on a Baltimore street.) Political scientists estimate that in many urban areas, fixers routinely manipulated 10 to 15 percent of the vote. A 1929 study by the Brookings Institution, looking back on U.S. elections in the nineteenth century, observed: "Indifference, fraud, corruption, and violence have marked the operation of our electoral system."

The corruption influenced national as well as local politics. Both major parties stole votes with abandon in the 1876 presidential election between Republican Rutherford Hayes of Ohio and Samuel Tilden of New York. The race ended in a deadlock, resolved only after a congressionally created commission delivered the presidency to Hayes by a single disputed electoral vote. At least three other presidential elections—in 1880, 1884, and 1888—proved so close that fraud may have played a role in their outcomes too.

As the century closed, however, fraud gradually began to diminish as popular disgust with vote rigging spurred reforms. States began to require voters to register before Election Day. Today's "reformers" who want to get rid of voter registration or implement instant same-day registration have conveniently forgotten that voter registration was developed to prevent the type of fraud that was so common in elections.

In Massachusetts, Richard Henry Dana III, son of the author of the classic *Two Years Before the Mast*, persuaded the Massachusetts legislature to adopt the "Australian" ballot, a government-printed ballot that would list all candidates and that voters would cast in secret in a booth. It became a model for reformers elsewhere. As changes spread to other states, voter "turnout" fell precipitously. Historians Gary Cox and Morgan Krause point out that turnout in New York State elections dropped some 15 percent after the anti-fraud measures took effect.

Election fraud didn't vanish from American politics, of course. Jokes still circulate about the late Chicago mayor Richard Daley's uncanny ability to get the dead to vote for him. But first prize for twentieth-century electoral corruption goes to Mayor Frank "I Am the Law" Hague, whose political machine controlled gritty Jersey City, New Jersey, across the Hudson River from New York, from 1917 to 1947. His desk had a special drawer that opened in the front, allowing visitors to deposit bribes that then disappeared inside the desk. On a yearly salary of $8,000, he amassed a fortune of at least $10 million.

Hague's career began inauspiciously, as you might expect. Expelled from school after sixth grade as incorrigible, he became a ward heeler for the Jersey City Democratic machine. In 1908, he entered city employment as a janitor. Ten years later, he was mayor, and through his control of the Hudson County vote, he became the leader of the state Democratic Party and the man who could dictate who would become governor or a judge. In 1939, so great was Hague's power that he could order his hand-picked governor to appoint his son, Frank Hague, Jr., to the state supreme court even though the young man had never graduated from law school.

The Hague machine turned election fraud into a science. On the Sunday before an election, the mayor would gather his ward heelers into a Jersey City arena (called the Grotto) and give his orders. "Three hundred and sixty-four days a year you come to me wanting favors.... Now, one day in the year I come to you." Hague fielded roughly one worker per hundred voters, and boy did he get results. In 1937, the Democratic candidate in the First District of the First Ward won 433 votes, the Republican only 1. This struck some people as odd since a short time earlier, the district had recorded 103 Republican votes. An investigation found torn ballots, others with unmistakable erasure marks, and still others altered by pencil. The single Republican ballot, marked with a red pencil, "could not have been erased without doing definite damage to the ballot," investigators noted.

Reformers were always trying to clean up Jersey City elections, but they faced an uphill fight. In 1935, the Honest Ballot Association sent 245 Princeton students to monitor a city election. Hague's ruffians beat up five of them within an hour of their arrival. Several others, ejected from a polling place, went to see the mayor to protest. "Well, you fellows go back there if you wish, but if you get knocked cold it will be your own hard luck," he told them. Later, Hague explained to *Collier's* magazine that the roughing-up involved "animal spirits, that's all. I told my boys to lay off, but it was a pretty dull election, and they couldn't resist the temptation to have a little fun."

In 1937, the *Jersey Journal* asked in a disgusted editorial: "Where was Election Superintendent Ferguson's 1,300 deputies when the new irregularities now charged occurred last Tuesday?" In response, the superintendent issued a public statement that read, in part: "Where were my deputies? Some of them were locked up in the police stations; some were stuck on corners, with a threat that if they moved from them, a night stick would be wrapped around their necks.... The only way to have an honest election in Hudson County under present conditions is with the militia."

Mayor Hague retired from office in 1947, turning over the job of mayor to his nephew. Gradually, his machine lost control of the city, though Jersey City's politics remain far from pristine to this day. Nevertheless, Hague's flagrant vote rigging was extreme for post-Tammany American politics.

Yet if Hague's ghost, or Boss Tweed's, took a look at a recent newspaper, he'd smile in recognition. Wholesale vote fraud is on the rise again. In Jersey City, a former mayor named Gerald McCann, who had left office due to a fraud conviction, tried for a comeback in 2007. Initially, he won a school board seat by 21 votes. But then one of his opponents sued, and it was uncovered in court that as many as 216 suspect votes had been cast, most of them from 'incompetent or otherwise elderly or ill" residents of nursing homes who had been hoodwinked into casting absentee ballots of McCann.

Of course, Democrats will often retort that all the stories of potential electoral abuses pale beside the Republican shenanigans that helped deliver Florida to George W. Bush in 2000. Media recounts that showed that Bush would have won Florida under any reasonable recount standard are beside the point, they say. Election officials, they claim, wrongly identified thousands of people as felons, most of them minorities, thus preventing them from voting under the state's election laws. If those votes had counted, Democrats charge, Al Gore would have become president.

But both the *Miami Herald* and the *Palm Beach Post* found that, if anything, election officials were too permissive in whom they allowed to cast ballots. A *Post* analysis discovered that 5,600 people voted whose names matched those of convicted felons. "These illegal voters almost certainly influenced the down-to-the-wire presidential election," the *Post* reported. "Of the likely felons identified by the *Post*, 68 percent were registered Democrats."[5]

Democrats such as their super lawyer Marc Elias believe that all the ambiguities in election law that are being increasingly exploited work to their benefit, allowing them to litigate every single close race. Unfortunately, if "anything goes" continue to be the ballot bywords that they became in 2020, the nation may soon wake up to a crisis even bigger than our most recent nightmare.

Perhaps then the public will demand to know who subverted the election laws. But wouldn't it be better if we did something about the problem now? We should reform the system now so we never again divide the country the way it was riven in two by the 2020 election.

## CHAPTER TWELVE

# HOW TO FIX THE FLAWS IN OUR ELECTION PROCESS

W e have both been working on election integrity for more than three decades. When we published *Who's Counting? How Fraudsters and Bureaucrats Put Your Vote at Risk* in 2012, we made a series of election reform recommendations. These recommendations were based on our extensive experience, research, and interviews with many election and government officials, prosecutors, voters, candidates, and organizations concerned with election integrity.

As we said in 2012, reforms are necessary "to address the chaos, incompetence, and outright fraud that menaces our election systems." The recommendations we made then, and the recommendations we make now, could fix many of the vulnerabilities in the system we use to elect our mayors, city council members, state legislators, governors, members of Congress, and the president of the United States. They are intended to ensure that everyone who is eligible is able to vote and that their vote is not diluted or stolen through mistakes, errors, or fraud.

While some states have made things even worse since then, such as when California legalized vote trafficking of absentee ballots in 2018, a number of states have tried to implement many of these reforms. Yet powerful, well-funded, radical, left-wing advocacy organizations like the ACLU, the League of Women Voters, and the Lawyers Committee for Civil Rights have worked with the Democratic National Committee to wage a major war in the media and in the courts to stop these needed reforms.

They have pushed the false narrative that there is no fraud in our elections or that it is so minimal that we should not be concerned about it. They have also, with their willing allies in the mainstream media, falsely labeled any efforts to implement needed reform as "voter suppression." This despite the fact that turnout has steadily increased in states that have implemented many of these reforms, which are overwhelmingly supported by the American public. It is hard to see their intent as anything other than to make it easy to cheat and manipulate election results and to do so without getting caught or prosecuted.

As we have extensively outlined in this book, errors, mistakes, and misbehavior by election officials, careless and shoddy election practices and procedures, and outright fraud by voters, candidates, election officials, and political operatives can cause and have caused problems in elections throughout our history. It is simply indisputable that this is a continuing problem in too many elections for us to simply ignore it. There are far too many instances of such problems occurring that demonstrate the weaknesses in our current patchwork system across the states.

The rules governing the conduct of elections, which since our founding have been administered by the states through laws implemented by state legislatures, should not be changed shortly before an election, as occurred in 2020. It confuses voters, candidates, and election officials and provides opportunities for mischief. The laws especially should not be changed by a few officials with no lawful authority to do so. This is antidemocratic, and it can lead to the manipulation of election rules that favor certain candidates or political parties.

Another antidemocratic tactic used in 2020 was collusive lawsuits filed by partisan advocacy organizations in coordination with state and local election officials and attorneys general who want to evade, alter, or ignore the laws the legislature adopted to govern elections.

Another new, corrupt development that occurred in 2020 was private interest groups with partisan affiliations and goals masquerading as "nonpartisan" and giving hundreds of millions of dollars to local election officials to fund election operations. No state should allow election officials and agencies to accept private funding, particularly when it is conditioned on those organizations dictating, directing, and interfering in the conduct of the election and providing unequal opportunities to vote to the residents of certain politically advantageous jurisdictions within those states.

The ultimate goal of our democratic election process must be to ensure that the public, political parties, and candidates trust the fairness and credibility of the outcome of our elections and that election officials ensure both access and security. That goal is elusive in large part because of the vulnerabilities that currently exist, which numerous individuals and organizations on the left want to make even worse.

State legislators and local officials can take many steps to safeguard their elections. While there are some steps that only Congress and the federal government can take, we recommend improvements to voter registration and election procedures that states can and should implement.

## VOTER REGISTRATION

**Maintain accurate voter registration lists.** It seems obvious that one of the most basic requirements for clean elections is up-to-date, accurate voter registration lists that are not full of multiple and duplicate registrations as well as ineligible individuals such as felons and aliens. Yet most states are not taking advantage of the wealth of information available to them from both their own databases and commercial databases.

Computerized statewide voter registration lists must be designed to be interoperable so they can communicate seamlessly with other state government databases to allow frequent exchanges and comparisons of information. There should be frequent comparisons of the statewide voter registration list with the databases maintained by the motor vehicle department for driver's licenses, the state corrections department files (for felons whose ability to vote has been taken away), state vital records to find registered voters who have died, and state welfare, public assistance, and unemployment benefit agencies. This will provide election officials with information relevant to registration such as address changes, deaths, citizenship status, and other factors affecting eligibility.

State officials should supplement data from state vital statistics agencies on deceased registrants with information from the Social Security Administration's Master Death File or independent audits of the voter registration file by commercial groups that identify deceased individuals.

Since the main source of funding for county governments is property taxes, counties have extremely detailed records on every property in a county. Yet few election officials are taking advantage of that to verify voter registration lists. Election officials should be checking the claimed residence address on all new voter registration forms against county tax records to find individuals who are falsely claiming commercial, industrial, and government addresses or vacant and undeveloped lots as a residence. Moreover, all new registrations should be checked against the entire voter registration list to verify how many individuals are registered at that address and then cross-checked with county tax records to find any anomalies.

For example, it seems obvious that if county tax records show that a registered address is a single family home yet the registration list shows that thirty individuals are registered at that address, such an anomaly should raise a red flag that needs to be investigated by election officials looking for fraudulent or out-of-date registrations. Similarly, individuals registered at the same address but with only slight differences in their names must be checked to ensure that these are not multiple registrations by the same individual.

List maintenance programs need to be required and funded for ongoing and comprehensive accuracy updates. Reports of list maintenance activity should be provided to the state legislative oversight committees each year detailing the extent and timing of list maintenance programs in each county and statewide.

States should be using the U.S. Postal Service's National Change of Address (NCOA) system several times a year to find voters who have moved and to learn if they are registered in more than one state. Since not all citizens inform the post office or election officials when they move to a new residence, states should supplement the NCOA system by using information from commercial data houses such as credit agencies. They often have much more current, detailed information than government agencies and can provide information not only on the current address of a voter but also other information important to eligibility such as citizenship.

State voter registration lists should be transparent, readily accessible, and freely available to candidates, political parties, nonprofit organizations, and the public (except for confidential information such as Social Security numbers and driver's license numbers).

The voter registration lists provided through electronic poll books to individual polling locations should include photographs of registered voters from their driver's licenses, voter ID cards, or any other state records.

We do not encourage states to allow online voter registration because of the dangers posed by hackers and cybercriminals. But to the extent that states allow online voter registration, it should be limited only to individuals for whom there is already an existing state record such as a driver's license that contains all the information required to register to vote, including a signature.

Verifying the citizenship of registered voters is a vital but missing component in our registration system. Only lawful citizens can vote in federal and state elections, although a handful of jurisdictions like San Francisco have authorized aliens to vote in local elections. States should require proof of citizenship to register to vote, and they should verify the citizenship of registered voters with the records of the U.S. Department of Homeland Security (DHS). They can also access the E-Verify system that is used by employers to check the citizenship status of new employees.

Unfortunately, DHS has for years put up administrative roadblocks and red tape in front of state election officials seeking access to the department's alien databases, which contain information on aliens legally in the country and any illegal aliens who have been detained with a record created for them. That is something Congress needs to stop.

State agencies such as Departments of Motor Vehicles should be prohibited from offering *any* individual the opportunity to register to vote who uses any foreign identification or other document that indicates the individual is not a U.S. citizen. When election officials discover that a registered voter is not a U.S. citizen, they should be required by state law to immediately remove that individual from the voter registration roll. They should also be required to send notification to the local district attorney, the state attorney general, the FBI, and the U.S. Departments of Homeland Security and Justice for investigation and possible prosecution under both state and federal laws that prohibit aliens from registering or voting.

State court clerks and jury commissioners should be required to notify election officials and state and federal law enforcement when an individual who is called for jury duty from the voter registration list is excused because the individual is not a U.S. citizen, is deceased, or has moved out of state. Similarly, states should condition requests from federal courts for a state's voter registration or DMV list to use for federal juries on an agreement by the federal courts to notify state election officials if an individual is excused from jury duty because he is not a U.S. citizen, is deceased, or has moved out of state.

## IN-PERSON AND ABSENTEE VOTING

**States should require a photo ID to vote both in person and absentee.** It seems obvious to everyone except the denizens of the left that requiring a photo ID to authenticate a voter's identity, whether they are voting in person or through an absentee ballot, is a basic requirement for a secure voting system. Although the overwhelming majority of Americans already have such an ID, states should issue a free photo ID to anyone who cannot afford one. As part of that effort, every driver's license or state photo ID issued should note prominently whether the individual is a citizen or noncitizen. Acceptable IDs would include driver's licenses, state non-driver's ID cards, U.S. passports, U.S. military IDs, tribal government IDs, and IDs issued by state colleges and universities but only if they prominently display whether the student is a citizen.

There should be no affidavit or other exceptions of any kind to the ID requirement as some states have implemented since this makes it too easy to evade the ID requirement. For individuals who are too disabled to go to a state office on their own to obtain a state ID, states should provide appropriate transportation for the individual from their residence to the state ID office and back to their residence. Or they should equip a mobile van as Alabama did to travel to the home of permanently disabled individuals to provide them with an ID to vote.[1]

Because absentee ballots, as we have discussed, are the most vulnerable to coercion, intimidation, theft, forgery, alteration, and misdelivery, they should be reserved for those individuals who are too disabled to vote in person or who will be out of town on Election Day and all early voting days. Given their security weaknesses, all absentee ballots should require notarization or the signature of a witness as well as the printed name, address, and telephone number of the witness so the witness can be contacted if questions arise over the authenticity of the ballot.

To prevent coercion and intimidation, no individual should be allowed to witness more than one absentee ballot of a voter who is unrelated to that individual. A person should be allowed to witness the absentee ballots of up to five immediate family members. This is a necessary precaution because as election fraud cases show, such as the Ninth Congressional District race in 2018 in North Carolina, without such a limitation, corrupt vote brokers can target numerous voters in their homes, apartments, condominiums, retirement communities, or assisted living centers.

In addition to requiring photocopies of a photo ID, the signatures of voters on absentee ballots should be compared to the signatures of the voters on their registration files. If signature comparison software with adjustable parameters is utilized, it should be set for the highest effective rate.

No completed absentee ballot received from a voter should be removed from its envelope until the verification process has been completed and subjected to observation by designated observers of the candidates or the major political parties. All voters wanting to vote with absentee ballots should be required to fill out a signed request, with no electronic signature accepted.

There should be no permanent absentee ballot lists and no automatic mailing to all voters of absentee ballots or absentee ballot request forms. The deadline for the receipt of all absentee ballots should be the closing of polls on Election Day to obviate any disputes about the timing of absentee ballots and problems with the U.S. Postal Service's failure to postmark an envelope. The deadline for a request for an absentee ballot should be based on U.S. Postal Service delivery standards for that state.

If a state insists on accepting absentee ballots that are post-marked by Election Day, voters should not be sent pre-stamped, pre-postmarked envelopes for the return of their ballots. Since the U.S. Postal Service is unlikely to restamp the envelopes, this risks absentee ballots not being mailed until after Election Day when early results are already being reported. This could lead to attempts to manipulate election results.

To avoid the same absentee ballot being counted more than once, all absentee ballots should have an embedded barcode. The barcode would not identify which voter is receiving the absentee ballot since that would compromise ballot secrecy. Instead, the purpose of the code would be to trigger software within the computer scanners to note that a specific ballot is being counted and cannot be counted again. This would prevent individuals being able to run the same ballot through a scanner multiple times to pad votes for particular candidates. It would also prevent others from photocopying the standard absentee paper ballot and sending in fraudulent votes.

In order to keep track of absentee ballots being delivered through the Postal Service, states should require a barcode on all envelopes containing blank absentee ballots being sent to voters who have requested an absentee ballot. They should have a similar code on the envelopes to be used to send voters' completed ballots back to election officials. This would allow ballot envelopes to be tracked through the mail.

The use of drop boxes for the deposit of absentee ballot envelopes, something that was greatly expanded in the 2020 election, should be severely limited because they introduce too many unknowns into the voting system. If authorized, states should require drop boxes to be located only in secure government buildings where they are under twenty-four-hour security and video surveillance. The video surveillance should be available to designated representatives of the candidates and major political parties.

To prevent the type of coercion and outright fraud that happens all too often in nursing homes and assisted living centers, county election officials should provide bipartisan teams of election officials to assist individuals seeking to cast an absentee ballot from such facilities in a supervised setting.

One of the most important steps for states to take is to ban vote trafficking of absentee ballots by third parties. This prohibition would ensure that candidates, campaign staffers, party activists, and political operatives would not be able to pressure or coerce vulnerable voters in their homes or mishandle, alter, or change absentee ballots they pick up from voters. States should only allow the voter, a member of his or her immediate family, or a designated caregiver to personally deliver an absentee ballot.

Any individual delivering a ballot should be required to complete a form that would be included with the voter's absentee ballot. That form would require the name, address, telephone number, and relationship of the individual delivering the ballot and be signed by both the voter and the deliverer. States should require that form be delivered to election officials along with the completed absentee ballot.

**States must allow election observers complete access to the voting and election process.** One reason so many doubts were raised by many Americans over the results of the 2020 election were claims that election officials in places like Detroit and Philadelphia unlawfully excluded observers. These actions were highly suspicious and should not be allowed to happen. Political parties, candidates, and third-party organizations should all be allowed to have observers watch every part of the election process, including procedures such as the opening and verification of absentee ballots. Transparency is essential to a fair and secure system and to maintaining public confidence in the election process.

The only limitation on observers should be that they cannot interfere with the voting and counting process. They must be legally authorized under state law to be in a position—exactly like election officials—to observe everything going on except the actual voting by individuals in the voting booth. Election officials should be prohibited from stationing observers so far away that they cannot meaningfully observe the process.

Moreover, some states have ill-advisedly banned observers from using cameras in carrying out their observer duties. In fact, the use of cameras can resolve disputes between observers and election officials over what actually happened inside a polling place or counting center. Cameras can prevent problems from becoming a he-said-she-said occurrence where authorities are unable to determine what happened.

Thus, states should allow observers to have cameras and recording devices wherever they are stationed but prohibit them from recording the actual votes cast by individuals. Beyond observers, cameras should be stationed in all polling locations, ballot counting centers, and election processing facilities so that the public can watch elections, canvassing, and the tabulation of ballots as these events are happening live on the Internet.

State law should demand that election officials who prevent legally qualified observers from viewing the election process be disciplined. Punishment should include suspension, termination, or civil fines. For this and many other reasons, all polling places should be run by a politically neutral polling official or jointly run by at least two officials representing the two major political parties. Furthermore, states should allow any registered voter to be an observer anywhere in the state and not limit observers to the specific county or township where they are registered to vote.

## COUNTING VOTES

**No state should allow the counting of ballots prior to Election Day.** The counting of ballots, including absentee and early votes, should not begin until the polls close at the end of Election Day. To do otherwise risks the premature release of election results to a particular candidate by election officials that could help that candidate. Or a public leak could discourage voters from turning out to vote if they see that the candidate they support is behind in the early returns.

If a state insists on beginning the count prior to Election Day, it should ban the release of results until the evening of Election Day, subject to criminal penalties. Once it begins, the counting of ballots should continue without pause until all votes have been tabulated. If extreme circumstances occur that require the suspension of the vote count, election officials should be required to notify the public of the suspension and the exact time it will resume.

To preventing hacking, no electronic voting machines placed in polling locations should be connected to the Internet; in fact, they should not be allowed to have any internal modems even present in the machines. Furthermore, the computers used in county and township election departments used to tabulate results should be stand-alone computers that are not connected to the Internet or a government-wide network that could allow hackers to interfere with the vote count.

## ELECTION LITIGATION

**State legislatures must be able to prevent election officials and executive branch officials from violating or waiving state election laws.** State legislatures must ensure that they have legal standing, either through a specific state law or a constitutional amendment if that is required, to sue other state officials such as governors or secretaries of state who make or attempt to make unauthorized changes in state election laws. For example, if a secretary of state extends the deadline set by state law for the receipt of absentee ballots, legislatures should have legal standing to immediately contest that unilateral and unauthorized change that overrides state law.

Governors and secretaries of state should have the authority to remove and replace county election officials who engage in similar behavior. And voters should be provided by state law with standing and the ability to immediately file a lawsuit against any state or local official who fails to abide by or enforce a state election law requirement.

**States should not implement automatic voter registration, same-day voter registration, or ranked-choice voting.** We have outlined the many problems with automatic voter registration, which will lead to multiple registrations by the same person as well as the registration of ineligible individuals like aliens. State legislatures should not implement it.

Nor should they implement same-day voter registration, which gives election officials no opportunity to verify the authenticity of the information provided by a voter. Registration should be required before Election Day to give election officials sufficient time to verify the accuracy of the registration information contained on a registration form and to confirm the eligibility and identity of the individual seeking to cast a vote in the upcoming election.

Ranked-choice voting is a confusing gimmick that potentially disenfranchises large numbers of voters. States should not even consider replacing runoff elections with ranked-choice voting.

Finally, states should prohibit election officials from receiving private funding from outside organizations or individuals. This would prevent potential conflicts of interest. Such funding may influence or change the outcome of elections and violate principles of equal protection since it may lead to unequal opportunities to vote in different areas of a state.

The objective that all of us should have is an election process that is fair, secure, and reliable. It should be transparent so that the public, candidates, political parties, and the news media have complete access to every aspect of the system as it is administered, as individuals register and vote, and as the ballots are counted and tabulated. You can guarantee both access and security through common sense and straightforward laws and rules that everyone understands and accepts.

At the end of the day, we need a system in which everyone involved, from the voters themselves to the candidates, has confidence that the individual with the most legitimate votes wins the election. While the candidates as well as their supporters who lose may be disappointed, we want them to accept that they lost fairly in a completely legitimate election. That is the key to maintaining our democratic republic and the well-being of self-government in the greatest nation for liberty and freedom in history.

# ACKNOWLEDGMENTS

Between us, John Fund and I have been working on election issues, particularly election integrity and security, for more than sixty years. I became passionate about this issue after witnessing voter intimidation in Atlanta, Georgia, while volunteering as a poll observer in a low-income-housing neighborhood in a local election at the very beginning of my legal career.

But I am also interested in protecting individuals' votes and the integrity of our elections because I am a first-generation American. I heard many stories from my Russian father and German mother when I was growing up about their experiences and the horrors of tyrannical dictatorships without the liberties and freedoms—and the ability to vote—that our election process helps ensure.

I have fought to guarantee that each eligible voter's ballot counts, including when I served as a county election official in Georgia and Virginia. I joined the Civil Rights Division of the U.S. Department of Justice in 2001 to enforce the Voting Rights Act and other federal voting laws in order to help safeguard our elections. Our job was to uphold the civil and constitutional rights of all Americans, and that's what I did even when we were attacked by liberals for enforcing voting laws on a race-neutral basis as intended by Congress.

What is astonishing and frankly shameful is the unfair, unjustified, personal attacks that John and I have been subjected to for years by biased reporters, uninformed members of Congress, and the boorish, rude leaders of so-called civil rights organizations. And why? Simply because we want the same thing that poll after poll shows the American people want: fair and secure elections where everyone who is eligible is able to vote and where their votes are not diluted or stolen through fraud or errors and mistakes made by election officials.

We have not been and never will be deterred from writing about and doing what we think is right by such malicious attacks. In fact, my favorite theme song is Tom Petty's "I Won't Back Down."

It has been a pleasure to be a friend and colleague of John Fund for more than twenty years. He is an outstanding journalist, a good writer, and a great friend. I also want to thank Roger Kimball and the editors at Encounter Books for giving us the opportunity, once again, to write about a very important topic.

The Heritage Foundation, where I have worked since I left the Federal Election Commission, is the greatest institution for freedom, liberty, economic prosperity, and the rule of law that exists in America today. My colleagues in the Edwin Meese III Center for Legal and Judicial Studies, including John Malcolm and Cully Stimson, are some of the best lawyers and legal minds I have ever worked with. Working for the greatest attorney general in many generations (if not ever), Ed Meese, a gentleman and a scholar, is something I would not trade for anything. They, along with the leadership of Heritage, from Ed Feulner to Kay Cole James, have done nothing but fully support my work on this very important issue.

Finally, this book could not have been written without the help and editing prowess of my best friend, partner, and wife of more than thirty years, Susan Burnell. Thanks to her for all her work, especially for putting up with long nights and working weekends.

There are many other good friends and colleagues I have not mentioned, but they know who they are, and I appreciate all their help and support over the years. What Harry Truman once said about getting a dog if you want a friend in Washington is something I have found is not true; I have found many good friends in the nation's capital who have been there when I needed them.

The survival of our democratic republic depends on Americans believing their vote counts and their continued faith in the fairness and security of our electoral process. John Fund and I will continue to work tirelessly to protect the integrity of our elections despite the unfair, unjustified, and dishonest attacks on our personal and professional work on this vital issue.

It is simply too important to let anything deter us.

—Hans von Spakovsky

Expressing appreciation to those who helped make a book possible is always a tricky endeavor. You are almost certain to forget someone, so apologies are offered in advance to anyone whom I inadvertently pass over.

Books are normally solitary labors. But for me this one had the advantage of a knowledgeable, judicious, and wise coauthor. I couldn't have asked for a better collaborator than Hans von Spakovsky.

I owe editor Rich Lowry and my colleagues at *National Review* my thanks for letting me write with complete freedom on issues of election integrity. Thanks also to James Taranto of the *Wall Street Journal* for allowing me to preview some of the arguments in this book on the *Journal's* op-ed page.

I am especially grateful to Roger Kimball of Encounter Books for believing in this project. Encounter's staff pulled off amazing feats to bring this book to you so soon after the 2020 elections. Amanda DeMatto, Mary Spencer, and Michael Totten made all the pieces fit just so.

I am also in debt to those in the think tank, public policy, and philanthropic worlds who provided helpful advice, including Christian Adams, Cleta Mitchell, Michael Thielen, Lisa Nelson of the American Legislative Exchange Council, state Rep. Shawnna Bolick, and Rick Graber of the Bradley Foundation. I will always be grateful to Clara Del Villar for her encouragement.

Many chapters were improved by conversations with Congresswoman Claudia Tenney, Republican National Committee member Shawn Steel, Grover Norquist, Dan Walters, Chris Ruddy, Jon Caldera, Michael Pack, Adam Laxalt, Gail Heriot, James and Heather Higgins, Henry Olsen, and Jameson Campaigne.

I also want to thank all of the people who contacted me, many of whom did not want their names mentioned, with tips, observations, and concerns about our fragile election system.

—John Fund

# NOTES

## INTRODUCTION

1 Alec Dent, "Did Edison Research Find That Dominion Deleted Trump Votes or Switched Votes to Biden?" *The Dispatch* (Nov. 12, 2020).

2 Jacob Shamsian, "Newsmax settles a defamation lawsuit from a Dominion executive at the center of election conspiracy theories and issues an apology," *Business Insider* (April 30, 2021), https://www.businessinsider.com/newsmax-settles-dominion-executive-eric-coomer-defamation-lawsuit-and-apologizes-2021-4.

3 Steve Kroft, "Vote Early, Vote Often," *60 Minutes*, Columbia Broadcasting System (1998), https://search.alexanderstreet.com/preview/work/bibliographic_entity%7Cvideo_work%7C2862229.

4 Interview, Glenn Garvin, *Miami Herald* (September 9, 2020).

## CHAPTER ONE

1 Peter Hasson, "125 Democrats And 1 Republican Vote To Lower Voting Age to 16," *Daily Caller* (March 8, 2019).

2 "Ruling That Delayed California Recall Vote Is Overturned," Associated Press (Sept. 23, 2003).

3 David Melmer, "Daschle accuses Republicans of voter harassment," *Indian Country Today* (Nov. 1, 2002).

4 Jason Snead, "Injecting Reality into the Election Reform Debate," Honest Elections Project (March 23, 2021).

5 Ibid.

6 Ibid.

7 "Toplines and Crosstabs April 2021 Election Reform," University of Massachusetts Amherst, UMass Poll (April 28, 2021), https://polsci.umass.edu/toplines-and-crosstabs-april-2021-election-reform.

8 "The Economist/YouGov Poll" (April 3–6, 2021), p. 84.

9 https://www.youtube.com/watch?v=rrBxZGWCdgs

10 John Fund, "Voter Fraud: We've Got Proof It's Easy," *National Review Online* (Jan. 12, 2014).

11 John Fund, "End the Left-Right Stalemate on Voter Rights," *National Review Online* (April 3, 2018); https://www.nationalreview.com/2018/04/voting-rights-social-security-voter-id-proposal/

12  Interview with Don Palmer (R), commissioner, U.S. Election Assistance Commission (July 23, 2020).

13  "Identity Theft and Your Social Security Number," Social Security Administration, https://www.ssa.gov/pubs/EN-05-10064.pdf.

14  John Gramlich, "Angering Their Own Party, Rhode Island Democrats Approve Voter ID," Stateline.org (July 20, 2011).

15  Christopher Hitchens, "Ohio's Odd Numbers," *Vanity Fair* (March 2005), https://www.vanityfair.com/news/2005/03/hitchens200503?utmsource=onsite-share&utmmedium=email&utmcampaign=onsite-share&utmbrand=vanity-fair.

16  Shayna Greene, "Fact Check: Did Democrats Object to More States For 2016 Than Republicans For 2020?" *Newsweek* (Jan. 13, 2021), https://www.newsweek.com/fact-check-did-democrats-object-more-states-2016-republicans-2020-1561407

17  Pat Beall, "Will your ballot be safe? Computer experts sound warnings on America's voting machines," *USA Today* (Nov. 2, 2020), https://thevotingnews.com/tag/voting-technologu/.

18  Melissa Quinn, "Sidney Powell tells court 'no reasonable person' would take her voter fraud claims as fact," CBS News (March 23, 2021).

19  Dan Firnbach, "Antrim County Election Results Corrected After Issue Skewed Initial Results," 9and10News.com (Nov. 6, 2020).

20  J. Alex Halderman, "Analysis of the Antrim County, Michigan November 2020 Election Incident" (March 26, 2021).

21  Scott Wolchok, Eric Wustrow, Dawn Isabel, and J. Alex Halderman, "Attacking the Washington, D.C. Internet Voting System," International Conference on Financial Cryptography and Data Security (Feb. 20212).

22  "Analysis of the Antrim County, Michigan, November 2020 Election Incident," p. 3.

23  Ibid. at p. 3.

24  Ibid.

25  Ibid. at p. 4.

26  Ibid.

27  Ibid. at p. 40.

28  Ibid. at 40–47.

29  Ibid. at 48.

30  Ray Duckler, "Audit of Windham, N.H., election continues with new vote totals," *Valley News* (May 18, 2021), https://www.vnews.com/Preliminary-numbers-from-audit-say-GOP-got-short-changed-40532482

**CHAPTER TWO**

1  Lila Hassan and Dan Glaun, "COVID-19 and the Most Litigated Presidential Election in Recent U.S. History: How the Lawsuits Break Down," PBS (Oct. 28, 2020).

2  See Hans von Spakovsky and J. Christian Adams, "COVID-19 and Ebola: What

We Can Learn from Prior Elections," Heritage Foundation Issue Brief No. 5066 (May 1, 2020).

3 Anthony Banbury, "Elections and COVID-19: What We Learned from Ebola," Devex (April 8, 2020).

4 The CDC reports that during the 2014–2016 Ebola epidemic in West Africa, there were 28,600 cases and over 11,000 fatalities. See Centers for Disease Control and Prevention, "Ebola (Ebola Virus Disease): 2014–2016 Ebola Virus Outbreak in West Africa," https://www.cdc.gov/vhf/ebola/history/2014-2016-outbreak/index.html.

5 News release, "Secretary-General's Remarks at Joint Press Conference with President Ellen Johnson Sirleaf of Liberia," Office of the Secretary-General of the United Nations, December 19, 2014, https://www.un.org/sg/en/content/sg/press-encounter/2014-12-19/secretary-generals-remarks-joint-press-conference-president.

6 United Nations, "U.N. Peacebuilding Commission Commends Liberia for Peaceful Elections," December 24, 2014, https://news.un.org/en/story/2014/12/487132-un-peacebuilding-commission-commends-liberia-peaceful-elections (accessed April 30, 2020).

7 "S. Korea Reported 4 Imported Virus Cases With Zero Local Infections," Yonhap News Agency (April 30, 2020).

8 "Election Day and COVID-19: Poll Worker Procedures for April 7, 2020" and "Election Day Checklist for COVID-19 Procedures," Wisconsin Elections Commission.

9 Kathy Leung, Joseph Wu, Kuang Xu, and Lawrence M. Wein, "No Detectable Surge in SARS-CoV-2 Transmissions due to the April 7, 2020, Wisconsin Election," (April 29, 2020).

10 Heather Paradis et al., "Notes from the Field: Public Health Efforts to Mitigate COVID-19 Transmissions During the April 7, 2020, Election—City of Milwaukee, Wisconsin, March 13–May 5, 2020," Morbidity and Mortality Weekly Report, Centers for Disease Control and Prevention (July 31, 2020).

11 "Considerations for Election Polling Locations and Voters," Interim Guidance, Centers for Disease Control and Prevention (June 22, 2020).

12 *Democratic National Committee v. Bostelmann*, 977 F.3d 639 (Seventh Cir. 2020).

13 *Democratic National Committee v. Wisconsin State Legislature*, 141 S.Ct 28 (2020).

14 *Common Cause Indiana v. Lawson*, 977 F.3d 663 (Seventh Cir. 2020).

15 *People First of Alabama v. Merrill*, 476 F.Supp.3d 1179 (S.D. AL 2020)

16 *Merrill v. People First of Alabama*, 141 S.Ct. 190 (2020).

17 *Andino v. Middleton*, 592 U.S. _____, 141 S.Ct. 9 (2020).

18 549 U.S. 1 (2006).

19 2020 WL 5739010 (Fourth Cir. 2020).

20 *Middleton v. Andino*, 990 F.3d 768 (Fourth Circ. 2020).

21 990 F.3d at 771.

22 990 F.3d at 771–772.

23  990 F.3d at 772.

24  990 F.3d at 773.

25  990 F.3d at 773.

26  990 F.3d at 773–774.

27  *Wise v. Circosta*, 978 F.3d 93 (Fourth Cir. 2020).

28  See North Carolina Alliance Leadership at http://nc.retiredamericansfund.org/north-carolina-alliance-leadership/.

29  *Moore v. Circosta*, 2020 WL 6063332 (M.D. N.C. 2020).

30  *Wise v. Circosta*, 978 F.3d at 104.

31  978 F.3d at 104–105.

32  978 F.3d at 117.

33  *Moore v. Circosta*, 141 S.Ct. 46 (2020).

34  *Carson v. Simon*, 2020 WL 6018957 (D. Minn. 2020).

35  *Carson v. Simon*, 978 F.3d 1051 (Eighth Cir. 2020).

36  *Michigan Alliance for Retired Americans v. Secretary of State*, 2020 WL 6122745 (Mich. Ct. App. 2020).

37  *Husted v. A. Philip Randolph Institute*, 584 U.S. _____, 138 S.Ct. 1833 (2018).

38  *Genetski v. Benson*, Case. No. 20-000216 (Mich. Ct. of Claims March 9, 2021); "Michigan Court Rules Secretary of State Violated Law," Keweenaw Report (March 17, 2021).

39  *Democratic Senatorial Campaign Committee v. Iowa Secretary of State*, 950 N.W.2d 1 (Iowa 2020)

40  950 N.W.2d at 5.

41  Peter Jackson, "Democrats gain control of Pennsylvania's Supreme Court," Associated Press (Nov. 4, 2015). Democrats control the court 5 to 2.

42  See 28 U.S.C. §1251(a) and Rule 17 of the U.S. Supreme Court.

43  *Texas v. Pennsylvania*, 141 S.Ct. 1230 (2020). Justices Alito and Thomas issued a short statement saying they believed the rule requiring states to first obtain the permission of the Supreme Court to file a lawsuit against another state is invalid because the court cannot "deny the filing of a bill of complaint in a case that falls within our original jurisdiction." They were referring to Article III, Section 2 of the Constitution that gives the Supreme Court sole jurisdiction over all "Controversies between two or more States."

44  In *Bush v. Gore*, the Supreme Court said the "state legislature's power to select the manner for appointing electors is plenary." 531 U.S. 98, 104 (2000).

45  *Penn. Democratic Party v. Boockvar*, 238 A.3d 345 (Pa. 2020).

46  *Texas v. Pennsylvania*, Bill of Complaint, p. 15.

47  *Republican Party of Pennsylvania v. Boockvar*, 141 S.Ct. 643 (2020).

48  *Republican Party of Pennsylvania v. Boockvar*, 141 S.Ct 1 (2020).

49  *Texas v. Pennsylvania*, Bill of Complaint, p. 21–22.

50  *Texas v. Pennsylvania*, Bill of Complaint, p. 26–29.

51  *Texas v. Pennsylvania*, Bill of Complaint, p. 29–35.

52  *Texas v. Pennsylvania*, Bill of Complaint, p. 2–3.

53  *Texas v. Pennsylvania*, Motion for Leave to File Bill of Complaint, p. 1–2.

54  *Republican Party of Pennsylvania v. Degraffenreid*, 141 S.Ct. 732.

55  141 S.Ct. at 732–733 (citations omitted and emphasis added).

56  141 S.Ct. at 734–735. The federal decision was *Ziccarelli v. Allegheny Cty. Bd. of Elections*, 2021 WL 101683 (W.D. Pa., Jan. 12, 2021).

57  141 S.Ct. at 735.

## CHAPTER THREE

1  "As America embraces early voting, GOP hurries to restrict it," Associated Press (April 16, 2021).

2  Ibid.

3  "The Court and Voter ID's," *New York Times* (Jan. 9, 2008).

4  Frank Lynn, "Boss Tweed Is Gone, But Not His Vote," *New York Times* (Sept. 9, 1984).

5  "G.O.P. and Allies Draft 'Best Practices' for Restricted Voting," *New York Times* (March 24, 2021).

6  Quin Hillyer, "Voter fraud has swung election outcomes, but narrative-obsessed media can't admit it," *Washington Examiner* (April 7, 2021).

7  See, e.g., Barack Obama, U.S. President, Remarks by the President at the National Action Network's 16th Annual Convention (Apr. 11, 2014), https://obamawhitehouse.archives.gov/the-press-office/2014/04/11/remarks-president-national-action-networks-16th-annual-convention; Jamelle Bouie, "Hillary Clinton Hits the GOP on Voter Suppression," *Slate*, (June 4, 2015); Attorney General Eric Holder Addresses the NAACP Annual Convention (July 16, 2013), https://www.justice.gov/opa/speech/attorney-general-eric-holder-addresses-naacp-annual-convention.

8  Ellen Kurz, "Registration is a voter-suppression too. Let's finally end it," *Washington Post*, (Oct. 11, 2018).

9  Hans A. von Spakovsky, "The Myth of Voter Suppression and the Enforcement Record of the Obama Administration," 49 *University of Memphis Law Review* 1147, 1158 (2018).

10  52 U.S.C. §§ 10301, 20501 (2012).

11  Valerie Richardson, "'Patronizingly racist': Jim Crow-election laws comparison blasted as 'insulting' to Blacks," *Washington Times* (April 5, 2021).

12  Ibid.

13  Jane C. Timm, "Georgia governor signs sweeping election regulations into law. There are even restrictions on snacks," NBC News (March 25, 2021).

14  2021 GA S.B. 202, 156th General Assembly (2021–2022), available at https://www.documentcloud.org/documents/20527915-sb-202-as-passed.

15  *Common Cause of Georgia v. Billups*, 504 F.Supp.2d 1333 (N.D. Georgia 2007),

order of dismissal vacated and reentered, 554 F.3d 1340 (Eleventh Cir. 2009); cert. denied, 556 U.S. 1282 (2009).

16 Hans A. von Spakovsky, "Lessons from the Voter ID Experience in Georgia," Heritage Foundation Issue Brief No. 3541 (March 19, 2012).

17 Ibid.

18 Enrico Cantoni and Vincent Pons, "Strict ID Laws Don't Stop Voters: Evidence From a U.S. Nationwide Panel, 2008–2018," National Bureau of Economic Research (2019).

18 O.C.G.A. § 21-2-417(c).

20 52 U.S.C. § 21083.

21 "Remarks by President Biden in Press Conference," whitehouse.gov (March 25, 2021).

22 "Remarks by President Biden Before Marine One Departure," whitehouse.gov (March 26, 2021).

23 O.C.G.A. § 21-2-414.

24 Sammie Purcell, "State Rep. Wilson accused of 2018 election violations for giving pizza to voters," Reporter Newspapers (March 3, 2021).

25 52 U.S.C. § 10307.

26 Richard C. Pilger et al. (editors), "Federal Prosecution of Election Offenses," U.S. Department of Justice (Eighth Ed. Dec. 2017), p. 44.

27 New York Elec. Law § 17-140.

28 Simon Lewis and Joseph Tanfani, "Special Report: How a small group of U.S. lawyers pushed voter fraud fears into the mainstream," Reuters (Sept. 9, 2020).

29 GianCarlo Canaparo and Hans von Spakovsky, "Lawyers Are Facing Reprisal for Representing Trump. This Is Un-American," *The Daily Signal* (Feb. 4, 2021).

30 Craig Mauger and Beth LeBlanc, "Whitmer, Nessel seek disbarment of lawyers in election challenge," *The Detroit News* (Feb. 1, 2021).

31 Hayden Ludwig, "Arabella Advisors' $600 Million Shadow Over the Election," Capital Research Center, Special Report (Sept. 10, 2020).

32 "Establishment of Presidential Advisory Commission on Election Integrity," Executive Order 13799, 82 FR 22389 (May 11, 2017). Hans von Spakovsky was appointed to serve as a member of the commission.

33 "New Presidential Advisory Commission on Election Administration Presents Recommendations to President Obama," U.S. Election Assistance Commission (Jan. 22, 2014).

34 "ACLU Response to Trump Election Commission Executive Order," ACLU (no date).

35 Roger Chesley, "Bipartisanship prevails in resistance to Trump's voter panel," *The Virginia Pilot* (July 10, 2017).

36 Client Services, Virginia Department of Elections, https://www.elections.virginia.gov/candidatepac-info/client-services/.

37 https://www.pfaw.org/blog-posts/pfaw-foundation-takes-out-full-page-nyt-advertisement-exposing-trumps-sham-election-integrity-commission/.

38 *"Dunlap v. PACEI*: Investigating the Voter Fraud Commission," *American Oversight* (June 29, 2020).

39 "Termination of Presidential Advisory Committee on Election Integrity," Executive Order 13820, 83 FR 969 (Jan. 3, 2018).

40 See Marina Vinneneuve, "Report: Trump commission did not find widespread voter fraud," Associated Press (August 3, 2018).

41 *U.S. v. Brown*, 494 F.Supp.2d 440 (S.D. Miss. 2007); *U.S. v. Brown*, 561 F.3d 420 (Fifth Cir. 2009).

## CHAPTER FOUR

1 "Voter Fraud Issues: A Florida Department of Law Enforcement Report And Observations," Florida Department of Law Enforcement (Jan. 5, 1998), p. 2, http://www.ejfi.org/Voting/Voting-9.htm.

2 For a complete listing of state statutes banning electioneering in or near polling places, see "State Laws Prohibiting Electioneering Activities Within a Certain Distance of the Polling Place," National Association of Secretaries of State (August 2016), https://www.nass.org/sites/default/files/surveys/2017-10/state-laws-polling-place-electioneering-2016.pdf.

3 The twelve states are Arkansas, Colorado, Georgia, Louisiana, Maine, Minnesota, Montana, Nebraska, New Jersey, North Dakota, South Dakota, and West Virginia.

4 Eric Eggers, "Ballot Fraud, American-Style...and Its Bitter Harvests," *RealClearInvestigations* (Dec. 13, 2018), https://www.realclearinvestigations.com/articles/2018/12/12/ballot_fraud_american-style_and_its_bitter_harvests.html.

5 Corey W. McDonald, "Developer's Conviction for Voter Fraud Reverberates Throughout Hoboken," *The Jersey Journal*, (June 26, 2019), https://www.nj.com/hudson/2019/06/developers-conviction-for-voter-fraud-raises-questions-of-vote-by-mail-ballots-in-hoboken.html (July 9, 2020).

6 For other Heritage case studies by this author on election fraud, including those that involve absentee ballots, see "Absentee Ballot Fraud: A Stolen Election in Greene Country, Alabama," Heritage Foundation Legal Memorandum, No. 31 (Sept. 5, 2008), https://www.heritage.org/election-integrity/report/absentee-ballot-fraud-stolen-election-greene-county-alabama; "Where There's Smoke, There's Fire: 100,000 Stolen Votes In Chicago," Heritage Foundation Legal Memorandum No. 23 (April 16, 2008), https://www.heritage.org/election-integrity/report/where-theres-smoke-theres-fire-100000-stolen-votes-chicago; "Stolen Identities, Stolen Votes: A Case Study in Voter Impersonation," Heritage Foundation Legal Memorandum No. 22 (March 10, 2008), https://www.heritage.org/report/stolen-identities-stolen-votes-case-study-voterimpersonation; and "Election Fraud in the 2008 Indiana Presidential Campaign: A Case Study in Corruption," Heritage Foundation Legal Memorandum No. 111 (Jan. 13, 2014), https://www.heritage.org/election-integrity/report/election-fraud-the-2008-indiana-presidential-campaign-case-study.

7 *Gooch v. Hendrix*, 5 Cal.4th 266 (1993).

8  Gooch, 5 Cal.4th at 285.

9  When third parties have access to completed absentee ballot request forms, it gives them a sample of a voter's signature, making forgery of the signature on an absentee ballot easy.

10  Ibid. at 272–273.

11  Ibid. at 281.

12  Gooch, 5 Cal.4th at 274.

13  Ibid. at 275–276.

14  Ibid. at 277. In discussing the applicable law, the court referenced another fraud case in which some votes were disqualified because the voters were nonresidents and others because voters had made illegal offers to city officials if they voted in favor of a city consolidation. *See Canales v. City of Alviso*, 3 Cal.3d 118 (1970).

15  Gooch, 5 Cal.4th at 285.

16  Joseph Tanfani and Karen Branch, "$10 Buys One Vote: Dozens Cast Votes in Miami Mayoral Race—for $10 Each," *Miami Herald*, (Jan. 11, 1998). One indicator of possible election fraud is when the ratio of absentee ballots cast for candidates is substantially different than the ratio of votes they received through in-person voting.

17  Will Lester, "Court: Carollo Is Mayor of Miami," Associated Press (March 11, 1998).

18  Final Report of the Miami-Dade County Grand Jury, State Attorney Katherine Fernandez Rundle, Circuit Court of the Eleventh Judicial Circuit of Florida in and for the County of Miami-Dade, Spring Term A.D. 2012 (Dec. 19, 2012), p. 1, https://www.miamisao.com/publications/grand_jury/2000s/gj2012s.pdf.

19  "In Re the Matter of the Protest of Election Returns and Absentee Ballots in the November 4, 1997, Election for the City of Miami, Florida," 707 So.2d 1170, 1171 (Third Dist. Ct. of Appeal of Fla. 1998).

20  Ibid. at 1172.

21  Ibid. at 1172.

22  Ibid. at 1172.

23  Will Lester, "Court: Carollo Is Mayor of Miami," Associated Press (March 11, 1998).

24  Donald P. Baker, "New Mayoral Election Is Ordered for Miami," *Washington Post*, (March 5, 1998).

25  707 So.2d at 1172.

26  1999 Pulitzer Prizes, https://www.pulitzer.org/prize-winners-by-year/1999.

27  This summary of the findings of the *Miami Herald*'s investigation are from the series of articles the newspaper published that were considered by the Pulitzer board, including Joseph Tanfani and Karen Branch, "$10 Buys One Vote: Dozens Cast Votes in Miami Mayoral Race—for $10 Each," (Jan. 11, 1998); Karen Branch et al., "The Outsiders: Voters Crossed the Line in Miami Non-residence No Bar at Polls," (Feb. 1, 1998); Karen Branch et al., "Dubious Tactics Snared Votes for Suarez, Hernandez," (Feb. 8, 1998); Karen Branch, Dan Keating, and

Elaine DeValle, "Some Miami Employees Crossed the Line to Vote," (Feb. 9, 1998); Herald Special Report, "Felons Vote, Too—But It's a Crime: Killers and Thieves Cast Miami Ballots," (Feb. 15, 1998); Joseph Tanfani, Karen Branch, and Manny Garcia, "Suarez Adviser Investigated in Vote Buying: He Supplied Cash, Ran Scheme, Witnesses Say," (Feb. 22, 1998); and Andres Viglucci, "Nonprofit Agency Collected Absentee Ballots," (April 5, 1998). All these articles are available at https://www.pulitzer.org/winners/staff-44. See also Manny Garcia and Tom Dubocq, "Unregistered Votes Cast Ballots in Dade; Dead Man's Vote, Scores of Others Were Allowed Illegally," *Miami Herald*, (Dec. 24, 2000).

28  Some states have what is termed in-person absentee balloting, where a person can vote using an absentee ballot at the county government's election department prior to Election Day.

29  In 1997, Miami was still using punch card voting machines. "Punching" the ballot means a hole is punched in the punch card with a stylus next to the candidate's name.

30  Karen Branch et al., "Dubious Tactics Snared Votes for Suarez, Hernandez," *Miami Herald*, (Feb. 8, 1998).

31  "In Re the Matter of the Protest of Election Returns and Absentee Ballots in the November 4, 1997, Election for the City of Miami, Florida," 707 So.2d, at 1174.

32  *Crawford v. Marion County Election Board*, 128 S.Ct. 1610, 1619 (2008).

33  *Pabey v. Patrick*, 816 N.E.2d 1138 (Ind. 2004).

34  Pabey, 816 N.E.2d at 1140.

35  Ibid.

36  Ibid. at 1144.

37  Ibid. at 1145–1146.

38  Ibid. at 1146.

39  Eric Shawn, "Voter Fraud 'a Normal Political Tactic' in Upstate NY City," Fox News (Jan. 17, 2012), https://www.foxnews.com/politics/voter-fraud-a-normal-political-tactic-in-upstate-ny-city.

40  Ibid.

41  Ibid. For another case in which minority voters were targeted with an absentee ballot fraud scheme, see Hans A. von Spakovsky, "Absentee Ballot Fraud: A Stolen Election in Greene Country, Alabama," Heritage Foundation Legal Memorandum No. 31 (Sept. 5, 2008), https://www.heritage.org/election-integrity/report/absentee-ballot-fraud-stolen-election-greene-county-alabama.

42  Pabey, 816 N.E.2d at 1146–1147.

43  Ibid. at 1147.

44  Ibid., footnote 3.

45  Pabey, 816 N.E.2d at 1150.

46  Ibid. at 1151.

47  In the Matter of Investigation of Election Irregularities Affecting Counties Within the 9th Congressional District, Before the State Board of Elections, State of North Carolina, Order (March 13, 2019) (hereafter "North Carolina Order"),

p. 3, https://www.democracydocket.com/wp-content/uploads/sites/41/2020/03/North-Carolina-Election-Contest-Order_03132019.pdf.

48  Ibid. at 10. The number of votes received by each candidate was as follows: Harris (139,246), McCready (138,341), and Jeff Scott (5,130).

49  Ibid. at 3.

50  Ibid. at 4.

51  N.C.G.S.A. §§ 163A-1298 and 1310.

52  In the Matter of Investigation of Election Irregularities Affecting Counties Within the 9th Congressional District, Before the State Board of Elections, State of North Carolina, Preview of Evidence, p. 2.

53  North Carolina Order at 2.

54  Ibid. at 9.

55  Ibid. at 10 and 12. See also Dan Kane and Ely Portillo, "'The Guru of Bladen County' Is at the Center of NC's Election Troubles," *The News & Observer*, (April 23, 2019), https://www.newsobserver.com/news/politics-government/article222806255.html.

56  This summary of the evidence is all from the North Carolina Order unless otherwise indicated.

57  Some may claim that the fraud did not work since his criminal conduct in this election was discovered, but there is evidence that he engaged in this same type of absentee ballot fraud in prior elections that were not overturned. In fact, North Carolina election officials "sought criminal charges after the 2016 election" against Dowless, "but prosecutors didn't indict him." If they had, he would not have been in a position to corrupt the 2018 election, an object lesson in what happens when prosecutors fail to prosecute election fraud. Michael Biesecker, Jonathan Drew, and Gary D. Robertson, "North Carolina Officials Sought to Charge Political Operator," Associated Press (Dec. 19, 2018), https://apnews.com/58695ada638841e58b8392e3c1d68528 .

58  North Carolina Order at 20–21.

59  Ibid. at 24–25, 37.

60  Ibid. at 41.

61  Ibid. at 42–44. In addition to the absentee ballot fraud, the board also found two other "irregularities" in the election: (1) disclosure of early voting results in Bladen and Robeson Counties, and (2) a lack of office security in the board of elections office in Bladen County. Ibid. at 10.

62  Alex Seitz-Wald and Leigh Ann Caldwell, "Republican Dan Bishop wins narrow victory in North Carolina special election," NBC News (Sept. 10, 2019), https://www.nbcnews.com/politics/2020-election/north-carolina-special-election-mccready-bishop-n1052021.

63  Carli Brosseau, Josh Shaffer, Dan Kane, and Will Doran, "Bladen County Political Operative Faces New Perjury, Obstruction of Justice Charges," *The News & Observer*, (July 30, 2019), www.newsobserver.com/article233308957.html.

64  Jonathan Dienst, "Paterson City Council Vice President Among 4 Charged

With Voting Fraud in May Special Election: NJAG," NBC4-New York (June 29, 2020); *McKoy v. Passaic County Board of Elections*, Docket No. PAS-L-1751-20 (Sup. Court of New Jersey, County of Passaic, August 19, 2020).

65  Jonathan Dienst, "Paterson City Council Vice President Among 4 Charged With Voting Fraud in May Special Election: NJAG," NBC4-New York (June 29, 2020).

66  "Alabama mayor convicted of voter fraud, removed from office," Associated Press (Jan. 17, 2019).

67  DeFiglio pleaded guilty to falsifying business records in an absentee ballot fraud scheme that involved fraudulent absentee ballot request forms and the submission of fake ballots with forged voter signatures; voters did not even know that ballots had been submitted in their names. Eric Shawn, "Voter Fraud 'a Normal Tactic' in Upstate NY City," Fox News (Dec. 17, 2012), https://www.foxnews.com/politics/voter-fraud-a-normal-political-tactic-in-upstate-ny-city; and Eric Shawn, "They Tried to Steal an Election, N.Y. Voter Fraud Scheme Case Heats Up," Fox News ( Dec. 20, 2009), https://www.foxnews.com/politics/they-tried-to-steal-an-election-n-y-voter-fraud-case-heats-up.

68  Eric Shawn, "Officials Plead Guilty in New York Voter Fraud Case," Fox News (Dec. 21, 2011), https://www.foxnews.com/politics/officials-plead-guilty-in-new-york-voter-fraud-case.

69  "Limestone County Social Worker Charged With 134 Felony Counts Involving Election Fraud," News Release, Office of Ken Paxton, Attorney General of Texas (Nov. 6, 2020).

70  Interim Report of the Miami-Dade County Grand Jury, Inquiry Into Absentee Ballot Voting, State Attorney Katherine Fernandez Rundle, Circuit Court of the Eleventh Judicial Circuit of Florida in and for the County of Miami-Dade, Fall Term A.D. 1997 (Feb. 2, 1998), p. 1, http://www.miamisao.com/publications/grand_jury/1990s/gj1997f-interim.pdf.

## CHAPTER FIVE

1  Encounter Books.

2  553 U.S. 181, 128 S.Ct. 1610, 1619 (2008).

3  Available at heritage.org/voterfraud.

4  Jeff Zeleny and Patrick Healy, "Obama Is Expected to Hit a Milestone in Today's Votes," *New York Times* (May 20, 2008).

5  Ibid.

6  Ibid.

7  2008 Democratic Popular Vote, *RealClearPolitics*, http://www.realclearpolitics.com/epolls/2008/president/democratic_vote_count.html.

8  "Obama Has Taken the Superdelegate Lead," Democratic Convention Watch (May 10, 2008), http://demconwatch.blogspot.com/2008/05/obama-takes-lead-in-dcw-sd-for-first.html.

9  Farhana Hossain and Archie Tse, "On Day of Last Primary, Obama's Superdelegate Surge," *New York Times* (June 3, 2008).

10   Erin Blasko, "Fake Signatures May Mean Obama Didn't Actually Qualify," *South Bend Tribune* (Oct. 13, 2011).

11   Eric Shawn, "Indian Dem Official Sentenced to Prison for '08 Ballot Fraud in Obama-Clinton Primary," Fox News (June 17, 2013).

12   Ibid.

13   Ibid.

14   David Sherfinski, "Virginia Man Pleads Guilty to Voter Fraud in Gingrich Case," *Washington Times* (June 19, 2013). Gingrich was unaware of what the signature gatherer had done.

15   Andy Giegerich, "Clackamas election worker gets jail time for election fraud," *Portland Business Journal* (April 25, 2013).

16   David Kennedy, "Woman found guilty in Canton polling place disturbance," WLBT-3 (Nov. 25, 2013).

17   "Former Philadelphia Judge of Elections Convicted of Conspiring to Violate Civil Rights and Bribery," Press Release, U.S. Department of Justice (May 21, 2020).

18   "Former Congressman Charged with Ballot Stuffing, Bribery, and Obstruction," Press Release, U.S. Department of Justice (July 23, 2020).

19   Hans A. von Spakovsky, "Holder Winks at Voter Intimidation," *Wall Street Journal* (June 9, 2009). Liberal activists were outraged that a voting rights lawsuit had been filed against black members of the Panthers for intimidating and threatening white poll watchers and other voters.

20   Jamie Satterfield, "Ex-deputy blames 'infamous dirty politics' for vote-buying scheme in Monroe sheriff's race," Knoxnews.com (April 16, 2019).

21   Ibid.

22   "3 sentenced to prison for 2014 Magoffin vote-buying scheme," Associated Press (Dec. 2, 2016)

23   "Leger Pleads Guilty to Vote Tampering," EvangelineToday.com (March 11, 2015); *Cloud v. Schedler*, 161 So.3d 831 (La. App. 3 Cir. 2014).

24   John Fritze, "Wendy Rosen reaches plea agreement on voting charges," *Baltimore Sun* (March 8, 2013).

25   Ibid.

26   Jennifer Vaughn, "21-year-old pleads guilty to voting in Mass. and NH in 2016 election," WMUR-9 (March 1, 2019).

27   Sophia Tareen, "Voter advocates push Illinois to exit multistate database," Associated Press (Oct. 21, 2007); Pema Levy, "Indiana Sued Over Its Aggressive New Voter Purge Program," *Mother Jones* (Oct. 31, 2017).

28   "Consultant to Real Estate Developers Pleads Guilty in White Plains Federal Court to Conspiracy to Corrupt the Electoral Process in Bloomingburg," Press Release, U.S. Department of Justice (June 19, 2018).

29   "Voter fraud found in Vernon election, new winner named," *Los Angeles Times* (Oct. 15, 2012).

30   52 U.S.C. § 10508.

31  "Crowley woman convicted on election fraud charge," KLFY-10 (Sept. 2, 2020).

32  "Identities released of six accused in voter fraud case," ValleyCentral.com (July 17, 2014); "Office of the Attorney General of Texas, Election Fraud Violations, Prosecutions Resolved, https://www.courthousenews.com/wp-content/uploads/2019/05/Election-Fraud-Prosecutions-14May18.pdf.

33  *U.S. v. City of Boston et al.*, Case No. 05-11598 (D. Mass. July 2005).

34  Ibid. Order of Oct. 18, 2005.

35  *Crawford v. Marion County Election Board*, 472 F.3d 949, 953 (Seventh Cir. 2007), affirmed 553 U.S. 181 (2008).

36  Mihir Zaveri, "Two poll workers plead guilty to illegal voting," *Houston Chronicle* (May 23, 2017).

37  Sam Newhouse, "Philly election officials plead guilty," Philly.metro.us (Jan. 14, 2016).

38  "D.A. Holtzman Announces Grand Jury Report Disclosing Systematic Voting Fraud in Brooklyn," Press Release, New York District Attorney's Office (Sept. 5, 1984); In the Matter of Confidential Investigation, No. R84011 (N.Y. Supreme Court, 1984).

39  "Report on the New York City Board of Elections' Employment Practices, Operations, and Election Administration," New York City Department of Investigations (Dec. 2013).

40  "Root out politics at the city Board of Elections," Staten Island Advance Editorial (Jan. 7, 2014).

41  Cindy Carcamo, "San Francisco will allow noncitizens to vote in a local election, creating a new immigration flashpoint," *Los Angeles Times* (Oct. 26, 2018).

42  Clint Berge, "Eau Claire man going to jail for voting illegally," WQOW-18 (Oct. 9, 2020).

43  "Felon Voter Fraud Convictions Stemming from Minnesota's 2008 General Election," Minnesota Majority (Oct. 13, 2011).

44  Sam Stanton, "Mexican citizen who voted for Trump found guilty of voter fraud in 5 U.S. elections," *Sacramento Bee* (August 23, 2019).

45  Lee Filas, "Third person accuse of voter fraud in Lake County pleads guilty," *Daily Herald* (July 11, 2018

46  "Physician Sentenced to 15 Months in Federal Prison for Passport Fraud— Ghanaian National Admitted Fraudulently Obtaining a U.S. Passport, Falsely Claiming American Citizenship, and Illegally Voting in Ten Federal Elections as an Alien," Press Release, District of Maryland, U.S. Department of Justice (Sept. 27, 2019).

47  "Nineteen Foreign Nationals Charged for Voting in 2016 Election," Press Release, Eastern District of North Carolina, U.S. Department of Justice (August 24, 2018); Gary D. Robertson, "NC federal attorneys: 24 more charged in voter-fraud probe," Associated Press (March 19, 2021).

48  Travis Fain, "Foreign nationals charged with illegal voting mostly got small fines," WRAL (Dec. 16, 2019).

49 "Dismissing the Election Contest Against Loretta Sanchez," Report of the Committee on House Oversight on H.R. 355, Report 105-416, 105th Cong., 2nd Session (Feb. 12, 1998).

50 See Publicinterestlegal.org. Hans von Spakovsky is a member of the board of the Public Interest Legal Foundation.

51 USCIS Form N-400.

52 See the following reports of the Public Interest Legal Foundation: "Motor Voter Mayhem—Michigan's Voter Rolls in Disrepair," (Oct. 2018); "Alien Invasion II—The Sequel to the Discovery and Cover-up of Non-citizen Registration and Voting in Virginia," (May 2017); "Garden State Gotcha—How Opponents of Citizenship Verification for Voting Are Putting New Jersey's Noncitizens at Risk of Deportation," (Sept. 2017); "Safe Spaces—How Sanctuary Cities Are Giving Cover to Noncitizens on the Voter Rolls," (August 2018).

53 "Motor Voter Mayhem," p. 1.

54 Available at https://www.eac.gov/sites/default/files/eac_assets/1/6/Federal_ Voter_Registration_ENG.pdf.

55 Julian Routh, "State review of voter registrations narrows list of potentially ineligible voters to 8, 598," *Pittsburgh Post-Gazette* (July 27, 2018).

56 They were subjected to relentless personal and public attacks by liberal academics and media elites for daring to publish a study on this issue.

57 Jesse T. Richman, Guishan A. Chattha, and David C. Ernest, "Do Non-Citizens Vote in U.S. Elections?" Political Science & Geography Faculty Publications, No. 11, ODU Digital Commons, Old Dominion University (2014).

58 Ibid. at 4.

59 Ibid. at 13.

60 Ibid. at 14.

61 See 18 U.S.C. §§ 611, 911, and 1015(f).

62 "Elections: Additional Data Could Help State and Local Elections Officials Maintain Accurate Voter Registration Lists," U.S. Government Accountability Office, GAO-05-478 (June 2005), p. 42–43.

63 Hans von Spakovsky's experience as a career lawyer at the Justice Department demonstrated to him that the DEOs view their designation mostly as a ceremonial post and that they take almost no steps to actually investigate and prosecute election fraud or take advantage of sources of information about fraud such as the jury lists and citizen applications.

64 Jason Snead and Kaitlynn Samalis-Aldrich, "Good News: Mississippi Woman Convicted After Trying to Win Votes Via Bribes," *Daily Signal* (Oct. 10, 2019); John North, "Ex-deputy in vote-buying scheme gets 5 years of probation," WBIR-10 (April 10, 2019).

65 "America The Vulnerable: The Problem of Duplicate Voting," Government Accountability Institute (2017).

66 "Critical Condition—American Voter Rolls Filled With Errors, Dead Voters, and Duplicate Registrations," Public Interest Legal Foundation (September 2020).

67  Andrew Bahl, "Former Congressman Steve Watkins agrees to diversion deal, could avoid prosecution," *Topeka Capital-Journal* (March 3, 2021).

68  Hans von Spakovsky, "4 Votes Claiming NPR Residence Turn Up in Search of California Voting Records," *Daily Signal* (Sept. 17, 2020).

69  Video available at https://publicinterestlegal.org/blog/video-visiting-nevada-voters-registered-at-commercial-addresses/.

70  Interview with J. Christian Adams (April 13, 2021).

### CHAPTER SIX

1  "For the People Activist Training," Public Citizen and Declaration for American Democracy, March 23, 2021, https://www.facebook.com/DFADCoalition/videos/887493735126323.

2  Hans von Spakovsky served as a commissioner on the Federal Election Commission from 2006 to 2007.

3  Hans A. von Spakovsky, "H.R.1, the 'For the People Act of 2019,'" Testimony before Committee on the Judiciary, U.S. House of Representatives (Jan. 29, 2019), https://www.heritage.org/sites/default/files/testimony/2019-01/HR1%20Testimony%201-29-19.pdf.

4  Ella Nilsen, "House Democrats just passed a slate of significant reforms to get money out of politics," Vox.com (March 8, 2019).

5  Ibid.

6  Marisa Shultz, "Mississippi Rep. Bennie Thompson explains why he was only Dem to vote against massive HR 1 election bill," Fox News (March 4, 2021).

7  Section 1031.

8  Section 1004.

9  Section 1903.

10  Section 1601.

11  Sections 1011-1021. Individuals can opt out but only after they have become registered. Section 1012.

12  Section 1013.

13  52 U.S.C. § 20506(a)(5)(C).

14  Section 1015.

15  Sections 1001–1008.

16  "Beware: E-signatures can be easily forged," Cnet.com (Jan. 12, 2002); "Digital Signatures Can Be Forged in PDF Docs," Darkrading.com (March 1, 2019).

17  Section 1041.

18  Section 1041.

19  138 S.Ct. 1833 (2018).

20  Section 1201.

21  Section 2502.

22  Section 1071.

23  Section 1071.

24 Section 1201.

25 Section 1094.

26 See, for example, "Critical Condition—American Voter Rolls Filled With Errors, Dead Voters, and Duplicate Registrations," Public Interest Legal Foundation (September 2020).

27 Sections 1621–1624.

28 Section 1621.

29 See Hans A. von Spakovsky and Roger Clegg, "Felon Voting and Unconstitutional Congressional Overreach," The Heritage Foundation, Legal Memorandum No. 145 (Feb. 11, 2015).

30 Sections 2401–2455.

31 *NAACP v. Alabama*, 357 U.S. 449 (1958).

32 *Torcaso v. Watkins*, 367 U.S. 488 (1961).

33 Section 2412.

34 Section 2403. The Supreme Court ruled in *Evenwel v. Abbott* that including aliens does not violate the Equal Protection Clause but left open the question of whether states could use only citizen population in redistricting if they wanted to do so. 136 S.Ct. 1120 (2016).

35 Sean Trende, "The Most Important Redistricting Case in 50 Years," *RealClear-Politics* (June 3, 2015).

36 "Senate Testimony: S. 1 Would Suppress Speech, Violate the First Amendment," Institute for Free Speech, Press Release (March 24, 2021).

37 Sections 6001–6011.

38 Letter on Feb. 9, 2021, to Rep. Nancy Pelosi, Rep. Keven McCarthy, Sen. Chuck Schumer, and Sen. Mitch McConnell from Thomas J. Josefiak, Bradley A. Smith, Matthew S. Petersen, Darryl R. Wold, Michael E. Toner, Caroline C. Hunter, David M. Mason, Lee F. Goodman, and Hans A. von Spakovsky, https://www.ifs.org/wp-content/uploads/2021/02/2021-02-09_Former-FEC-Commissioners-Letter_Concerns-With-HR-1-And-S-1.pdf.

## CHAPTER SEVEN

1 Kenneth P. Vogel and Patricia Mazzei, "In Florida Recount Fight, Democratic Lawyer Draws Plaudits and Fire," *New York Times* (Nov. 14, 2018).

2 Kirk A. Bado, "New congressional maps reapportion Marc Elias's responsibilities," *National Journal* (April 29, 2021).

3 Adam Entous, Devlin Barrett, and Rosalind S. Helderman, "Clinton campaign, DNC paid for research that led to Russia dossier," *Washington Post* (Oct. 24, 2017).

4 Chuck Ross, "Carter Page Sues DNC and Its Law Firm Over The Steele Dossier," *Daily Caller* (Oct. 15, 2018).

5 Hans A. von Spakovsky, "Dissent is Criminal," *National Review Online* (Nov. 18, 2009); available at https://www.nationalreview.com/corner/dissent-criminal-hans-von-spakovsky/.

6   Vogel and Mazzei, *New York Times.*

7   https://www.perkinscoie.com/en/professionals/marc-e-elias.html.

8   Vogel and Mazzei, *New York Times.*

9   Vogel and Mazzei, *New York Times.*

10  Cleta Mitchel and Hans von Spakovsky, "Hillary Clinton, the DNC and the Law," *Wall Street Journal* (Nov. 12, 2017).

11  Mark Tapscott, "Looking to 2020, Kamala Harris Hires Heavy Hitter Lawyer Involved With Russian Dossier," *The Epoch Times* (Jan. 22, 2019).

12  For a more extensive explanation of what happened, see John Fund and Hans von Spakovsky, *Who's Counting? How Fraudsters and Bureaucrats Put Your Vote at Risk*, Encounter Books (2012), pages 20–24.

13  Jacob Ogles, "Norm Coleman advises Rick Scott not to get 'out-lawyered' in recount," FloridaPolitics.com (Nov. 10, 2018).

14  Editorial, "The 'Absentee' Senator," *Wall Street Journal* (July 2, 2009).

15  Fred Lucas, "6 Big Election Hits by Marc Elias, Democrats' Recount King," *Daily Signal* (Nov. 14, 2018).

16  Colton Lochhead, "Lawsuit aims to stop recall attempts targeting 3 Nevada state senators," *Law Vega Review-Journal* (Oct. 16, 2017).

17  *Luna v. Cegavske*, Case No. 2:17-02666 (D. Nevada Oct. 16, 2017), Complaint; available at https://publicinterestlegal.org/files/Nevada-Complaint.pdf. The case was mooted when the organizers of the petition drive failed to get enough signatures to qualify for the ballot.

18  *Luna v. Cegavske*, Case No. 2:17-02666, (D. Nevada Oct. 16, 2017), Complaint at paragraph 42; available at https://publicinterestlegal.org/files/Nevada-Complaint.pdf.

19  Interview with J. Christian Adams, President and General Counsel, Public Interest Legal Foundation (May 1, 2021).

20  "Lt. Gov. Mark Robinson Explains Why It's Not Racist to Require ID for Voting," *Daily Signal* (April 23, 2021).

21  Christine Ravold, "Political Law Personified: Marc Elias & Perkins Coie," Capital Research Center (Dec. 13, 2018).

22  Ibid.

23  Maggie Haberman, "George Soros Bankrolls Democrats' Fight in Voting Rights Cases," *New York Times* (June 5, 2015).

24  Hans von Spakovsky, "Shades of Jim Crow at the Justice Department," *National Review Online* (Oct. 22, 2014).

25  831 F.3d 204 (Fourth Cir. 2016).

26  *See N.C. State Conf. of the NAACP v. McCrory*, 182 F. Supp.3d 320 (M.D.N.C. 2016).

27  *North Carolina v. N.C. State Conf. of the NAACP*, 137 S. Ct. 1399 (2017) (Roberts, C. J., concurring).

28  Robert Barnes, "The crusade of a Democratic superlawyer with multimillion-dollar backing," *Washington Post* (August 7, 2016).

29  *Shelby County v. Holder*, 570 U.S 529, 552-553 (2013).

30  "A Review of the Operations of the Voting Section of the Civil Rights Division," Office of the Inspector General, U.S. Dept. of Justice (March 2013).

31  *Johnson v. Miller*, 864 F. Supp. 1354 (S.D. Ga. 1994), affirmed, *Miller v. Johnson*, 515 U.S. 900 (1995).

32  *Texas Alliance for Retired Americans v. Hughs*, Case No. 20-40643 (Fifth Cir. March 11, 2021).

33  Marc Elias, "Four Pillars to Safeguard Vote by Mail," DemocracyDocket.org (March 18, 2020).

34  Robert Barnes, "The crusade of a Democratic superlawyer with multimillion-dollar backing," *Washington Post* (August 7, 2016).

## CHAPTER EIGHT

1  Hayden Ludwig, "Mark Zuckerberg Meddled in Battleground State Elections: Here's How," Capital Research Center (March 3, 2021); https://capitalresearch. org/article/mark-zuckerberg-meddled-in-battleground-state-elections-heres-how/

2  Jesse McKinley and Luis Ferré-Sadurni, "N.Y. Officials Need Money. They Were Told To Go To Zuckerberg," *New York Times* (Oct. 2, 2020); https://www. nytimes.com/2020/10/02/nyregion/voting-absentee-ballots-ny.html.

3  "Building Confidence in U.S. Elections—Report of the Commission on Federal Election Reform (Sept. 2005); https://www.legislationline.org/download/id/1472/ file/3b50795b2d0374cbef5c29766256.pdf.

4  Steve Coll, "Battling Anxiety Over Making Sure Your Vote Gets Counted," *The New Yorker* (Sept 4, 2020); https://www.newyorker.com/news/daily-comment/ battling-anxiety-over-making-sure-your-vote-gets-counted.

5  Scott Walter, "Zuckerberg's Return on Investment in Pennsylvania," Capital Research Center (Jan. 5, 2021); https://capitalresearch.org/article/zuckerbergs-return-on-investment-in-pennsylvania/

6  twitter.com/AOC/status/1230333195060859286.

7  Interview with Scott Walter, President, Capital Research Center (April 8, 2021).

8  See Schedule I of IRS Form 990.

9  J. Christian Adams, "The Real Kraken: What Really Happened to Donald Trump in the 2020 Election," *PJ Media* (Dec. 2, 2020); https://pjmedia.com/ jchristianadams/2020/12/02/the-real-kraken-what-really-happened-to-donald-trump-in-the-2020-election-n1185494.

10  Brian Fung, "Inside the Democratic party's Hogwarts for digital wizardry," *Washington Post* (July 8, 2014); https://www.washingtonpost.com/news/the-switch/ wp/2014/07/08/inside-the-democratic-partys-hogwarts-for-digital-wizardry/.

11  Hayden Ludwig, "The *New* New Organizing Institute," Capital Research Center (Jan. 14, 2021); https://capitalresearch.org/article/the-new-new-organizing-institute/.

12  Hayden Ludwig, "How CTCL Helped Biden in Arizona and Nevada," Capital

Research Center (Jan. 22, 2021); https://capitalresearch.org/article/how-ctcl-helped-biden-in-arizona-and-nevada/.

13 Interview with state Rep. Shawnna Bolick (R), April 8, 2020.

14 "The Restriction of Political Campaign Intervention by Section 501(c)(3) Tax-Exempt Organizations," Internal Revenue Service; https://www.irs.gov/charities-non-profits/charitable-organizations/the-restriction-of-political-campaign-intervention-by-section-501c3-tax-exempt-organizations.

15 Sasha Issenberg, *The Victory Lab: The Secret Science of Winning Campaigns* (New York: Crown, 2012), p. 305.

16 Molly Ball, "The Secret History of the Shadow Campaign That Saved the 2020 Election," *Time* (Feb. 4, 2021); https://time.com/5936036/secret-2020-election-campaign/.

17 John Fund, *Stealing Elections*, New York, Encounter Books, 2008), p. 120.

18 See M. D. Kittle, "Special Investigation: Infiltrating the Election," *Wisconsin Spotlight* (March 9, 2021); https://wisconsinspotlight.com/special-investigation-infiltrating-the-election/.

19 Dan O'Donnell, "Green Bay's City Attorney Accidently Incriminates the City of Green Bay," MacIver Institute (April 23, 2021); https://www.maciverinstitute.com/2021/04/green-bays-city-attorney-accidentally-incriminates-the-city-of-green-bay/.

20 See Joshua Peguero, "Former Brown County Clerk testifies at hearing over Green Bay elections report," 2 First Alert WBAY (March 10, 2021); https://www.wbay.com/2021/03/10/former-brown-county-clerk-testifies-at-hearing-over-green-bay-elections-report/

21 See National Vote at Home Institute, https://voteathome.org/.

22 https://www.maciverinstitute.com/2021/04/green-bays-city-attorney-accidentally-incriminates-the-city-of-green-bay/.

23 Ben Christopher, "'We'll get that paid'; Newsom and Padilla vow to fix controversial election contract," CalMatters (Dec. 23, 2020); https://calmatters.org/politics/2020/12/newsom-padilla-skdknickerbocker-contract-gotv/.

24 "Top Republicans Raise Alarm Over Election Assistance Commission's Ability to Protect Taxpayers," Press Release, Committee on Oversight and Reform, U.S. House of Representatives (March 18, 2021).

25 Fred Lucas, "Zuckerberg money could affect DeSantis relection campaign," Fox News (April 29, 2021); https://www.foxnews.com/politics/zuckerberg-money-florida-desantis-reelection.

26 Interview with J. Christian Adams, February 5, 2021.

27 Interview with Phillip D. Kline, Associate Prof. of Law, Liberty University School of Law, March 26, 2021.

## CHAPTER NINE

1 "State Board Unanimously Orders New Election in 9th Congressional District," North Carolina State Board of Elections, Press Release (Feb. 25, 2019); https://

www.ncsbe.gov/Press-Releases?udt_2226_param_detail=229 (accessed Sept. 19, 2019).

2  John Wildermuth and Tal Kopan, "California's Late Votes Broke Big for Democrats. Here's Why GOP Was Surprised," *San Francisco Chronicle* (Nov. 30, 2018), https://www.sfchronicle.com/politics/article/California-s-late-votes-broke-big-for-13432727.php (accessed Sept. 19, 2019).

3  "Report: Political Weaponization of Ballot Harvesting in California," Ranking Member Rodney Davis, Comm. on House Admin., U.S. House of Representatives (May 14, 2020).

4  Ibid.

5  See Hans A. von Spakovsky, *Elections Exclusively by Mail: A Terrible Idea Whose Time Should Never Come*, Heritage Foundation Legal Memorandum No. 51 (April 21, 2010); https://www.heritage.org/election-integrity/report/elections-exclusively-mail-terrible-idea-whose-time-should-never-come.

6  Arizona, Massachusetts, Michigan, Missouri, Nevada, New Hampshire, New Mexico, North Carolina, and Ohio allow a family member to return the ballot, with some other exceptions. The states that do not address this issue are Delaware, Hawaii, Idaho, Mississippi, New York, Oklahoma, Rhode Island, Tennessee, Utah, Vermont, Washington, Wisconsin, and Wyoming.

7  "Returning Absentee Ballots," National Conference of State Legislatures; http://www.ncsl.org/research/elections-and-campaigns/returning-absentee-ballots.aspx.

8  Dustin Waters, "Mail-in ballots were part of a plot to deny Lincoln reelection in 1864," *Washington Post* (August 22, 2020).

9  "True Confessions of Texas Vote Harvesters," *RealClearInvestigations* (Feb. 19, 2019); https://www.realclearinvestigations.com/articles/2019/02/19/true_confessions_of_texas_vote_harvesters.html.

10  Ryan Gillespie, "Former Eatonville Mayor Found Guilty of Voting Fraud, Election Violations," *Orlando Sentinel* (May 19, 2017); http://www.orlandosentinel.com/news/breaking-news/os-anthony-grant-trial-verdict-20170519-story.html.

11  "Former Mayor of Martin Sentenced to 90 Months for Civil Rights Offenses, Fraud, Vote Buying, and Identity Theft," Press Release, Office of the U.S. Attorney for the Eastern District of Kentucky (Dec. 16, 2014); https://www.fbi.gov/contact-us/field-offices/louisville/news/press-releases/former-mayor-of-martin-sentenced-to-90-months-for-civil-rights-offenses-fraud-vote-buying-and-identity-theft.

12  In the 2018 California election, a family's doorbell camera caught a vote harvester saying that she was there to collect absentee ballots as part of a "new service, but only to, like, people who are supporting the Democratic Party." Miranda Morales, "CA Dem Party Sinking to New Lows to 'Harvest' Absentee Ballots," RedState (Oct. 16, 2018); https://www.redstate.com/mirandamorales/2018/10/16/ca-dem-party-sinking-new-lows-harvest-absentee-ballots/.

13  Steve Miller, "Why Ballot Fraud Is as Big as Texas, Despite Local Enforcers," *RealClearInvestigations* (March 18, 2019); https://www.realclearinvestigations.com/

articles/2019/03/18/why_ballot_fraud_is_as_big_texas_despite_local_enforcers.html.

14  Jon Levine, "Confessions of a voter fraud: I was a master at fixing mail-in ballots," *New York Post* (August 29, 2020). Although the political operative was not named, the newspaper confirmed his "long work as a consultant" for numerous candidates in campaign records.

15  Ibid.

16  Ibid.

17  "Voter Fraud Issues: A Florida Department of Law Enforcement Report and Observations," Florida Department of Law Enforcement (Jan. 5, 1998), p. 2; www.ejfi.org/Voting/Voting-9.htm.

18  "Final Report of the Miami-Dade County Grand Jury," Circuit Court of the Eleventh Judicial Circuit of Florida, County of Miami-Dade (Dec. 19, 2012), p. ii–iii; https://miami.cbslocal.com/wp-content/uploads/sites/15909786/2012/12/grandjuryreport.pdf.

19  Ibid. at 16 (emphasis in original).

20  State Board Unanimously Orders New Election in 9th Congressional District, supra note 2.

21  Morgan Krakow, "New Indictments Handed Down for N.C. Political Operative at Center of Election Fraud Scheme," *Washington Post* (July 30, 2019); https://www.washingtonpost.com/politics/2019/07/30/new-indictments-handed-down-nc-political-operative-center-an-election-fraud-scheme/?noredirect=on; "Dowless, 7 Others Indicted in NC 9th District Absentee Ballot Investigation," WCNC (July 30, 2019); https://www.wcnc.com/article/news/crime/dowless-7-others-indicted-in-nc-9th-district-absentee-ballot-investigation/275-7bedeae8-e46c-4e41-98d0-bc29ed7b6869.

22  Leigh Ann Caldwell, "Republican Candidate's Son Shakes Up North Carolina Hearing with Surprise Testimony," NBC News (Feb. 20, 2019); https://www.nbcnews.com/politics/elections/republican-candidate-s-son-shakes-north-carolina-hearing-surprise-testimony-n973836.

23  "In re. Investigation of Election Irregularities Affecting Counties Within the 9th Congressional District," North Carolina State Board of Elections, p. 11; https://www.documentcloud.org/documents/5743744-NC-BOE.html.

24  Ibid. at 10.

25  Jason Snead and Hans von Spakovsky, "North Carolina Election Fraud Should Be a Wake-Up Call for the Left," *Daily Signal* (March 5, 2019); https://www.dailysignal.com/2019/03/05/north-carolina-election-fraud-should-be-a-wake-up-call-for-the-left/.

26  Texas Election Code § 86.006. Texas Government Code § 573 defines relationships based on affinity and consanguinity.

27  See Election Fraud Cases, Heritage Foundation; https://www.heritage.org/voterfraud/search?state=TX.

28  "True Confessions of Texas Vote Harvesters."

29 Peter Tapsak and Jason Snead, "Voter Fraud Is Real. Here Are 4 More Cases," Daily Signal (August 18, 2016); https://www.dailysignal.com/2016/08/18/voter-fraud-is-real-here-are-4-more-cases/.

30 Deanna Boyd and Anna M. Tinsley, "Former Democratic Party Leader Paid Women in Alleged Tarrant Voter Fraud Ring, AG Says," Fort Worth Star-Telegram (Oct. 24, 2018); https://www.star-telegram.com/news/politics-government/election/article220540115.html.

31 Steve Miller, "Why Ballot Fraud Is as Big as Texas, Despite Local Enforcers," *RealClearInvestigations* (March 18, 2019); https://www.realclearinvestigations.com/articles/2019/03/18/why_ballot_fraud_is_as_big_texas_despite_local_enforcers.html

32 Ibid.

33 "Former Postal Employee Convicted of Soliciting Bribes During Election," Press Release, U.S. Attorney's Office, Southern District of Texas, U.S. Department of Justice (March 7, 2017); https://www.justice.gov/usao-sdtx/pr/former-postal-employee-convicted-soliciting-bribes-during-election.

34 "True Confessions of Texas Vote Harvesters."

35 Ibid.

36 Those states are Arizona, California, Hawaii, Montana, New Jersey, and Utah. See "Absentee and Early Voting," National Conference of State Legislatures; http://www.ncsl.org/research/elections-and-campaigns/absentee-and-early-voting.aspx.

37 "Inaccurate, Costly, and Inefficient: Evidence That America's Voter Registration System Needs an Upgrade," The Pew Center on the States, Issue Brief (Feb. 2012), p. 1; https://www.pewtrusts.org/~/media/legacy/uploadedfiles/pcs_assets/2012/pewupgradingvoterregistrationpdf.pdf.

38 Ibid.

39 "Final Report of the Miami-Dade County Grand Jury," p. 12.

40 Ibid.

41 Victor Joecks, "Clark County election officials accepted my signature—on 8 ballot envelopes," *Las Vegas Review-Journal* (Nov. 12, 2020).

42 See e.g., 52 U.S.C. § 10508.

43 Andy Kroll, "Revealed: The Massive New Liberal Plan to Remake American Politics," *Mother Jones* (Jan. 9, 2013).

44 Thomas Perez, Assistant Attorney General for Civil Rights, U.S. Department of Justice, "Address at the George Washington University Law School Symposium (Nov. 16, 2012).

45 Scott Malone and David Ingram, "U.S. Should Automatically Register Voters: Attorney General," Reuters (Dec. 12, 2012).

46 "7 Ways to Universal Voter Registration," FairVote, http://www.faivote.org/7-ways-to-universal-voter-registration.

47 See, for example, Thom File and Sarah Crissey, "Voting and Registration in the Election of November 2008," U.S. Census Bureau, U.S. Department of

Commerce (July 2012), Table 6 (Reasons for Not Registering and Voting, by Selected Characteristic: 2008). Since this is a survey of registration and turnout as reported by voters, it may vary from actual registration and turnout reported by state election officials.

48 "Voting and Registration in the Election of November 2010," U.S. Census Bureau, U.S. Department of Commerce, Table 10 (Reasons for Not Voting, by Selected Characteristics: November 2010); "Voting and Registration in the Election of November 2016," U.S. Census Bureau, U.S. Department of Commerce (May 2017), Table 10 (Reasons for Not Voting, by Selected Characteristics: November 2016).

49 "Voting and Registration in the Election of November 2010," U.S. Census Bureau, U.S. Department of Commerce, Table 10 (Reasons for Not Voting, by Selected Characteristics: November 2010); "Voting and Registration in the Election of November 2016," U.S. Census Bureau, U.S. Department of Commerce (May 2017), Table 10 (Reasons for Not Voting, by Selected Characteristics: November 2016).

50 "Voter Registration Modernization," Brennan Center for Justice (2009), p. 5.

51 "Voter Registration Modernization," Brennan Center (2009), p. 1.

52 Randal D. Lloyd, "Motor Voter: A Dismal Failure," 7 *Nevada Journal* (Feb. 1999).

53 See H.R.1, the For the People Act.

54 "Automatic Voter Registration," National Conference of State Legislatures (Feb. 8, 2021).

55 Bryan Anderson, "Did non-citizens vote last year? California officials still can't say," *The Sacramento Bee* (Jan. 4, 2019).

56 Ibid.

57 Mark Osborne, "1,500 noncitizens may have been registered to vote in California DMV error," ABC News (Oct. 9, 2018).

58 Nathaniel Rakich, "What Happened When 2.2 Million People Were Automatically Registered to Vote," Fivethirtyeight.com (Oct. 20, 2019).

59 Sophia Tareen, "Illinois: Error registered a possible 545 noncitizens voters," Associated Press (Jan. 23, 2020).

60 See for example *Arcia v. Detzner*, 908 F. Supp. 2d 1276 (S.D. Fla. 2012).

61 *Florida State Conference of the NAACP v. Browning*, 522 F.3d 1153, 1155 (Eleventh Cir. 2008).

62 "Voting Rights Advocates Challenge Florida Registration Law in Federal Court, Press Release, BerlinRosen Public Affairs, Brennan Center for Justice, Advancement Project, and Project Vote (Sept. 17, 2007.

63 *Washington Association of Churches v. Reed*, 492 F. Supp. 2d 1264 (W.D. WA. 2006).

64 Justin Levitt, Wendy Weiser, and Ana Munoz, "Making the List: Database Matching and Verification Processes for Voter Registration," Brennan Center for Justice (March 24, 2006), page iii.

65 See Elections Canada, http://www.elections.ca.

66 "Voter Turnout at Federal Elections and Referendums," Elections Canada,

https://www.elections.ca/content.aspx?section=ele&dir=turn&document=in dex&lang=e.

67  "Voter Turnout at Federal Elections and Referendums," Elections Canada, https://www.elections.ca/content.aspx?section=ele&dir=turn&document=ind ex&lang=e; "Voter Turnout Data," United States Elections Project, http://www. electproject.org/.

68  John Ibbitson, "The Alarming Decline in Voter Turnout," *The Globe and Mail* (Oct. 14, 2011).

69  Ella Nilsen, "Maine Voters Blew Up Their Voting System and Started From Scratch," *Vox* (June 12, 2018). Ranked choice voting only applies to federal elections, not state elections, because the Maine Supreme Judicial Court held that the law conflicts with the state's constitution. *Opinion of the Justices*, 162 A.3d 188, at 209–211 (Me. 2017). Alaska implemented ranked choice voting for both state and federal elections through a ballot measure approved by voters in 2020. Some municipalities in states like California, Minnesota, and Washington state also use ranked choice voting. Simon Waxman, "Ranked-Choice Voting Is Not the Solution," *Democracy Journal* (Nov. 3, 2016).

70  H.R. 4464, "Rep. Raskin, House Democrats Introduce Ranked Choice Voting Bill," Press Release, Rep. Jamie Raskin (Sept. 25, 2019).

71  David Sharp, "Ranked Choice as Easy as 1, 2, 3? Not So Fast, Critics Say," Associated Press (Oct. 9, 2016).

72  Craig M. Burnett and Vladimir Kogan, "Ballot and Voter 'Exhaustion' Under Instant Runoff Voting: An Examination of Four Ranked-Choice Elections," *Electoral Studies* Vol. 37 (2015), pp. 41–49.

73  Ibid., p. 42.

74  Jeff Jacoby, "Why ranked choice is the wrong choice," the *Boston Globe* (Sept 20, 2020). Fortunately, Massachusetts voters rejected ranked choice voting.

75  Waxman, "Ranked-Choice Voting Is Not the Solution."

76  Sharp, "Ranked Choice as Easy as 1, 2, 3?"

77  *Baber v. Dunlap*, 376 F.Supp.3d 125, footnote 6 (D. Maine 2018) ("Whether RCV is a better method for holding elections is not a question for which the Constitution holds the answer...To the extent that the Plaintiffs call into question the wisdom of using RCV, they are free to do so but...such criticism falls short of constitutional impropriety." *Baber*, at 135).

78  Ibid., at 131.

79  Ibid., at 132. Thousands of ballots were discarded in the Second Congressional District race that was being litigated in this case, illustrating, according to Prof. Gimpel, that those voters guessed wrong due to an information deficit.

80  Burnett and Kogan, "Ballot and Voter 'Exhaustion' Under Instant Runoff Voting," p. 49.

81  Ibid.

82  Ibid., p. 44.

83  Jason Sorens, "The False Promise of Instant Runoff Voting," *CATO Unbound*

(Dec. 9, 2016). Sorens argues that ranked choice voting is worse than "the status quo because it neuters third parties" by eliminating their "blackmail power." Under our current system, Sorens contends, major parties have "an incentive to cater a bit to ideological minorities" to avoid those third parties fielding a candidate in a race that will take votes away from the major party candidate.

## CHAPTER TEN

1 Mark Niesse, "Inquiry shows 1,000 Georgians may have voted twice, but no conspiracy," *Atlanta-Journal-Constitution* (Sept. 30, 2020).

2 Ian W. Karbal, "How careful local reporting undermined Trump's claims of voter fraud," *Columbia Journalism Review* (Nov. 3, 2020).

3 John Hinderaker, "Do Trump's Lawyers Know What They Are Doing?" Powerlineblog.com (Nov. 19, 2020).

4 Zachary Evans, "Pro-Trump Lawyer Lin Wood Donated To Democrats For Years," *National Review* (Dec. 3, 2020)

5 Charlie Nash, "Pro-Trump Attorney Calls on Republicans To Withhold Votes In Georgia Runoffs That Will Decide Senate," *Mediate* (Nov. 23, 2020)

6 James Wooten, *Dasher: The Roots and Rising of Jimmy Carter*, Summit Books (1978), p. 244.

7 Trump v. Raffensperger, Case No. 2020-343255 (Fulton County Sup. Ct.).

8 Joseph A. Wulfsohn, "Liberal media teamed up for 'smear campaign' to dismiss The Post's Hunter Biden story," *New York Post* (Dec. 11, 2020)

9 Hans von Spakovsky served on the Fulton County Registration and Elections Board from 1996 to 2001.

10 Everett Catts, "Fulton Board of Commissioners again delays votes on Barron's firing," *The Neighbor* (May 5, 2021).

11 Ibid.

12 "DeKalb County elections manager fired for errors found in ballot audit," WSB-TV (Nov. 20, 2020).

13 Interview, February 15, 2021.

14 Interview, May 1, 2021.

15 Mark Niesse and David Wickert, "Georgia House speaker takes aim at state's top election official," *Atlanta Journal-Constitution* (Dec. 10, 2020).

16 Hans von Spakovsky, "The Left's 'Jim Crow' Rhetoric is Absurd, Insulting and Dishonest," *The Daily Signal* (March 30, 2021).

## CHAPTER ELEVEN

1 Sami Edge, "No, voter fraud actually isn't a persistent problem," *Washington Post* (Sept. 1, 2016)

2 Tim Alberta, "The Inside Story of Michigan's Fake Voter Fraud Scandal," *Politico* (Nov. 24, 2020)

3 553 U.S. 181, 128 S.Ct. 1610, 1619 (2008)

4   *Crawford v. Marion County Election Board*, 472 F.3d 949, 953 (7th Cir. 2007).

5   *Palm Beach Post*, May 28, 2001, p. 1

## CHAPTER 12

1   https://www.sos.alabama.gov/alabama-votes/voter/request-mobile-unit.

# INDEX

Abrams, Stacey, 1, 208

absentee ballots, 6, 13, 84–86; Al Franken, Marc Elias and, 137–138; changes to, under H.R.1, 124–126; Congressional election, Ninth District, North Carolina, 2018, 79–83; COVID-19 pandemic and changes made regarding, 29, 30, 32, 39–48; Democratic mayoral primary election, East Chicago, Indiana, 2003, 75–79; Marc Elias proposals for, 148–149; mayoral election, Miami, Florida, 1997, 69–75; permanent lists, 180–182; rules regarding delivery by voter or family member, 172; safeguarding elections with accurate photo ID for, 229–234; school board election, Fresno County, California, 1991, 67–73; as tool of choice for voter fraud, 65; vote trafficking and, 175–176

Acadia Parish, Louisiana, 98–99

ACLU, 12, 30, 97, 105, 140, 145, 212, 224; reaction to the Presidential Advisory Commission on Election Integrity, 60, 61

Adams, J. Christian, 57, 60, 113–114, 139, 154–155, 168

Advancement Project, 190

AFL-CIO, 36

African Americans and Hispanics: negative stereotyping of, by early voting advocates, 140–143; voter registration increases among, 54–55

Agee, Steven, 33–35, 36

Alabama, 31–32, 35, 129; absentee ballot return rules, 172; John Lewis Voting Rights Advancement Act proposal by Joe Biden and, 144

Alaska, 192

Alberta, Tim, 212

aliens: allowed to vote under H.R.1, 120–121; redistricting under H.R.1 including, 130–131; voting by, 104–109, 189–190, 228

Alito, Samuel, 37, 43

Allied Security Operations Group, 22, 24

altering of vote counts, 93–94

Amanpour, Christiane, 201–202

Amero, Brian, 209

Antrim County, Michigan, 2–3, 20, 21–26

A. Phillip Randolph Institute, 39

Arizona: audit of Maricopa County 2020 election, 25–26; banning of private funding of county election offices by, in 2021, 157; Center for Tech and Civic Life (CTCL) in, 156–157; new voting law, 2021, 50; redistricting commission in, 128

Armstrong, Chad, 103

Associated Press (AP), 49, 57, 61, 62–63, 154

*Atlanta Journal-Constitution*, 199

Atlantic Philanthropies, 155

audits, election: Antrim County, Michigan, 21–26; Maricopa County, Arizona, 25–26; Windham, New Hampshire, 26

Australia, ranked choice voting in, 194

automatic voter registration, 119–121, 182–192, 228–229; alien voting and, 189–190; in Canada, 191; nonvoters and, 184–187; safeguarding election integrity by prohibiting, 235–236; unreliable federal databases and, 190–191

Baako, Michael Nana, 104

Baker, James, 5

Ball, Molly, 158–159

ballot petition fraud, 90–93

Baltimore, Maryland, 218

Barnett, Mark, 13

Barr, Bob, 192

Barron, Richard, 203

Bauer, Bob, 136

Benson, Jocelyn, 39–40, 45, 58

Best, Betty Jane, 94

Biden, Hunter, 201